How Great Leaders of UAE Shaped a Great Country

By: Mustafa Nejem

Copyright © 2023

Preface

When you view the map of the Middle East, you might see a wide region of the Arabian Desert. However, through the stretching of the golden sands of this region, a modern marvel has also evolved that is now known as the United Arab Emirates (UAE). The nation living in the emirates has been born through the visionary directions and dreams of its leaders that have shaped a great country. The leaders have transformed the country from a barren land to a thriving oasis of innovation and technological advancement. The book 'How Great Leaders of UAE Shaped a Great Country' highlights the extraordinary journey of this unique and hardworking nation that has been led by its visionary leaders who defined and shaped the destiny of the UAE.

In this book, as I explore the leadership achievements of the UAE transformation, I will delve into the rich cultural and historical heritage of the country. The tales of leadership make the core foundation of this book that highlight how the great leaders of the UAE became the visionary architects and developed a nation with determination, foresight, and unwavering commitment.

The key motivation for writing this book is to acknowledge the profound contribution of the founding father of the UAE, Sheikh Zayed bin Sultan Al Nahyan. The modern transformation of the UAE can truly be attributed to his compassion, wisdom, and resolute spirit. When the union of the emirates initially formed, he envisioned the development of a nation that will transcend the limitations typically associated with the people of desert origins. This book also chronicles the achievements of the successors of His Excellency. The successors also continued the visionary leadership style of the founding father and they include Sheikh Khalifa bin Zayed Al Nahyan, Sheikh Mohamed bin Zayed Al Nahyan, Sheikh Mohammed bin Rashid Al Maktoum, and other key personalities. All these leaders have made a lasting impression in shaping the UAE's history and enabling continued progress in a short duration.

The book is written in the backdrop of the changing dynamics of the world, where economic and political factors are affecting the work of progress and development. The UAE has been able to achieve success even in these testing times and turn the sands into gold. It has been made possible by the forward-thinking policies and strategic decision-making of the UAE leaders. They have a relentless pursuit of diversification and they create a fine balance between the economic growth and a sustainable environment. The pages in this book will lead you to the heart and core of the economic transformation of the UAE and role of the great leaders in achieving this remarkable success. You will come to know that the UAE leaders often introduced bold initiatives to position the UAE as the global powerhouse for the economic activity.

As you navigate through the chapters of this book, each chapter will reveal a new layer and a unique dimension of the transformational era of the UAE. The underlying themes will inspire you. The leadership narrative of the UAE is a global testament that even a desert area has boundless opportunities. A visionary leadership can convert the challenges into opportunities and motivate the nation to work with a clear vision and determination.

The book is a narrative of innovation, resilience, steadfastness, and a commitment to excellence from the lens of the leadership. I hope that this book will not only become an authentic, historical reference but also become a source of inspiration for the policymakers, leaders, and corporate professionals across the globe.

Table of Contents

List of Figures

1. Introduction

1.1. Introduction to the United Arab Emirates (UAE)

The United Arab Emirates (UAE) is a West Asian country located in the Middle East. In the Arabic language, it is also called Al Imarat al Arabiyah al Muttahidah. The countries bordering the UAE are Saudi Arabia and Oman. The country also has maritime borders with Iran and Qatar. The capital of the UAE is Abu Dhabi and the most populous city of the UAE is Dubai. The total area of the UAE is 83,600 square kilometers.[i] The country mostly observes desert climate, and the cooler winds can only be experienced in the eastern mountains. The country possesses large resources of petroleum and natural gas. The population of the UAE is 9,973,449 (approximately 10 million) and the country ranks 92 in the world population index.[ii] Arabic is the official language of the UAE. As the country hosts immigrants from multiple countries, you will also find people speaking Hindi, English, Urdu, Malaya, Tagalog, Pashto, and Persian. During the 19th century, the Trucial States of the Persian Gulf surrendered the control of their defense to the United Kingdom. Six of these states merged in 1971 and formed a collected entity known as the UAE. Another state Ra's al Khaymah joined the federation in 1972. As of today, there are 7 UAE states namely Abu Dhabi, Dubai, Sharjah, Ajman, Umm Al-Quwain, Fujairah, and Ras Al Khaimah as shown in Figure 1 below. Most of the population of the UAE is concentrated on the three largest emirates Dubai, Abu Dhabi, and Sharjah. These three emirates are home to approximately 85% of the population.[iii]

Figure 1: Map of the UAE[iv]

The UAE is one of the largest host of immigrants in the world. The immigrants account for 87.9% of the total population. The local Emiratis are only 11.6% of the total population. South Asians are the majority population of the UAE making up 59.4% of the total population.[v] South Asians include Pakistanis, Indians, and Bangladeshis. Other ethnic groups include Egyptians and Filipinos. The UAE is a Middle Eastern country with majority Muslim population. The Muslims are 76% of the total population.[vi] People with other religious communities include Christians, Buddhist, Parsi, Sikh, and Jews.

The oil and the global finance remained the key pillars of the UAE economy for more than three decades. The global financial crisis of 2008 hit the UAE hard due to the collapse of the real estate market, declining oil prices, and the crisis in the international banking system.

However, the leadership of the UAE still inspired and motivated the citizens. It was particularly observed during the Arab Spring in 2010-2011 where the UAE was not affected by this political revolution. At that time, the UAE leaders had introduced a $1.6 billion infrastructure plan for improving the living conditions of the poorer northern emirates.[vii] It helped in keeping the faith and confidence of the people on the leadership of the UAE.

In the recent years, the UAE has transformed itself into the leadership role in solving the issues at the national, regional, and international level. The country spent billions of dollars for providing the financial assistance and providing an enabling living environment in Egypt. The country also joined the international forces in the Defeat-ISIS coalition. The country also participates in Saudi-led military campaigns to fight the terrorists in Yemen. In September 2020, the UAE also signed a peace agreement with Israel. Bahrain was also part of this peace agreement. This agreement is popularly known as the Abraham Accords.[viii] Under this agreement, both Bahrain and the UAE recognized Israel. They were the third and fourth countries recognizing Israel after Egypt and Jordan.

The government system in the UAE is that of a federation of monarchies. The country got independence from the UK on December 02, 1971. The latest constitution of the country was first drafted in 1971 and it was enforced as a permanent constitution in May 1996. The legal system of the country is a combination of civil laws and Islamic sharia laws. The foreigners in the UAE cannot acquire the nationality of the UAE. The citizenship by birth is also not permitted in the UAE. An individual is a citizen of the UAE if his/her father is the citizen of the UAE. Only in those exceptional circumstances, where the father of a new-born individual is unknown, the citizenship may be granted if the mother is a UAE citizen.[ix] For the purpose of naturalization, the country has a residency requirement of 30 years.

The executive branch of the UAE is run by several key dignitaries. The current chief of state is President Muhammad Bin Zayid Al Nuhayyan. He became president in May 2022 following the demise of President Khalifa bin Zayid Al nNuhayyan. The head of government is Prime Minister Muhammad Bin Rashid Al Maktum. He assumed this office in January 2006. The cabinet of the UAE consists of the Council of Ministers. These ministers are appointed by the Prime Minister with the approval of the President. The president is elected by the Federal Supreme Council (FSC). The rulers of the seven emirates of the UAE are members of the FSC. At the time of the death of President Khalifa bin Zayid Al-Nuhayyan, the FSC held unscheduled elections in May 2022. The council selected Muhammad Bin Zayid Al Nuhayyan as the next President.[x] The President is appointed for a 5-year term. Therefore, the next elections will be held in 2027. The Prime Minister of the UAE is appointed by the President. Conventionally, the ruler of the Emirate of Dubai becomes the Prime Minister. In the UAE, the FSC is regarded as the highest constitutional authority. The authority not only formulates general policies but also gives approval to the federal legislation. The FSC meetings are scheduled four times a year. The rulers of Abu Dhabi and Dubai can exercise veto power in the decision-making process of the UAE. As the government system in the UAE is that of a federation of monarchies, no political party exists in the country, and the formulation of a political party is banned in the country. Figure 2 explains the current governmental setup of the UAE.

Executive Branch of the UAE

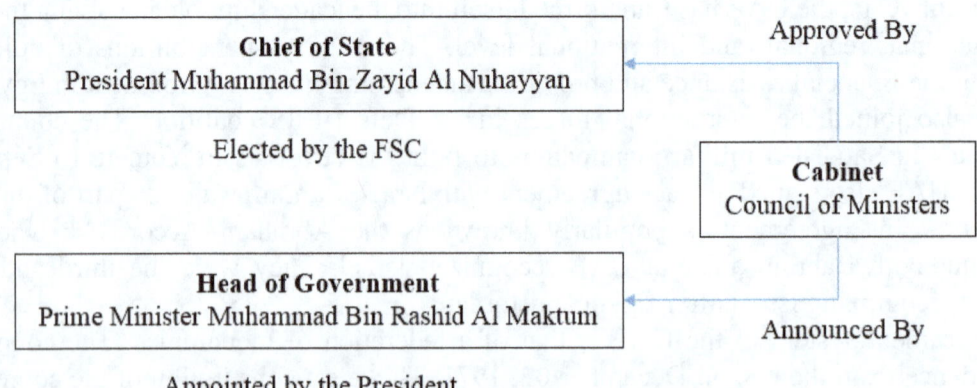

Figure 2: Executive Branch of the UAE

1.2. Historical Evolution of the Modern UAE

As I mentioned in the previous section, the UAE got independence from the Great Britain in 1971. Therefore, the country has a comparatively short history after getting independence. I also highlighted in the previous section that the highest authority in the UAE is the chief of the state, which is the president. The president is also the army chief in the UAE. Since the UAE got independence, only three presidents have assumed the office of the chief of the state. These three presidents are Zayed bin Sultan Al Nahyan, Khalifa bin Zayed Al Nahyan, and Mohamed bin Zayed Al Nahyan. Both second and third presidents are the sons of Zayed bin Sultan Al Nahyan that indicates the monarchy style of government in the UAE.

At the first glance, it may appear that the UAE is following an authoritarian style of leadership. However, this leadership style also has its advantages that can clearly be seen in how great leaders of UAE shaped a great country. The great transformation of the dessert region highlights that the country has progressed well under the leadership of the three chiefs of state. The nation has followed the guidelines of the leadership and the unity of command has expedited the decision-making process. The Arab nation is historically linked and attached to the Bedouin culture where the head of the family makes decisions for the welfare and benefit of the entire family. In this context, the leadership style of the rulers of the UAE is the most appropriate style for the country. Despite running the country as a federation of monarchies, the UAE has respect for democratic and pluralistic values. There is more freedom and liberties in the UAE compared to other Arab countries in the Middle East. The professionals, businesses, and celebrities prefer the UAE for hosting international matches, contests, conferences, and expos. Dubai Expo is one of the most famous exhibition featuring the state-of-the-art technologies, products, and services.

BBC has summarized some of the key dates when landmark developments were made in the history of the UAE.[xi] The Islam spread in the region in the decade of 630s. In 1892, Trucial states came under the protection of the UK. In the 19th century, the pearling industry dominated the economy of the entire region. The oil exploration activities began in the UAE in 1935. The oil reserves were first found in Abu Dhabi in 1958. A landmark development was made in 1968 when the UK announced that the military forces will be withdrawn from the East of Suez.

The UAE got independence in 1971 and joined the UAE and the Arab League. In 1981, the UAE was one of the founders in the establishment of the Gulf Cooperation Council. The first national elections in the UAE were held in 2006 and the voters elected the participants of the

Federal National Council. In 2015, the UAE joined the forces of Saudi Arabia for the air strikes to fight the rebels in Yemen. In 2020, the UAE made diplomatic relations with Israel along with Bahrain. In 2021, the UAE gained the distinction of being the first Arab and Muslim country to send its Hope spacecraft to the Mars mission as shown in Figure 3 below:

Hope, the United Arab Emirates' Mars mission

Highlights

- Hope is a United Arab Emirates Mars orbiter that arrived in February 2021.

- Hope is studying Mars' climate to help us understand what Mars was like when its atmosphere could have supported life.

- Hope is the Arab world's first mission to another planet. More countries exploring our Solar System means more discoveries and opportunities for global collaboration.

Figure 3: Hope Mission[xii]

The UAE also plans to launch MBZ-SAT satellite in 2024 as shown in Figure 4 below, where MBZ denotes the name of the President. The launch of this satellite will be a significant contribution to the space research initiatives of the UAE. It will strengthen the collaboration of the UAE in world space science. The satellite will provide images with a very high quality and the scientists and researchers will be able to utilize these images in their academic endeavors at the global level.[xiii]

Figure 4: MBZ Satellite[xiv]

1.3. Remarkable Transformation from a Desert to a Global Powerhouse

The UAE got independence in 1971, and in a short time, through the great efforts and contributions of the UAE leaders, the country has now become a global powerhouse. The question arises how the UAE achieved such brilliance despite the war-like situations in the Middle East and the tensions among the neighboring countries.

The World Economic Forum (WEF) has highlighted several factors that enabled this remarkable transformation of the UAE from a fishing village to a modern metropolis.[xv] According to WEF, Dubai, one of the main emirates of the UAE started the process of economic diversification as early as in the decade of 70s. Due to this factor, the UAE has achieved more economic growth than the neighboring countries. In comparison, Abu Dhabi has a much higher reliance on oil revenues at present. But Dubai has reduced its reliance on oil exports to less than 1% as shown in Figure 5 below:

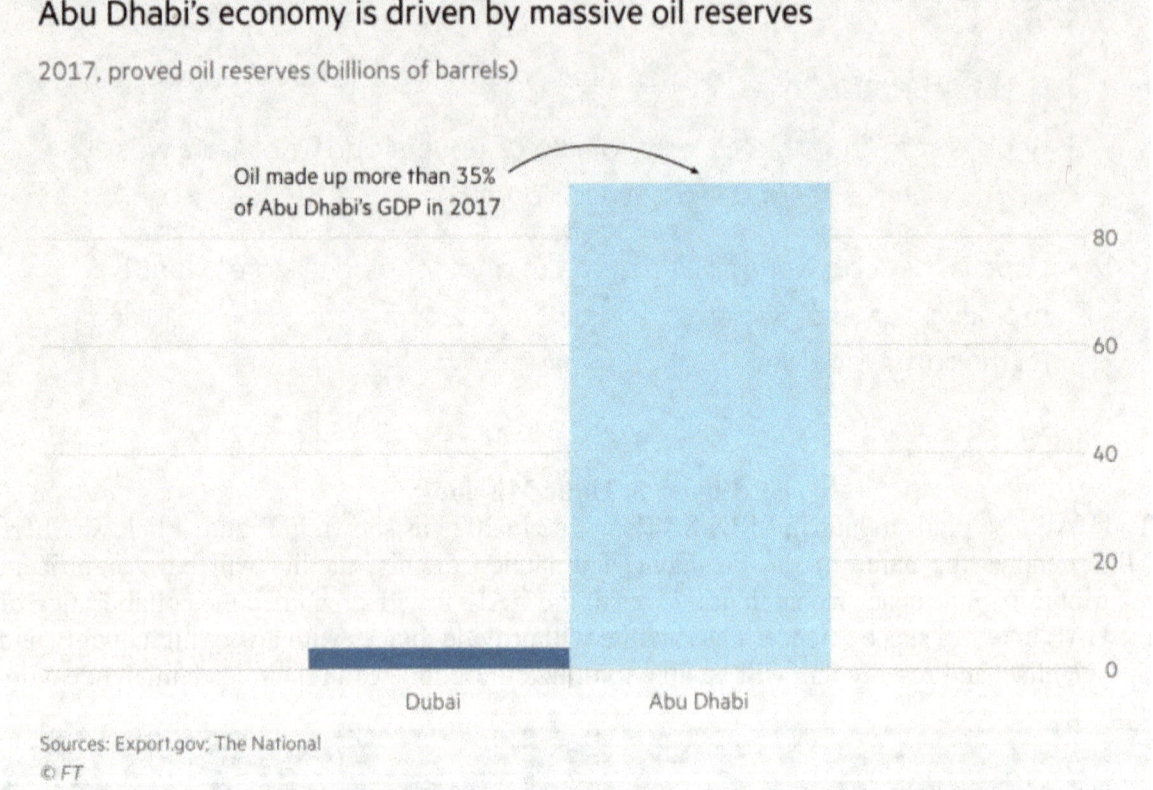

Figure 5: Higher Economic Diversification by Dubai than Abu Dhabi[xvi]

According to WEF, Dubai has also established a target that by 2050, it will extract at least half of the energy requirements from the renewable sources.

Another initiative that helped the UAE in achieving the remarkable progress is the Ghadan 21 reforms.[xvii] Through this reform package, the ruler of the Abu Dhabi promoted business and ecotourism in the emirate. As per the reform package, a new licensing regime was introduced in the UAE. The technology developers can now apply for an instant license and they will be allowed to conduct technology-led businesses in the emirate and contribute to the technological advancement of the emirate.

If you had to visit Dubai in the decade of 50s, you would struggle finding a place to stay. There were no hotels developed at that time in Dubai. Dubai was just a fishing village in 1960.

In 1999, a major development project completed in the UAE and the Burj Al-Arab was constructed. It was one of the major hotels in the Arab World as shown in Figure 6 below.

Figure 6: Burj Al-Arab built in 1999[xviii]

Burj Al-Arab was designed by a British Architect Tom Wright. He had been asked by the UAE leaders to create an iconic building for the UAE. The building is developed in the form of a ship and reflects the seafaring heritage of the UAE. Moreover, the building was constructed with a modernist look to emphasize the transformation of the UAE from a fishing village to a global city. This building was constructed in a duration of five years. The building had 202 hotel suites, and each suite had two floors.

It was not just another project in the UAE. Instead, the building became a trendsetter for initiating further development projects in the UAE. The real estate investors began making investments in the vanity projects in the UAE. Until the 21st century, the pace of growth of the UAE was slow and the UAE leaders were trying hard to make the UAE a global powerhouse.

Another landmark project initiated in the UAE was Palm Jumeriah that was completed in 2007. The emirate of Dubai particularly got the attention of the world not just because of developing iconic buildings but also developing islands. In the case of Palm Jumeriah, the islands were developed in the shape of a palm tree. An overarching circle covers the area of all the islands. When the building is viewed from the sky, it gives a magnificent look as shown in Figure 7 below. The work on this project had started in 2001 and the people of the UAE started living there in 2007.

Figure 7: Palm Jumeriah completed in 2007[xix]

Another significant milestone was achieved in 2009, when Dubai Metro was introduced. This project was completed in 2009. At that time, Dubai was the first city in the Arab world to have an urban train network. This metro line was being managed by a French company Keolis. A British architectural firm Aedas designed the structure of the metro line. This project also gained a huge prominence in the world because it was one of the longest driverless train lines in the world.

Figure 8: Dubai Metro completed in 2009[xx]

Another milestone was achieved by the UAE in 2010, when Burj Khalifa was completed and opened for the general public. It gained the distinction of being the world's tallest building. The height of this building is 828 meters. Its height is almost three times to that of Eiffel Tower. As the building elevates, the width of the building decreases that assists the building in keeping its shape as shown in Figure 9 below. The building was completed in a duration of six years.

Figure 9: Burj Khalifa completed in 2010[xxi]

Another milestone project in the UAE was completed in 2013, when Al Maktoum International Airport was opened for the general public. It was the second international airport in the Dubai emirate. The UAE has a strategic location in the Middle East where its geographical boundaries are located between Asia and Europe. The UAE leaders realized that the UAE can become an ideal stop-off place for connecting flights between different countries. Dubai International Airport was already fulfilling this purpose, but still, the need of another airport was felt by the UAE leaders to accommodate the large inflow of passengers. The airport first began cargo freight in 2010 and then the passengers' travel was allowed in 2013 as shown in Figure 10 below. The airport has the capability to serve 250 million passengers.

Figure 10: Al Maktoum International Airport[xxii]

In the above section, I have mentioned some of the examples that led to the remarkable transformation of the UAE from a desert area to a global powerhouse. These examples highlight the visionary approach of the UAE leaders where they made aggressive investments in the infrastructure projects to transform the image of the country. All of the projects were remarkable success that indicates that the experience, commitment, and steadfastness of the UAE leaders are the main factors that have shaped a great country.

1.4. Leadership and Development

All the UAE leaders followed a strategy of development and progress and they believe that the success of the nation is possible only when a true leadership is available to them. In 2008, Sheikh Mohammed bin Rashid developed an institutional mechanism so that the work of progress and development in the UAE could be linked to the leadership development. The prime minister launched a leadership program known as the UAE Government Leaders Program.[xxiii] The primary objective of this program is develop the leadership potential among the best national talent in the UAE. The program aims to develop the leaders that could implement the strategic directions of the UAE as mentioned in the Vision 2021 document and Centennial 2071 document.

One of the unique features of the leadership development program launched by the prime minister is that it provides a unified platform through which the leadership skills can be developed at federal level, private sector level, and local level.

The current leadership model of the UAE government focuses on three key aspects[xxiv] to lead the country in the 21st century. These three pillars are futuristic outlook, leadership spirit, and making an impact. An official website[xxv] has also been developed by the UAE government through which the aspiring candidates can join the leadership program.

1.5. Strategic Location and Geographical Advantages

As I explained in the historical evolution of the modern UAE, the economy of the country was dependent on pearl diving and fishing in the earlier days. However, after the discovery of oil and gas reserves, the country observed economic prosperity. The higher revenues and inflows made it possible for the UAE leaders to launch projects of infrastructure development as well that eventually shaped a great country and a modern UAE.

Besides oil and gas reserves and high-rise buildings, the UAE also enjoys a geographical advantage that makes it an ideal location for the international visitors, businesses, and investors. The location of the UAE is at the crossroad of Asia, Africa, and Europe. Due to this strategic location, a significant number of international trades and businesses have made the UAE their business hub. The UAE leaders have also offered tax incentives and free trade zones to facilitate the foreign investors. The airports and seaports of the UAE are well-connected and well-established and logistics and shipping operations can be carried out in a hassle-free manner through airport and maritime regions. The UAE leaders have also made the UAE a multicultural and cosmopolitan society and the UAE welcomes people from all backgrounds, ethnicities, and cultures. The respect for diversity and pluralism can be leveraged by the investors to tap into global markets and customer segments. According to the country profile of the BBC, although the UAE government follows a conservative style of government rooted in its tradition, yet the country can be regarded as the most liberal country in the Arab world.[xxvi] There is a good level of tolerance for the differing beliefs, cultures, and religious communities.

1.6. What this Book Covers

This book provides a distinctive leadership narrative combining the threads of UAE vision, history, and the great transformation that define the modern UAE. The book is a detailed exploration of the leadership journey and initiatives that continued the progress and development of the UAE and transformed the country from a desert area to a global powerhouse.

The book begins by highlighting the contributions of the founding fathers, chiefs of state, and the prime minister of the UAE. The book highlights why and how the UAE reduced its reliance on oil and gas exports and achieved a miracle in the development of the UAE through economic diversification and the sustainable growth. The book also describes the technology infrastructure and projects of the UAE that provided a global leadership to the UAE in the technological advancement.

The book also highlights the strategic location of the UAE and how great leaders of UAE capitalized on this opportunity for the global connectivity of the UAE. The investment climate and the business friendly policies of the UAE leaders are also discussed. The book explains how the tax incentives, flexible regulatory environment, and free trade zones encouraged the foreign investments to select the UAE for their businesses.

The book also highlights the efforts of the UAE leaders in the education sector and developing a knowledge-based economy. The contributions of the leaders are also mentioned to position the UAE as a global destination for tourism. The book also describes the preference of the UAE leaders regarding religious tolerance, pluralism, and developing a multicultural environment. The role of the new ministries is also discussed including the ministry of happiness and artificial intelligence.

When you begin reading the subsequent chapters of this book, you will realize that each chapter uncovers a new dimension of the efforts of the UAE leaders to make UAE a great and exemplary country for the rest of the world. This book is not just a historical account of the contribution of the great leaders of the UAE. The book also highlights the principles and strategies used by these great leaders and how the world leaders can take inspirations from these strategies and principles. I welcome you to a leadership narrative that transcends borders and is a true depiction of the role of visionary leaders in shaping the destiny of a nation. The book will expand your knowledge regarding the contribution of the UAE great leaders in shaping a great country. The book will also let you know how the leaders addressed the challenges in their leadership journeys and how they were successful even when the other countries in the world were struggling in maintaining their economic and political outlook.

2. Visionary Leadership of UAE

This book aims at highlighting the notable contributions of the great leaders of the UAE as to how they shaped a great country. Therefore, I am highlighting below the brief accounts and contributions of the three chiefs of state of the UAE and the current prime minister of the UAE.

2.1. The Foundational Role of Sheikh Zayed bin Sultan Al Nahyan

Figure 11: First Chief of State[xxvii]

Figure 11 is the picture of the founding father and the first chief of state of the UAE, His Highness Sheikh Zayed bin Sultan Al Nahyan. When the UAE got independence in 1971, he was the first president of the country. He had become the ruler of Abu Dhabi Emirate in 1966. One cannot understand the historical evolution of the modern UAE without understanding the life and success stories of the first president. He was a symbol of great determination, exemplary hard work, visionary approach, and deep religious faith. He was born in Abu Dhabi in 1918.

Sheikh Zayed was the youngest son of a ruler of Abu Dhabi, Sheikh Sultan bin Zayed Al Nahyan. The Abu Dhabi emirate was underdeveloped and the people were living with a lower quality of life at that time. The economy of the country was dependent on pearl diving and fishing. Some farmers were also using basic agricultural techniques in scattered oases. The literacy rate was very low and the acquisition of knowledge was limited to reading and writing. The local preachers used to impart teachings of Islam. The key modes of transportations were camels and boats. The survival of the families was challenging due to the harsh climatic conditions.

During the decades of 20s and 30s, Sheikh Zayed was engaged in acquiring knowledge from the people he knew and the environment. In 1946, Sheikh Zayed was appointed as the representative of the Abu Dhabi emirate in the eastern region in the area of Al Ain. He had to supervise six villages and the adjacent areas. During the decades of 40s and 50s, Sheikh Zayed made a significant contribution in improving the quality of life and living conditions of the people of Al Ain. He developed the first modern school in emirate and also enabled small-scale developments in the area. He also ensured equitable distribution of water resources because there was a water scarcity in that area. His excellent planning and exemplary leadership made Al Ain the predominant market center and one of the greenest cities in the Middle Eastern region.

Sheikh Zayed was appointed as the ruler of Abu Dhabi in 1966.[xxviii] He used his vast experience of leadership in Al Ain and led the emirate with a vision of progress and development. His steadfastness and committed efforts had enabled Abu Dhabi to export Abu Dhabi crude for the first time in 1962. He capitalized on this success and achieved economic prosperity of the emirate by enabling oil exports on a mass scale. He also introduced various programs of infrastructure development under which various schools, roads, hospitals, and housing facilities were developed.

In 1968, the UK government announced that it will withdraw its occupation in the Arabian Gulf by 1971. Sheikh Zayed considered it as a brilliant opportunity of developing the emirate because the withdrawal of the Great Britain had provided more autonomy and freedom to the UAE rulers. Sheikh Zayed worked in collaboration with the ruler of the Dubai emirate, Sheikh Rashid bin Saeed Al Maktoum. Both of these rulers wanted that a federation after the withdrawal of the UK should not only be based on the seven emirates but it should also include Bahrain and Qatar.[xxix] However, these efforts could not be materialized, and the current UAE is composed of seven emirates. This federation was announced on December 2, 1971.

When the federation came into being, Sheikh Zayed was elected as the first UAE president by all emirate rulers. This post is for a five-year duration. However, the fellow rulers re-elected him after every five years till his death in November 2004.

Sheikh Zayed is particularly remembered for his leadership philosophy and statesmanship. He believed that the resources of the UAE should be fully utilized and everyone should work for the betterment and the progress of the UAE. This philosophy of Sheikh Zayed also ensured women empowerment and gender equality. The UAE women got good opportunities of education, employment, and entrepreneurship.

Although the UAE follows a monarchist model of leadership, Sheikh Zayed incorporated good aspects of the Arabian Bedouin traditions in the leadership fabric of the UAE. The two aspects that he particularly emphasized on were consultation and consensus. He replicated the majlis (council) model of this tradition in the UAE society. Under this model, an open-house discussion forum is held, and the decisions are made after discussions and deliberations.

In 1970, Sheikh Zayed institutionalized the concept of majlis (council) and developed a National Consultative Council for Abu Dhabi.[xxx] Main tribal leaders were made part of this council. When this initiative achieved a remarkable success, a similar council was developed for the entire UAE in 1971 and named the Federal National Council.[xxxi] This council was given the status of the parliament of the state. You can see in Figure 2 that Council of Ministers is still active. It is approved by the President and announced by the Prime Minister.

Other key areas of intervention of Sheikh Zayed were the conservation of wildlife and the natural environment. He built collaborations with the world organizations for the conservation of species such as sand gazelle and Arabian Oryx. For his contribution for the wildlife protection, he was awarded with the prestigious Gold Panda award by World Wildlife Fund.[xxxii]

As I explained earlier, the UAE is a Middle Eastern country with majority Muslim population. The Muslims are 76% of the total population. People with other religious communities include Christians, Buddhist, Parsi, Sikh, and Jews. Despite being a majority Muslim country, Sheikh Zayed was a firm believer of religious tolerance and religious harmony. He enhanced cooperation with other countries to resolve the long-unresolved disputes. During the decade of 90s, Sheikh Zayed also encouraged the UAE armed forces to be part of the international peacekeeping forces. The chief of state is also the chief of armed forces in the UAE. Therefore, his guidelines and directions were in line with his mandate and the trust bestowed upon him by the UAE population. The UAE forces were part of the deterrent force to end the civil war in Lebanon. The forces also participated in the reconstruction program in Somalia.

In 1999, the world witnessed a colossal war between Bosnia and Serbia. Under the leadership of Sheikh Zayed, the UAE forces took part in the aerial campaign that was aimed at stopping Serbia from the genocidal activities in Kosovo. In many NATO missions, the country UAE is often the only Arab country and the non-NATO state that actively takes part in the peacekeeping missions. Despite the increasing training and power gained through these international collaborations, Sheikh Zayed never believed in waging war against any country. He always reiterated that the efforts of the UAE armed forces are aimed at rehabilitation and relief processes. Sheikh Zayed also established charitable entities to help the disadvantaged, vulnerable, and underdeveloped countries. Even before the establishment of the UAE as a federation of seven emirates, Sheikh Zayed had established the Abu Dhabi Fund for Development and the Zayed Charitable and Humanitarian Foundation.[xxxiii] The country now also offers assistance in collaboration with the Red Crescent Society.

Sheikh Zayed ruled the UAE from its foundation till his death in 2004. He died in his late eighties. All Emiratis know well the contributions and achievements of this great leader for shaping the modern UAE. He is truly regarded as the Father of the Nation. After his death, his eldest son became the president, Sheikh Khalifa bin Zayed Al Nahyan. The successors continued the principles and policies of the founding father.

2.2.Leading Role of Sheikh Khalifa bin Zayed Al Nahyan

Figure 12: Second Chief of State[xxxiv]

HH Sheikh Khalifa bin Zayed Al Nahyan (Figure 12) became the second president of the UAE after the demise of the first president in November 2004. He was the eldest son in the family. He led the country with his visionary approach for almost 18 years and passed away on May 13, 2022.

While leading the country as the President, HH Sheikh Khalifa initiated major restructuring projects at the federal level and at the level of the emirate Abu Dhabi. After his accession in November 2004, he appointed a new council of ministers in February 2006. As highlighted in Figure 2, the head of government in the UAE is appointed by the president. Therefore, the current prime minister of the UAE, HH Sheikh Mohammed bin Rashid Al Maktoum has also been appointed by HH Sheikh Khalifa. With this appointment, some major changes were made in the existing structure of the government. New ministries were added to shape a great country and modernize the approach to the government. There was also more focus on introducing reforms at the political front and increase the contribution of the UAE for the community development. There were also indirect elections introduced in the UAE for the membership of Federal National Council.

HH Sheikh Khalifa made drastic changes in the current mode of government of the UAE for encouraging public-private collaborations and foreign investment. He believed that the government alone cannot meet the needs of all citizens, and the collaboration with the private sector and the civil society will be a prudent strategy.

HH Sheikh Khalifa continued the policies of the previous chief of state to offer assistance to underdeveloped and vulnerable countries. In 2017, the UAE provided emergency assistance to Hurricane Irma that helped in the recovery process for the citizens of the US and the Caribbean.[xxxv] The relief efforts of the UAE were also offered during a major earthquake in Indonesia in 2018. In 2018, the Organization for Economic Cooperation and Development announced the UAE as the major donor of humanitarian assistance across the globe.[xxxvi]

In 2007, HH Sheikh Khalifa established a foundation for improving the accessibility of the utility services in the Northern Emirates. This foundation was named as Khalifa Bin Zayed Al Nahyan Foundation.[xxxvii] The foundation improved the accessibility in the areas of education, health, electricity, housing, water services, and transport services. In 2008, the UAE published a conceptual, policy document under the leadership of HH Sheikh Khalifa for the peaceful use of the nuclear power. Through this document, the UAE showed its strong commitment to safety, security, and transparency. The people of the UAE were highly inspired by the contributions and leadership of HH Sheikh Khalifa. As a symbol of their appreciation, in 2010, they renamed Burj Dubai to Burj Khalifa.

HH Sheikh Khalifa was also concerned by the fact that the local Emiratis are only 11.6% of the total population. South Asians are the majority population of the UAE making up 59.4% of the total population. He wanted that the local citizens also get good employment opportunities and do not lag behind in the competitive landscape of the UAE. Therefore, in 2012, HH Sheikh Khalifa announced a new program known as Absher to increase the proportion of the Emiratis in the local workforce.[xxxviii] Similar to other Middle Eastern countries, the phenomenon of localization is now a strategic direction employed by the UAE so that the local Emiratis also get good employment opportunities in the country.

Under the leadership of HH Sheikh Khalifa, the UAE had realized that relying on oil and gas export revenues will not be a good strategy, and the country should opt for the notion of economic diversification. With this strategic direction, in 2015, HH Sheikh Khalifa marked the whole year as the Year of Innovation for the UAE.

In 2017, HH Sheikh Khalifa also endeavored to increase the participation of the UAE in fulfilling its social responsibilities. Therefore, the year 2017 was marked as the Year of Giving in the UAE. During this year, HH Sheikh Khalifa focused on highlighting the spirit of volunteering and promoting the concept of service. The year 2019 was a landmark year in the history of the UAE concerning the women empowerment. In this year, HH Sheikh Khalifa issued a presidential resolution that made it mandatory that the representation of the women in the Federal National Council will be 50%.[xxxix]

A brief account of the contributions of HH Sheikh Khalifa makes it evident that he was a visionary leader and his efforts were not restricted to a particular domain or area. He continuously analyzed the needs of the UAE in the contemporary context and introduced those initiatives that can lead the UAE to the path of progress and development. Although, constitutionally, HH Sheikh Khalifa was independent and autonomous in the decision-making for the UAE, however, he always consulted with the rulers of all the emirates before introducing new initiatives and programs.

2.3. Leading Role of Sheikh Mohamed bin Zayed Al Nahyan

Figure 13: Current Chief of State[xl]

The current chief of state and the president of the UAE is His Highness Sheikh Mohamed bin Zayed Al Nahyan. He became the president in May 2022 after the death of HH Sheikh Khalifa. He also served as the ruler of Abu Dhabi up to 2022. He is a firm believer of people empowerment and letting the people choose their own destiny. He is leading the country through a servant leadership model where the leaders are always available for the betterment of the people and improving their living conditions. He is not fixated in a leadership belief and interacts with citizens and residents on a continued basis. HH Sheikh Mohamed is married to Her Highness Sheikha Salama bint Hamdan bin Mohamed Al Nahyan. The marriage took place in 1981. He has five daughters and four sons. HH Sheikh Mohamed has also adopted two daughters namely Salha and Amina.[xli] HH Sheikh Mohamed is fond of falconry and also takes interest in poetry. He is particularly passionate about the Nabati style of poetry, which is a native style and has gained a huge prominence in the region.[xlii]

HH Sheikh Mohamed has set several key targets for the betterment of the UAE and all these key targets have been highlighted on the official website of the UAE embassy.[xliii] The first of these targets is the development of a secure and robust society. HH Sheikh Mohamed believes that the wellbeing of the UAE people is closely linked to the infrastructure development and regional security. He takes a keen interest in the promotion of Compulsory Military Initiative of the UAE that was introduced in 2014. He also believes in an inclusive and pluralistic society and developed Abu Dhabi Strategy for People of Determination.[xliv] HH Sheikh Mohamed also believes that the gulf region today is highly threatened by external environment, and therefore, he encourages investments that are aimed at improving the military industries of the country such as Edge and Tawazun. He has also introduced an accelerator program for encouraging the startups and entrepreneurial activities. This program is known as Ghadan 21.[xlv] The program was launched in 2018 with an investment of 50 billion dirhams.

Another area of focus of HH Sheikh Mohamed is the development of a sustainable future. The sustainable economic development is at the core of the UAE's vision. The UAE hosted COP28 in 2023 for highlighting the contributions of the UAE for the sustainable development and an inclusive climate. HH Sheikh Mohamed has also supported the industries in the UAE to invest in renewable energy, biotechnology, food security, water security, and robotics.

HH Sheikh Mohamed also launched an initiative known as Masdar to promote the investment and research in the renewable energy sector.[xlvi] In 2016, HH Sheikh Mohamed transformed the government oil company ADNOC for fulfilling a broader aim of renewable energy and energy management. A new energy policy of the UAE was announced in 2021 in which the target of net zero emissions has been set for the entire country to be accomplished by 2050. The UAE has also appointed the first climate envoy so that the progress and development concerning net zero emissions could be tracked by the concerned authority.

HH Sheikh Mohamed is also credited to developing the first nuclear power plant of the UAE that is named Barakah.[xlvii] Under his leadership, the UAE also supports the initiatives of arts and culture and preserves the local heritage for the inspiration of the future generations.

Following the footsteps of his successors, HH Sheikh Mohamed has also built collaborations for contributing to the humanitarian assistance and the relief work. The UAE has always been a part of the International Security Assistance Forces and NATO-led missions. Through these missions, the UAE offered assistance in Afghanistan, Syria, Lebanon, and other war-affected countries. The UAE also provided relief assistance to the Ukrainian refugees who have arrived in Moldova, Bulgaria, and Poland.[xlviii] HH Sheikh Mohamed realized the sensitivity of the Ukrainian crisis and in October 2022, he announced that additional $100 million will be provided to the civilians that have been affected by the war between Ukraine and Russia.

HH Sheikh Mohamed also believes in religious harmony, religious tolerance, and inter-faith dialogues. As part of this vision, he welcomed Pop Francis in the emirate of Abu Dhabi. It was the first ever visit of a Christian leader in the Arabian countries. A joint declaration of Human Fraternity was signed during the visit.[xlix] The UAE also played an active role during the covid-19 pandemic and provided logistics support and medical supplies across the globe under the leadership directions of HH Sheikh Mohamed.

HH Sheikh Mohamed also built collaborations with Bill and Melinda Gates Foundation for polio eradication. Under this collaboration, the UAE has contributed $327 million for removing polio from all over the world.[l] A project, known as Special Olympics, promoted inclusive education for the educational attainment of differently-abled people. The UAE also supports this initiative under the leadership of HH Sheikh Mohamed and has so far pledged $25 million for this project.

Another key area of focus of HH Sheikh Mohamed is early education and schooling. His own education was a unique blend of the acquisition of all forms of knowledge. He also spent a significant time in the father's majlis and learned from the tribal leaders and elders besides his formal education. HH Sheikh Mohamed spent his formal education days in Al Ain, Abu Dhabi, and the Royal Academy in Rabat. His own experience made him believe that every child possesses unique talents and skills. Therefore, he always advocates a student-centered learning approach in the academic institutions.

2.4. Leading Role of Sheikh Mohammed bin Rashid Al Maktoum

Figure 14: The Current Prime Minister[li]

The second President of the UAE, Sheikh Khalifa bin Zayed Al Nahyan, appointed His Highness Sheikh Mohammed bin Rashid Al Maktoum as the Prime Minister of the UAE in January 2006. He became the prime minister after the death of his brother as the prime minister. The new cabinet under the leadership of Sheikh Mohammed bin Rashid took oath on February 11, 2006.[lii] Sheikh Mohammed bin Rashid has introduced various revolutionary initiatives after assuming the office of the premiership.

Sheikh Mohammed bin Rashid continued the focus of his predecessors on achieving sustainable development goals. Under his leadership, the UAE government introduced UAE Vision 2021 and then the UAE Vision 2030.[liii] The vision sets the future journey of the UAE and provides strategic directions to all commercial and industrial establishments.

In 2014, Sheikh Mohammed bin Rashid presented a seven-year agenda for the UAE for accomplishing the true vision of the UAE. The prime minister has also launched the UAE Centennial 2071 that provides the visionary directions for the UAE leaders for almost 5 decades.[liv]

The year 2021 was a landmark year in the history of the UAE when Sheikh Mohammed bin Rashid directed the government institutions and agencies to implement the 10 core principles of the UAE in all their plans and strategies. These 10 principles were named as Principles of the 50 because Sheikh Mohammed bin Rashid believes that these 10 principles will be applicable and relevant for the next 50 years.[lv] These 10 principles are mentioned in Figure 15 and Figure 16.

UNITED ARAB EMIRATES

Principles of the 50
The UAE's 10 Principles for the Next 50 Years

As the United Arab Emirates (UAE) approaches its Golden Jubilee, the country is entering a new phase in its history, a new era of its development path, and a new cycle of economic, political and social growth. This document summarises the new guidance for the UAE in its upcoming historical phase as directed by His Highness Sheikh Khalifa bin Zayed Al Nahyan, President of the UAE, and envisioned by His Highness Sheikh Mohammed bin Rashid Al Maktoum, Vice President and Prime Minister of the UAE and Ruler of Dubai, and His Highness Sheikh Mohamed bin Zayed Al Nahyan, Crown Prince of Abu Dhabi and Deputy Supreme Commander of the UAE Armed Forces.

This document sets forth 10 principles for the UAE, which all government agencies, including the legislative system, the police and security institutions as well as the scientific entities, must adhere to and use as guidelines for all their decisions, and strive to implement through their frameworks and strategies. These principles are as follows:

The First Principle

The major priority shall remain the strengthening of the union, its institutions, legislations, capacities and budgets. The urban, developmental and economic development of all parts of the country is the fastest and most effective way to consolidate the union of the UAE.

The Second Principle

To completely focus, over the upcoming period, on building the best and most dynamic economy in the world. The economic development of the country is the supreme national interest, and all state institutions, of all sectors and across different federal and local levels, shall bear collectively the responsibility of building the best global economic environment and maintaining the gains achieved over the past 50 years.

The Third Principle

The UAE's foreign policy is a tool that aims to serve the higher national goals, the most important of which is the UAE's economic interests. The goal of our political approach is to serve the economy. And the goal of the economy is to provide the best quality of life for the people of the UAE.

The Fourth Principle

The main future driver for growth is human capital. Developing the educational system, attracting talents, retaining specialists and continuously building skills are what shall keep the UAE at the top.

Figure 15: Ten Principles (Principle 1 to 4)[lvi]

UNITED ARAB EMIRATES

The Fifth Principle

Good-neighbourliness is the basis of stability. The geographical, social and cultural vicinity of the country is the first line of defence for its security, safety and its future development. Developing stable and positive political, economic and social relations with this vicinity is one of the most important priorities of the country's foreign policy.

The Sixth Principle

Cementing the reputation of the UAE globally as one nation is a national mission for all institutions. The UAE is one economic destination, one tourist destination, one industrial destination, one investment destination, and one cultural destination. Our national institutions must combine their efforts, and together benefit from the capabilities, and work to build global enterprises and partnerships across the world.

The Seventh Principle

The digital, technical and scientific excellence of the UAE will define its new development and economic frontiers, and the solidification of its position as a capital for talent, companies and investments in these sectors will make it the capital of the future.

The Eighth Principle

The value system in the UAE shall remain based on openness and tolerance, the preservation of rights, the consolidation of the rule of law, the preservation of human dignity, the respect of cultures, the strengthening of human fraternity, and the respect of national identity. The country will remain supportive, through its foreign policy, of all initiatives, pledges and international organizations that promote peace, openness and human fraternity.

The Ninth Principle

The UAE's foreign humanitarian aid is an essential part of its own vision and moral duty towards less fortunate nations. Our foreign humanitarian aid is not tied to religion, race, colour or culture. Political disagreement with any country should not stop us from providing swift relief for those in need.

The Tenth Principle

Calling for peace, harmony, negotiations and dialogue to resolve all political disputes is the basis of the UAE's foreign policy, and striving with regional partners and global friends to establish regional and global peace and stability is a fundamental driver of our foreign policy.

Figure 16: Ten Principles (Principle 5 to 10)[lvii]

According to the first principle, the major priority of the UAE leaders will be to strengthen the UAE as a union of the seven emirates. The second principle states that the nation will have a forward-looking approach and a dynamic approach will be adopted for strengthening the economy of the country. According to the third principle, the foreign policy of the UAE should be inspired by higher national goals of the UAE. The economic interests of the UAE should be protected in all foreign policy-related decisions. The fourth principle highlights that the human capital will be valued and respected as the key driver of the economic growth of the country. The educational system of the country will develop a highly skilled workforce that will ensure the leading position of the UAE in the Middle East and the global level.

According to the fifth principle, the UAE will keep friendly ties with all neighboring countries. It will be considered as the first line of defense for the country. The sixth principle highlights that the UAE will be made as a single hub and one stop destination for tourists, industrialists, celebrities, cultural initiatives, and investment ventures. The seventh principle mentions that the future development of the UAE will be powered by the advanced tools and technologies.

According to the eighth principle, the UAE will promote religious tolerance, openness, and human dignity as the key values of the UAE. The country will promote and encourage all those initiatives that encourage human fraternity and openness. The ninth principle indicates that the UAE will continue its policy of providing humanitarian aid in testing times to all nations regardless of the race, religion, culture, and color. As per the tenth principle, the UAE will support those global initiatives that call for peace and harmony at the regional and international levels. The rival countries will be encouraged to resolve their disputes through dialogue and negotiations.

These 10 key principles were introduced by Sheikh Mohammed bin Rashid when the UAE was approaching its golden jubilee. According to the document, these 10 principles should be adhered by all government agencies, scientific entities, and security institutions of the UAE.

2.5. Leadership for a Prosperous and Inclusive Society

This book is meant to describe you the strategies and directions through which the great leaders of UAE shaped a great country. One of the strategies that truly stand out in this regard is the respect for diversity and creating an inclusive society. The UAE is regarded as a cosmopolitan society in the world where people from multiple backgrounds, countries, and orientations live together peacefully and harmoniously and they achieve economic success and prosperity exclusively based on their hard work and efforts. In the UAE, the local Emiratis are only 11.6% of the total population. South Asians are the majority population of the UAE making up 59.4% of the total population. South Asians include Pakistanis, Indians, and Bangladeshis. Other ethnic groups include Egyptians and Filipinos. The UAE is a Middle Eastern country with majority Muslim population. The Muslims are 76% of the total population. People with other religious communities include Christians, Buddhist, Parsi, Sikh, and Jews. From these statistics, it is very clear that the UAE leaders have a deep respect for other ethnicities and religious communities.

HH Sheikh Mohamed also believes in religious harmony, religious tolerance, and inter-faith dialogues. As part of this vision, he welcomed Pop Francis in the emirate of Abu Dhabi as shown in Figure 17 below. It was the first ever visit of a Christian leader in the Arabian countries. A joint declaration of Human Fraternity was signed during the visit as shown in Figure 18 below.

Figure 17: Pop Francis Visit of the UAE[lviii]

[AR · DE · EN · ES · FR · HR · IT · PL · PT · ZH_CN · ZH_TW]

APOSTOLIC JOURNEY OF HIS HOLINESS POPE FRANCIS
TO THE UNITED ARAB EMIRATES
(3-5 FEBRUARY 2019)

A DOCUMENT ON

HUMAN FRATERNITY

FOR WORLD PEACE AND LIVING TOGETHER

[Multimedia]

INTRODUCTION

Faith leads a believer to see in the other a brother or sister to be supported and loved. Through faith in God, who has created the universe, creatures and all human beings (equal on account of his mercy), believers are called to express this human fraternity by safeguarding creation and the entire universe and supporting all persons, especially the poorest and those most in need.

This transcendental value served as the starting point for several meetings characterized by a friendly and fraternal atmosphere where we shared the joys, sorrows and problems of our contemporary world. We did this by considering scientific and technical progress, therapeutic achievements, the digital era, the mass media and communications. We reflected also on the level of poverty, conflict and suffering of so many brothers and sisters in different parts of the world as a consequence of the arms race, social injustice, corruption, inequality, moral decline, terrorism, discrimination, extremism and many other causes.

Figure 18: Human Fraternity Document[lix]

2.6. Nation-Building and the Role of a Visionary Leadership

The UAE follows a leadership style that is rooted in the Arab culture of the country. The country is a federation of monarchies and seven rulers have been appointed to rule each of the seven emirates of the country. The current chief of state is President Muhammad Bin Zayid Al Nuhayyan. He became president in May 2022. The head of government is Prime Minister Muhammad Bin Rashid Al Maktum. He assumed this office in January 2006. The cabinet of the UAE consists of the Council of Ministers. These ministers are appointed by the Prime Minister with the approval of the President. The president is elected by the Federal Supreme Council (FSC). The rulers of the seven emirates of the UAE are members of the FSC. The President is appointed for a 5-year term. Therefore, the next elections will be held in 2027. The Prime Minister of the UAE is appointed by the President. In the UAE, the FSC is regarded as the highest constitutional authority. The authority not only formulates general policies but also gives approval to the federal legislation. The FSC meetings are scheduled four times a year. The rulers of Abu Dhabi and Dubai can exercise veto power in the decision-making process of the UAE.

With the above executive setup, the UAE leaders have played a pivotal role in the nation building. They also believe that the current era is that of standardization and data-driven decision-making. Therefore, they have also developed a vision document in which the key pillars highlight the forward directions of the country. I will explain these vision documents in the last section of this chapter. The visionary leadership has been provided by the great leaders of the UAE by translating the vision document approaches into a comprehensive national agenda for the UAE. Based on the concepts of the vision document, the targets and indicators have also been setup that should be accomplished by the UAE within the stipulated time.

2.7. Key Leadership Strategies

The UAE leaders have adopted various leadership strategies that eventually shaped a modern UAE. All the UAE leaders have a futuristic approach and they envision how the UAE will look in the next 10 to 25 years. The vision documents of 2021 and 2031 are clear reflections of this leadership strategy. Moreover, the leaders possess self-confidence. They believe that whatever decisions they have made after consulting with all the stakeholders are in the best interest of the nation, and these indicators should be achieved with the set time and deadline. They also believe in the talent and skills of the UAE nation and do not hesitate to acquire the assistance of the foreign workforce if the project execution demands such expertise.

The third strategy pursued by the UAE leaders is a continued focus on innovation. They believe that the technological advancements will guide the outlook of the future cities. Therefore, significant investments have been made in the technology and infrastructure development projects. The current prime minister established the Dubai Internet City, as part of this leadership strategy, in October 1999.[ix] The establishment of Dubai Media City was also announced in 2000.

The UAE leaders also believe in learning as a continued process. They have established higher institutions of learning with the great academic facilities to develop a highly knowledgeable and skilled workforce. The leaders are also attached with their followers and they continuously engage with representatives of communities, business leaders, and corporate professionals to know their issues and resolve them at the earliest.

The UAE leaders also believe in effective communication. The leaders have their presence on social media so that they could reach the wider audience through the social networking sites. The UAE government and all UAE ministries have their websites that provide up-to-date information regarding the government activities. Another leadership approach of the UAE leaders is their focus on unity. They are believers of teamwork and collaboration and have never tried to wage war against any neighbor country. Instead, the leaders have always assisted in resolving the disputes of other countries as well.

Another unique quality of the UAE leaders is that they take calculated risks. When it comes to prosperity and development of the UAE, they do not believe in a conservative approach. When the UAE was just a fishing village, the UAE leaders focused on the oil exploration activities because they knew that the oil can be a major contributor to their country exports. As a result, the UAE became a prosperous country and this prosperity was visible in the emirates even before achieving independence in 1971. The UAE leaders have also encouraged the technology startups and technology projects even when other countries are fearful in taking risks in the projects based on emerging technologies. As an example, the UAE leaders permitted various projects based on blockchain technology and artificial intelligence.

The Dubai Land Department also launched a project to convert the real estate systems of the Dubai into blockchain technologies as shown in Figure 19 below:

DUBAI LAND DEPARTMENT REAL ESTATE BLOCKCHAIN

DETAILS OF THE ORGANIZATION
NAME
Dubai Land Department

COUNTRY
United Arab Emirates

WEBSITE (URL)
http://www.dubailand.gov.ae

TYPE
Governments

NATIONAL IMPLEMENTATION MECHANISM
- The organization has a strategy for coordinating WSIS Implementation at the national level: Yes
- The organization has a national e-strategy: Yes

INFORMATION ABOUT THE PROJECT

PROJECT TITLE
Dubai Land Department Real Estate Blockchain

TITLE ACRONYM
DLDRE Blockchain

DESCRIPTION
DLD provides outstanding services to all its customers whilst developing the necessary legislation to propel the real estate sector in Dubai, organizing and promoting real estate investment, and spreading industry knowledge. DLD has active organizations that include: RERA, the regulatory arm, Real Estate Investment Management & Promotion Center, Dubai Real Estate Institute, the educational arm, and Rental Dispute

Figure 19: Real Estate System based on Blockchain[lxi]

The description of the leadership strategies of the UAE leaders indicate that the leaders have a clear vision regarding the future directions of the UAE. They are committed and focused in their efforts. They encourage and welcome the new initiatives and believe that a nation can progress when all the citizens work towards the accomplishment of the overall objectives and the national priorities of the country.

2.8. UAE Vision

During the decade of 2020, there was an increased prominence of the new form of a gas known as shale gas. It was promoted as a good alternative of oil and a less expensive, environmentally friendly fuel source. The news quickly made headlines across the globe and the oil prices observed a significant decline. The oil prices also showed a decline during the covid-19 pandemic because the travelling through all means had reduced during the pandemic. As most of the countries in the Middle East were relying on oil exports for strengthening their economies, the decline in oil prices was a major source of concern for them. It was the leading reason that the Arab leaders realized that they need to change the strategic and economic directions of their countries and opt for economic diversification.

Another area of consideration was the leading inflow of immigrants. The Arab countries do not provide nationalities to foreign immigrants. However, still many foreigners come to these countries for better employment opportunities and better living conditions. It has been a win-win situation for the Arab countries because the technical jobs such as oil exploration activities and other labor work can be accomplished more effectively by utilizing foreign workforce. With the passage of time though, it also made it challenging for the local workforce to get good employment opportunities. Therefore, the UAE leaders in the new vision document have also considered the phenomenon of localization where the companies have been restricted to recruit a certain proportion of local workforce in all areas of operations.

The third area of consideration is the sustainability initiatives and the sustainable development goals of the United Nations. Under this vision, the UAE leaders also encouraged and promoted the use of renewable sources of energy to clean the environment and improve the carbon footprints of the country. The UAE has huge reserves of oil and gas that can easily meet the energy requirements of the country and also provide valuable foreign exchange to the country.

However, oil, gas, and coal increase carbon emissions in the environment. Due to the environmental pollution, the countries across the globe are encouraged to use the renewable sources of energy such as solar energy and wind energy. The UAE leaders have also focused on increasing the contribution of renewable energy in the industrial and commercial environment of the UAE.

These three factors; the economic diversification, the localization, and sustainability initiatives made the UAE leaders realize that a new strategic directions of the country should be developed in the form of a vision statement and document. Therefore, a formal document known as 'UAE Vision 2021' was developed. The development of a vision document is a proven and successful leadership strategy that is also being followed by Arab leaders of other countries. For example, a Saudi Vision 2030 document has also been developed.[lxii]

The UAE leaders have placed such a huge emphasis on vision development that a separate Vision 2021 website has been developed by the UAE government.[lxiii] The website shows UAE vision, national agenda, timeline of key events, team structure, and publications as shown in Figure 20 below:

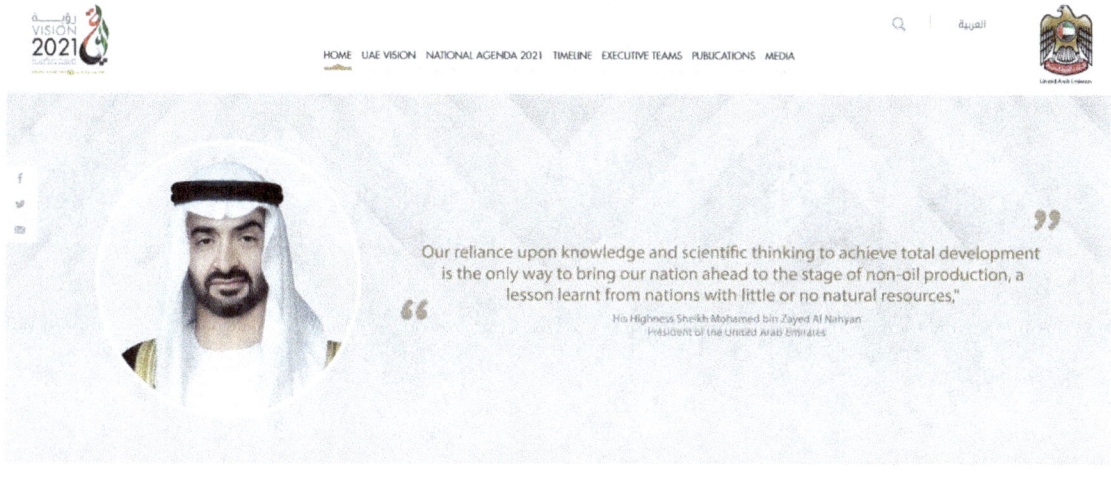

Figure 20: UAE Vision Website[lxiv]

UAE Vision was first presented by the prime minister. It was presented in 2010 in a cabinet meeting and the future directions of the UAE were presented in this vision document. The prime minister named the vision document Vision 2021 because the UAE got independence in 1971 and the year 2021 was the golden jubilee year for the UAE. Through the vision document, the UAE leaders set six key priorities for the UAE as shown in Figure 21 below:

NATIONAL PRIORITIES

Figure 21: Six National Priorities of the UAE[lxv]

According to the UAE leaders, the future directions of the UAE will be set as a competitive knowledge economy. To accomplish this objective, the quality of healthcare will be improved and world-class healthcare facilities will be provided. The economic diversification will be achieved by developing a competitive, knowledge-based economy. The judicial system will be based on fairness and speedy delivery of justice. An inclusive society will be promoted in the UAE and there will be a respect for the people with diverse cultural and religious orientations. The education system will meet the global standards and world class leaders will be developed in the institutions of higher learning. Efforts will be made for the development of a sustainable environment and a sustainable structure.

The targets of the UAE Vision 2021 were required to be accomplished by the golden jubilee of this great nation in 2021. After that, the UAE leaders felt that significant changes have occurred in the local and national outlook, and therefore, the strategic directions of the UAE should also be optimized accordingly. Therefore, a new vision document was developed that is known as 'We the UAE 2031' visionary approach.[lxvi]

The new vision document highlights that the UAE leaders always believe in a visionary approach and optimize the strategies based on the changing circumstances and ground realities. As shown in Figure 22 below, the new document has been introduced after a set of documents presented earlier by the UAE leaders:

33

Figure 22: Visionary Directions at Different Time Pointslxvii

The work program, aimed at introducing reforms in the corporate sector, was introduced in 2005. A comprehensive government strategy was announced in 2007. The vision for the next 10 years was announced in 2011. The conversion of vision concepts into the national agenda was accomplished in 2014. The year 2017 was a landmark year in the UAE history when the centennial document was presented by the UAE leader to highlight the strategic directions of the country up to the centennial year 2071 (UAE independence year 1971). The principle document for all the government and private entities was announced in 2021. Then the new vision document was announced in 2022.

In this vision document, the UAE leaders have set the strategic directions of the UAE for the next 10 years. Similar to six national priorities presented in the 2021 document, this document highlights the four national priorities for the UAE as shown in Figure 23 below:

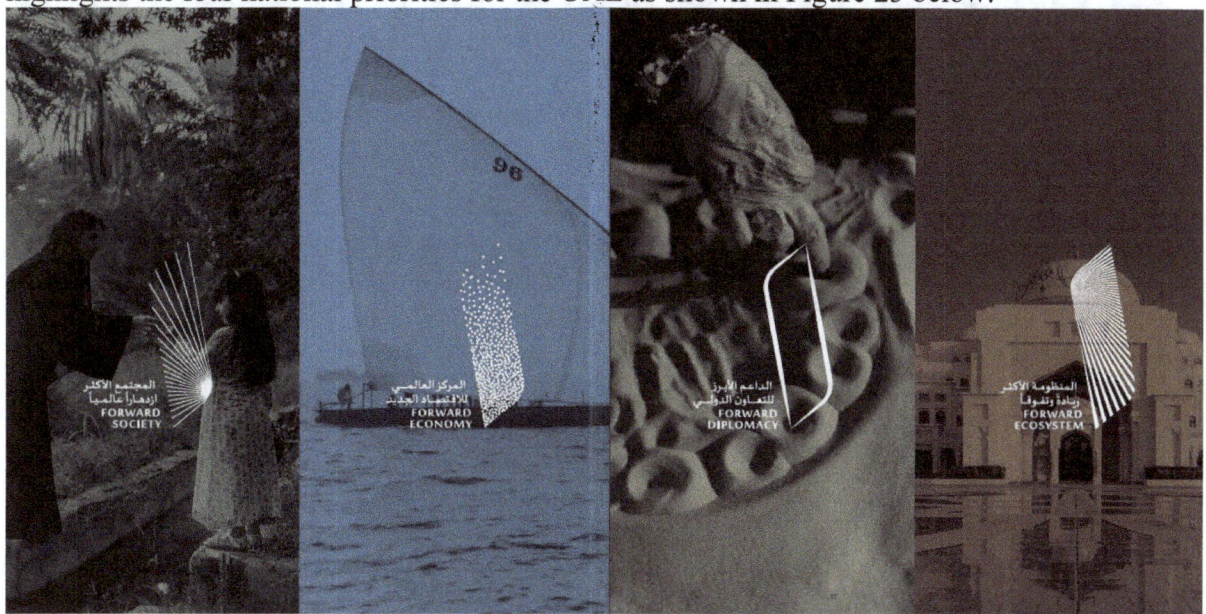

Figure 23: Four Pillars of the Vision Documentlxviii

The first pillar is called forward society. Under this visionary approach, the UAE leaders will focus on human capital development and build a tolerant, harmonic, and cohesive society. Advanced healthcare and education facilities will be accessible to all the citizens. The promise made in the vision document regarding forward society is shown in Figure 24 below:

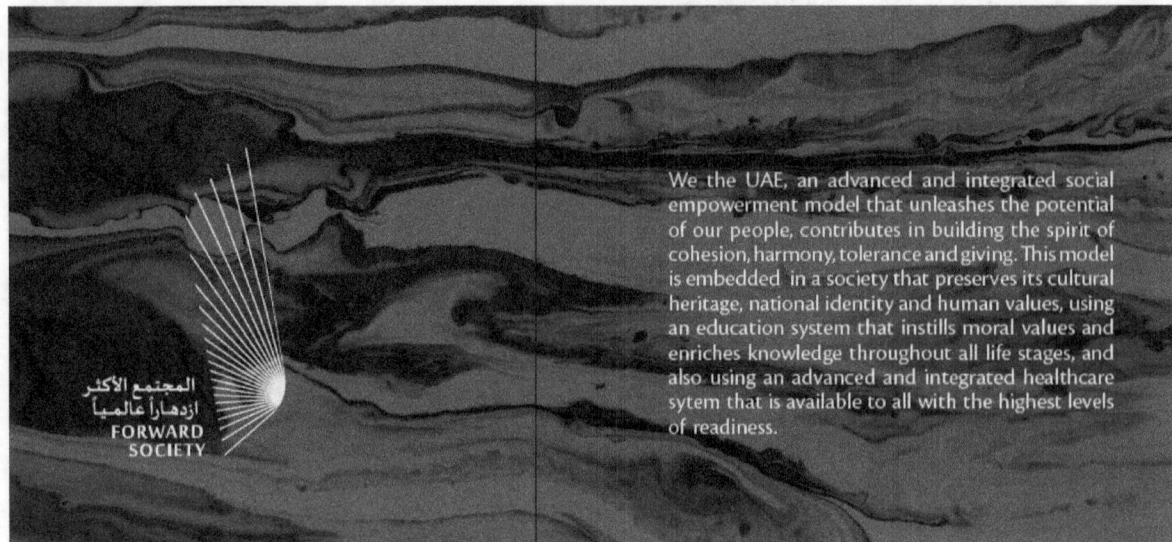

We the UAE, an advanced and integrated social empowerment model that unleashes the potential of our people, contributes in building the spirit of cohesion, harmony, tolerance and giving. This model is embedded in a society that preserves its cultural heritage, national identity and human values, using an education system that instills moral values and enriches knowledge throughout all life stages, and also using an advanced and integrated healthcare sytem that is available to all with the highest levels of readiness.

المجتمع الأكثر
ازدهاراً عالمياً
FORWARD
SOCIETY

Figure 24: Forward Society – The First Pillar[lxix]

The second pillar is called forward economy. Under this visionary approach, the UAE leaders will promote a competitive economy that will be based on the notion of diversification and the growth in the strategic areas. The innovation and technological advancement will be promoted at all levels and a global talent pool will be nurtured. The entrepreneurial activities and the role of the private sector will also be promoted in the UAE. The promise made in the vision document regarding forward economy is shown in Figure 25 below:

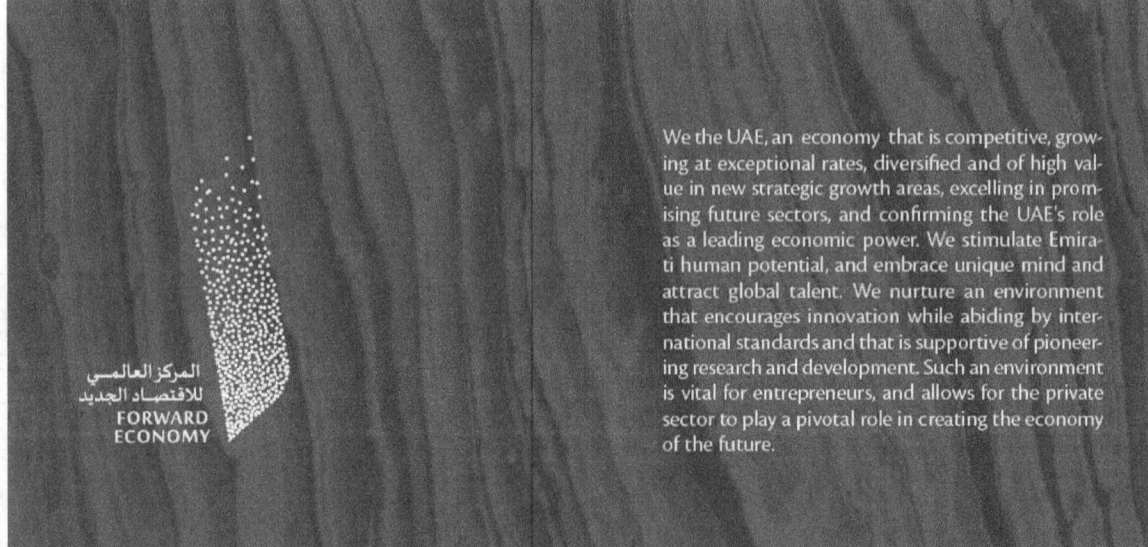

We the UAE, an economy that is competitive, growing at exceptional rates, diversified and of high value in new strategic growth areas, excelling in promising future sectors, and confirming the UAE's role as a leading economic power. We stimulate Emirati human potential, and embrace unique mind and attract global talent. We nurture an environment that encourages innovation while abiding by international standards and that is supportive of pioneering research and development. Such an environment is vital for entrepreneurs, and allows for the private sector to play a pivotal role in creating the economy of the future.

المركز العالمي
للاقتصاد الجديد
FORWARD
ECONOMY

Figure 25: Forward Economy – The Second Pillar[lxx]

The third pillar is called forward diplomacy. The UAE leaders will consider the national and regional interests in the national and global diplomacy. The international trade and partnerships will be executed with mutual trust and cooperation. The UAE will also play a leading role in the sustainability initiatives and ensure an emissions-free future for the country. The promise made in the vision document regarding forward diplomacy is shown in Figure 26 below:

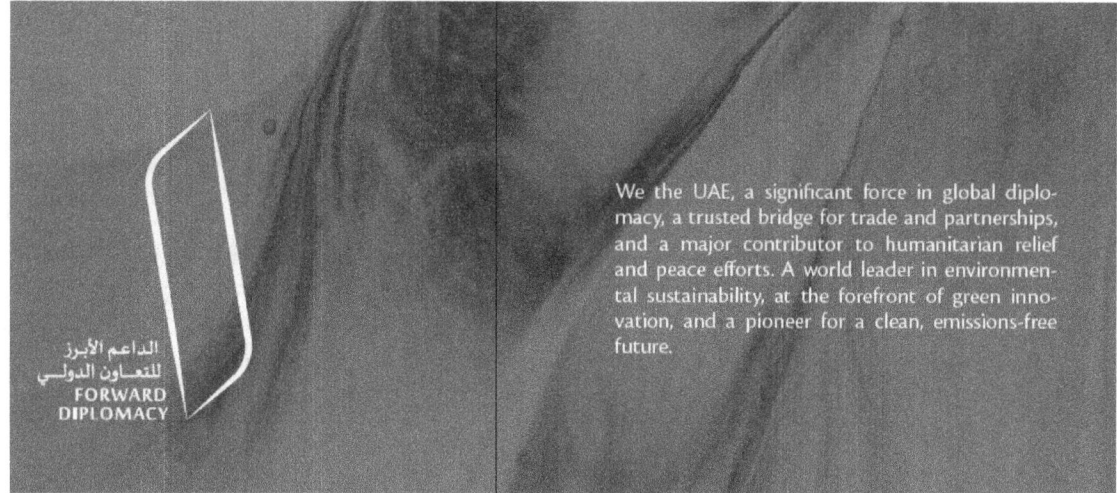

We the UAE, a significant force in global diplomacy, a trusted bridge for trade and partnerships, and a major contributor to humanitarian relief and peace efforts. A world leader in environmental sustainability, at the forefront of green innovation, and a pioneer for a clean, emissions-free future.

الداعم الأبرز
للتعاون الدولي
FORWARD
DIPLOMACY

Figure 26: Forward Diplomacy – The Third Pillar[lxxi]

The fourth pillar is called forward ecosystem. Under this visionary approach, the UAE leaders will ensure that UAE is the safest, secure, and the most connected country of the entire globe. The smart technologies and surveillance systems will be used in all the government and private sector domains and systems. The judicial system of the country will also be technologically equipped to preserve the human rights and dignity in a technology-advanced and a connected world environment. The promise made in the vision document regarding forward ecosystem is shown in Figure 27 below:

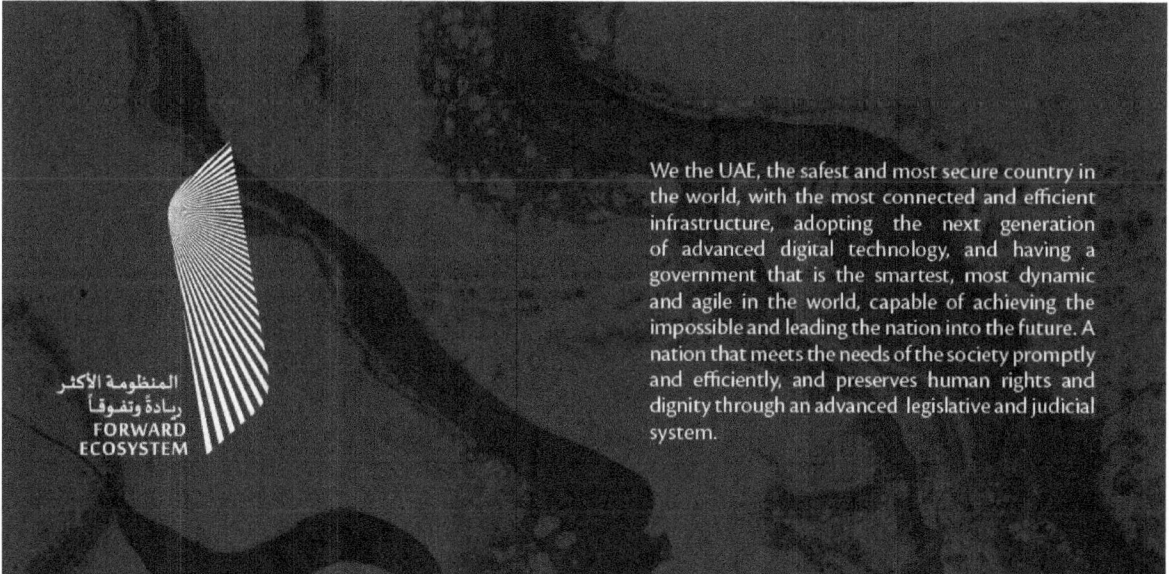

We the UAE, the safest and most secure country in the world, with the most connected and efficient infrastructure, adopting the next generation of advanced digital technology, and having a government that is the smartest, most dynamic and agile in the world, capable of achieving the impossible and leading the nation into the future. A nation that meets the needs of the society promptly and efficiently, and preserves human rights and dignity through an advanced legislative and judicial system.

المنظومة الأكثر
ريادةً وتفوقاً
FORWARD
ECOSYSTEM

Figure 27: Forward Ecosystem – The Fourth Pillar[lxxii]

According to the document, based on the four pillars, the vision document will be translated into a national agenda. The UAE leaders will guide the nation through this national agenda for the next 50 years. These factors highlight that the vision document is a highly significant document in the UAE context. Any individual who is interested in knowing how great leaders of UAE shaped a great country, and how they will lead the country over the next 50 years can get an idea from this vision document regarding the strategic directions of the UAE. The vision document was launched in November 2022 and the year mentioned on the document is vision 2031. Therefore, you can clearly anticipate the leadership approaches of the UAE through a comprehensive reading of the vision document.

The UAE leaders presented a vision document based on four pillars. The vision of the leaders is not limited to presenting the conceptual framework. The key national indicators have also been setup under this visionary approach so that the progress made on following the vision could be tracked through tangible outcomes. The key indicators presented based on the vision are mentioned in Figure 28 below:

Key national indicators of the vision

'We the UAE 2031' vision aims to:

- O   double the country's gross domestic product (GDP) from AED 1.49 trillion to AED 3 trillion

- O   generate AED 800 billion in non-oil exports

- O   raise the contribution of the tourism sector to the GDP to AED 450 billion

- O   raise the value of the UAE's foreign trade to AED 4 trillion

- O   rank the UAE as:

  - O   1st globally in developing proactive legislations for new economic sectors

  - O   oone of the top 10 countries globally in the 'Human Development Index'

  - O   oone of the top 10 countries globally in the quality of healthcare

- O   position the Emirati cities among the best 10 cities globally in the quality of life

- O   position the UAE globally

  - O   among the top 10 countries in attracting global talent

  - O   as first in the 'safety' index

  - O   as one of the top 10 countries in the 'Global Food Security Index'

  - O   as one of the top three countries in the 'Global Cybersecurity Index'.

Figure 28: Key Indicators based on the Vision 2031[lxxiii]

As highlighted in the figure above, the strength of any country in today's world is closely linked to its economy prosperity. Therefore, the first indicator is to double the GDP of the UAE in the next 10 years. The second target is based on the concept of economic diversification, whereby the UAE leaders want to increase the contribution of non-oil exports in the country. A large number of tourists visit the UAE each year, and the contribution of the tourism sector is expected to reach AED 450 billion.

The contribution of the foreign trade and investments will further be raised in the coming years. As the vision document is based on a forward-looking approach, the UAE leaders also want to improve the ranking of the UAE in various global indices. The UAE should lead in the development of regulatory frameworks for new areas of economic activity. It should stand among 10 countries in the global development index. It should also rank among the top countries for providing quality healthcare facilities.

The Emirati cities should be smart cities and rank among the top cities concerning the quality of life indicators. The global talent should also be attracted in the UAE universities, corporations, and other commercial sectors. The safety and security is the topmost priority of the UAE leaders and they want the UAE to be the first country in the global safety index. Regarding the food security, the UAE should stand among the top countries and its ranking should be among the top three in the cybersecurity index of the world.

The national theme for the UAE's Independence Day has been 'Spirit of the Union'.[lxxiv] The day is celebrated to remember the union of the emirates into an independent state from the UK rule. The founding father of the country always gave the message of unity. His kind-hearted behavior built a relationship of trust and confidence among the member emirates. This hospitality and courteous behavior can now be seen throughout the UAE. The residents meet with the people with great respect and often offer traditional dates and the Arabic tea. The UAE leaders believe that one can earn respect if one reciprocates the same. The leaders believe in providing equal opportunities and rights even to the minorities. In the UAE, you will not only find great mosques but also temples and churches. The leaders are the strong believers of tolerance, acceptance, and celebrating all cultures and colors.

3. Economic Transformation

The UAE leaders have always realized the significance of the economic strength of the country. The second pillar of the vision of the country is to build a forward economy. The first indicator of the UAE based on the four pillars of vision is to double the GDP of the UAE in the next 10 years. The second target is based on the concept of economic diversification, whereby the UAE leaders want to increase the contribution of non-oil exports in the country.

The UAE was once a fishing village and at that time too, the UAE leaders had realized that the country cannot prosper by relying on just one sector. The oil producing countries gain huge foreign revenues through oil exports but these revenues are not sustainable. When there is growth of using the alternate sources of energy, the demand for the oil will reduce. Moreover, when the price of oil increases sharply, people and businesses reduce the use of oil as the energy source due to the affordability factor. Therefore, the UAE leaders have envisioned that the country should explore alternate sources of income for a sustainable economy and continued revenue streams. In this chapter, I will highlight the emerging sectors that the UAE leaders are pursuing for investment and economic activity as part of their agenda of economic diversification.

3.1. Significance of Economic Diversification

The economic diversification is highly significant for the UAE in the current context because almost all of the Middle Eastern countries aim to reduce their reliance on oil exports. As I mentioned earlier, the UAE leaders have presented vision documents in different phases of their leadership journey. The presentation of multiple documents is aimed at optimizing the strategic directions based on the new and emerging realities. When the UAE was a fishing village and a pearling industry, the transformation to an oil-based economy was the need of the hour. However, the new realities demand diversification in other sectors of the economy. The economic experts have mentioned several areas where the economic activities can provide meaningful results to the UAE and other Middle Eastern countries. As shown in Figure 29 below, these emerging sectors are manufacturing sector, tourism sector, logistics and warehousing, pharmaceutical sector, renewable energy sector, and the technology sector. The UAE leaders have made investments in all of these sectors to provide more opportunities of businesses to the local and international investors.

Key Industries for Expansion

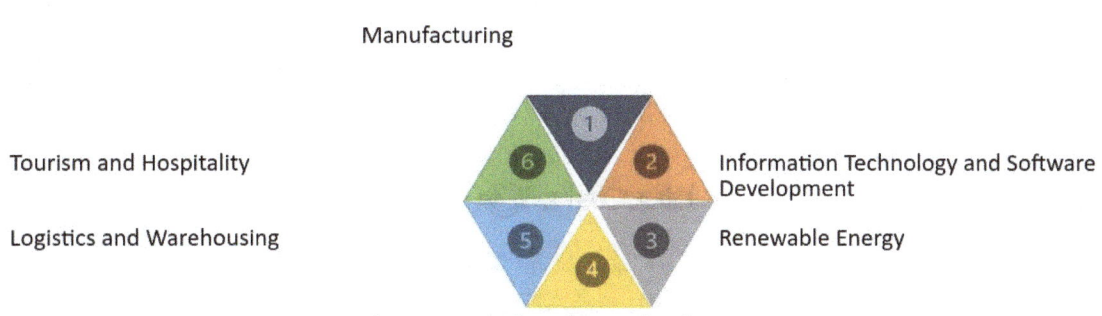

Figure 29: Key Industries for Economic Diversification[lxxv]

When the UAE leaders successfully achieve their agenda of economic diversification, the UAE will achieve various advantages and benefits as shown in Figure 30 below. There will be more job opportunities for the Emiratis and foreign immigrants. There will be an increased resilience in the UAE economy where the economy will not be affected by sudden fluctuations in the oil prices or the reduced demand of the oil. The UAE will be able to develop a knowledge-based economy as per the key pillars of the vision. The UAE leaders will be able to ensure the long-term growth of the country. The standard of living and quality of life indicators will be improved and the UAE will be able to improve its ranking as set forth in the key national indicators based on the new vision document.

Potential Impact of Economic Diversification on Local Economy and Employment

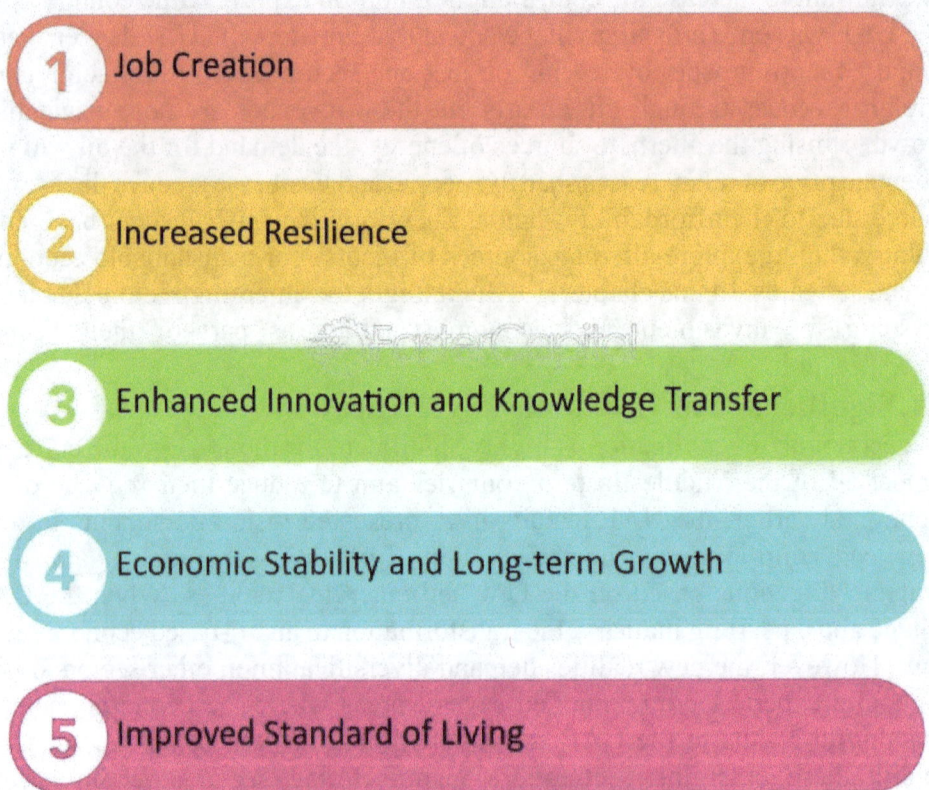

1. Job Creation
2. Increased Resilience
3. Enhanced Innovation and Knowledge Transfer
4. Economic Stability and Long-term Growth
5. Improved Standard of Living

Figure 30: Benefits of Economic Diversification[lxxvi]

One might argue that the economic diversification was needed in the Middle Eastern countries for quite long. Then, why the UAE leaders did not make hasty efforts in this domain. It is because the economic diversification is not a simple and easy task. The countries have faced various challenges and issues whenever they followed the path of economic diversification. Some of these challenges are highlighted in Figure 31 below:

Challenges and Solutions

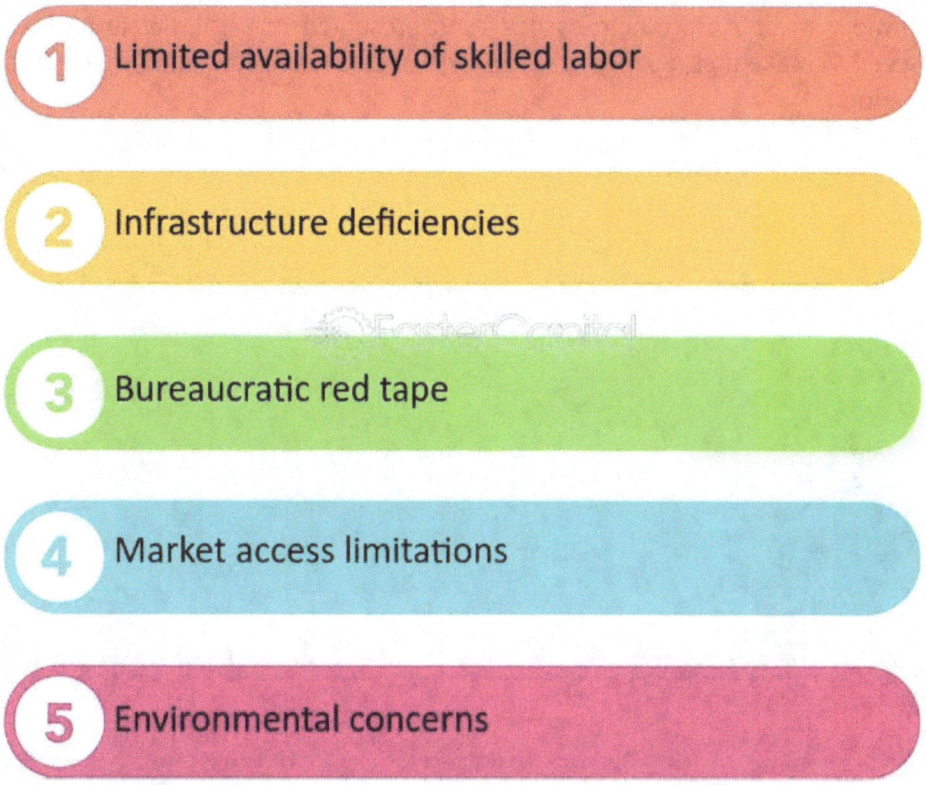

1	Limited availability of skilled labor
2	Infrastructure deficiencies
3	Bureaucratic red tape
4	Market access limitations
5	Environmental concerns

Figure 31: Challenges in Economic Diversification[lxxvii]

As highlighted above, when the countries pursue the path of economic diversification, they do not find an appropriate and skilled labor for the new business. It is because the academic institutes mostly offer specialization in those areas for which the students find a scope and viable job opportunities. The UAE might then have to rely on the foreign workforce that is not only quite expensive but also negates the spirit of localization ass the strategic direction of the country.

The second challenge is the deficiencies and limitations in the existing infrastructure. For example, one of the industries in which the UAE leaders have opted for economic diversification is the technology industry. The advanced technological systems are now based on AI-driven systems and Internet of Things concepts. These systems can only work when the underlying IT infrastructure provides a good level of connectivity and can process a large volume of data. Sensors may also be attached to the devices for predictive maintenance and identifying risks of failures. Therefore, infrastructure deficiencies can affect the initiatives of economic diversification.

The third challenge is bureaucratic hurdles. This is one area where the UAE will face the least challenge because as I explained to you earlier, all government and private entities have an active presence on their corporate websites and social media channels. The fourth challenge of market access limitations is also not going to affect the UAE much because the Middle Eastern region is itself a big market for all the industries and sectors where the UAE is pursuing economic diversification.

The fifth challenge of environmental concerns should also be viewed by the UAE leaders. When the reliance on oil exports and oil consumption are reduced, it will have a good impact on the environment. However, the penetration in the new markets can still pollute the environment. For example, the AI-based systems require fast-processing computers, systems, and even satellite-based internet connections. The use of these advanced systems may increase the carbon footprint of the UAE. The UAE leaders have set the target of net zero emissions in the next years. Therefore, the carbon footprints of the UAE should be regularly monitored by the environmental bodies of the UAE.

3.2. Transition from Oil-based to Diversified Economy

A projection of Arab countries has been presented in a journal article as to how they will proceed to make their economies, non-oil-based economics. The projection is shown in Figure 32 below:

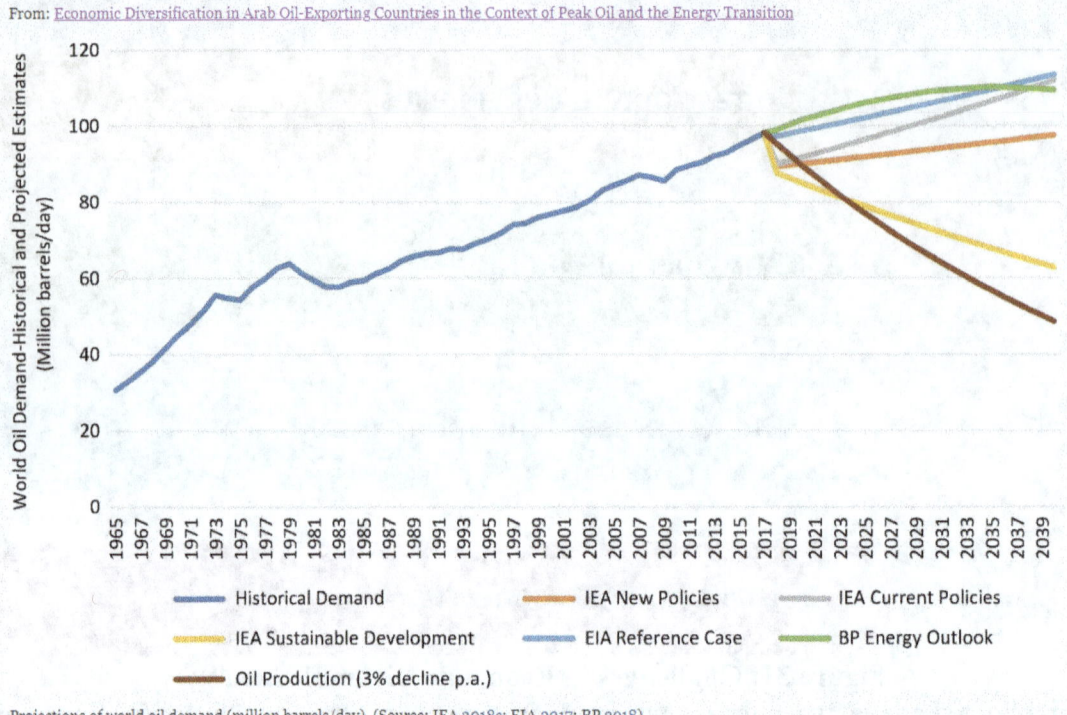

From: Economic Diversification in Arab Oil-Exporting Countries in the Context of Peak Oil and the Energy Transition

Projections of world oil demand (million barrels/day). (Source: IEA 2018c; EIA 2017; BP 2018)

Figure 32: Factors affecting the Oil Demand[lxxviii]

The above figure indicates that there will be a significant decline in the oil demand compared to the historical demand. The declining trend is being observed since 2017 and several factors have caused this decline. The new policies enforced by the International Energy Agency (IEA) have also restricted the quota of each oil-producing country including the UAE. The current policies of this agency have also emerged as a significant barrier to the oil demand. The sustainable development goals formulated by IEA have made a sharp decline in the oil demand because these goals promote the renewable sources of energy. The oil producing countries have also been asked to reduce their oil production (3% per annum) so that there is a level playing field for all oil-producing countries and the oil exports are not dominated by one country as the largest exporter to the world.

All these factors necessitate that the UAE also make a transition from an oil-based economy to a diversified economy. Significant efforts have been made on this front so far. However, as I explained earlier, there are also challenges associated with economic diversification. Therefore, the penetration in other sectors will take some time to be successful. It is a prudent strategy that the UAE leaders have incorporated the economic diversification in key national indicators so that the progress in this regard could be monitored periodically. The transition curves of different countries have been mentioned in a journal article as shown in Figure 33 below:

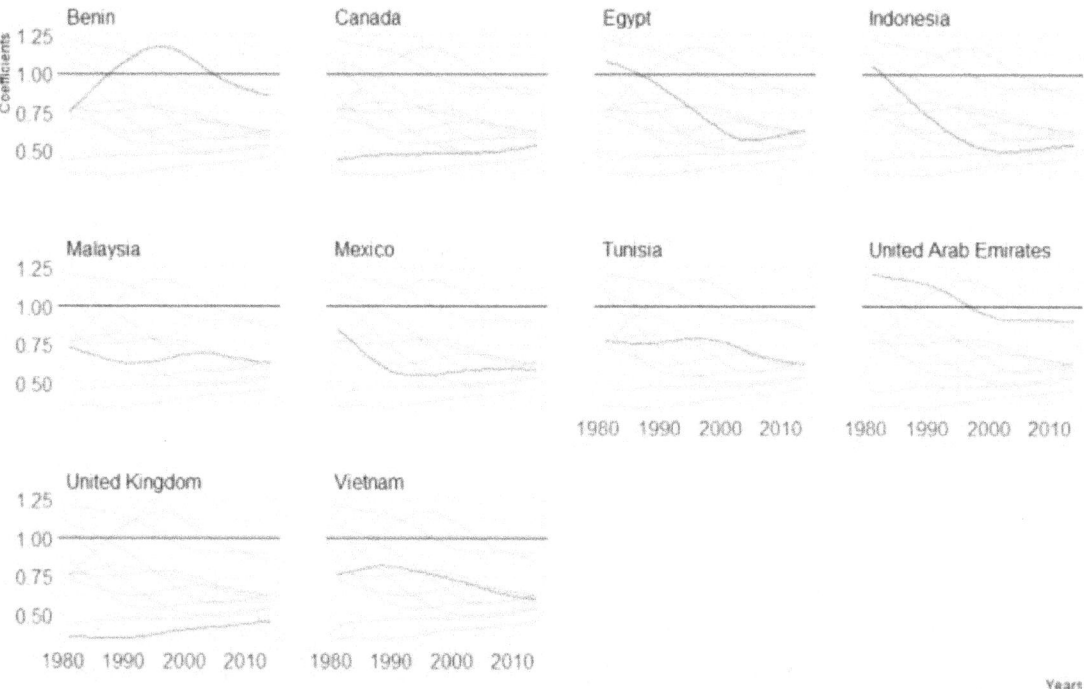

Figure 33: Transition to Oil-Based Economy[lxxix]

The above figure makes it evident that in 1980, the UAE was heavily reliant on oil exports and the value of coefficient was close to 1.25. However, up to 2010, the UAE has reduced this dependency and the level of reliance reduced to below 1.0. Ideally, the UAE leaders should develop the country close to Canada, where there is a reliance on oil exports close to 0.50, and this reduced reliance has been maintained over the years. The other lines in the case of Canada show that there are also many other sectors whose contribution in the economy has exceeded the coefficient value of 1.00. The same level of economic diversification should be achieved by the UAE.

The demand of oil is going to decline inevitably and some projections have reported a significant decline in the demand by 2040. Other agencies have showed a moderate level of decline; however, there is a consensus in all of these cases that the demand will decline, and no circumstances can maintain the demand of oil at current level as shown in Figure 34 below:

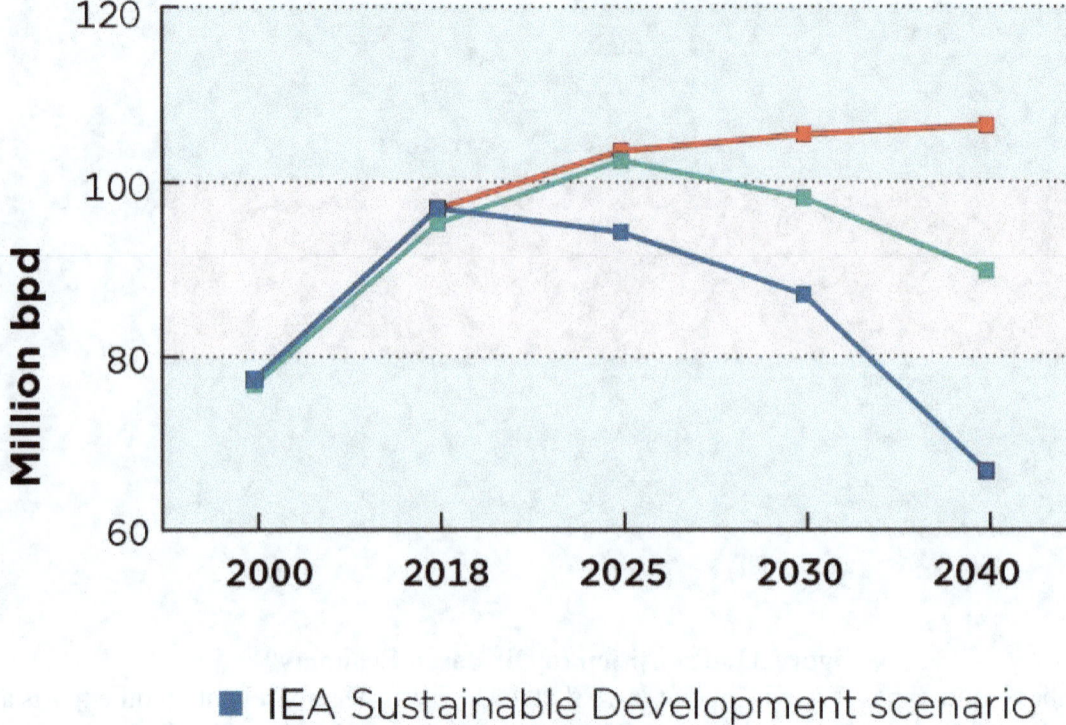

Long-term oil demand forecasts

- IEA Sustainable Development scenario
- Shell's Sky scenario
- IEA Stated Policies scenario

SOURCE: International Energy Agency and Shell

Figure 34: Oil Demand Forecasts[lxxx]

The above figure indicates a decline in demand based on the estimates of IEA Development, Shell, and IEA Stated Scenario. Therefore, as envisioned by the UAE leaders, the transition of the UAE economy and economic diversification is the only way forward for the UAE. When this transition occurs, the revenues of oil and gas companies in the Arab countries may also decline because the economic activities will be directed in other areas. Therefore, it will be prudent for oil and gas companies to focus on those areas that will remain profitable even in the new scenario. Figure 35 below shows some of these areas:

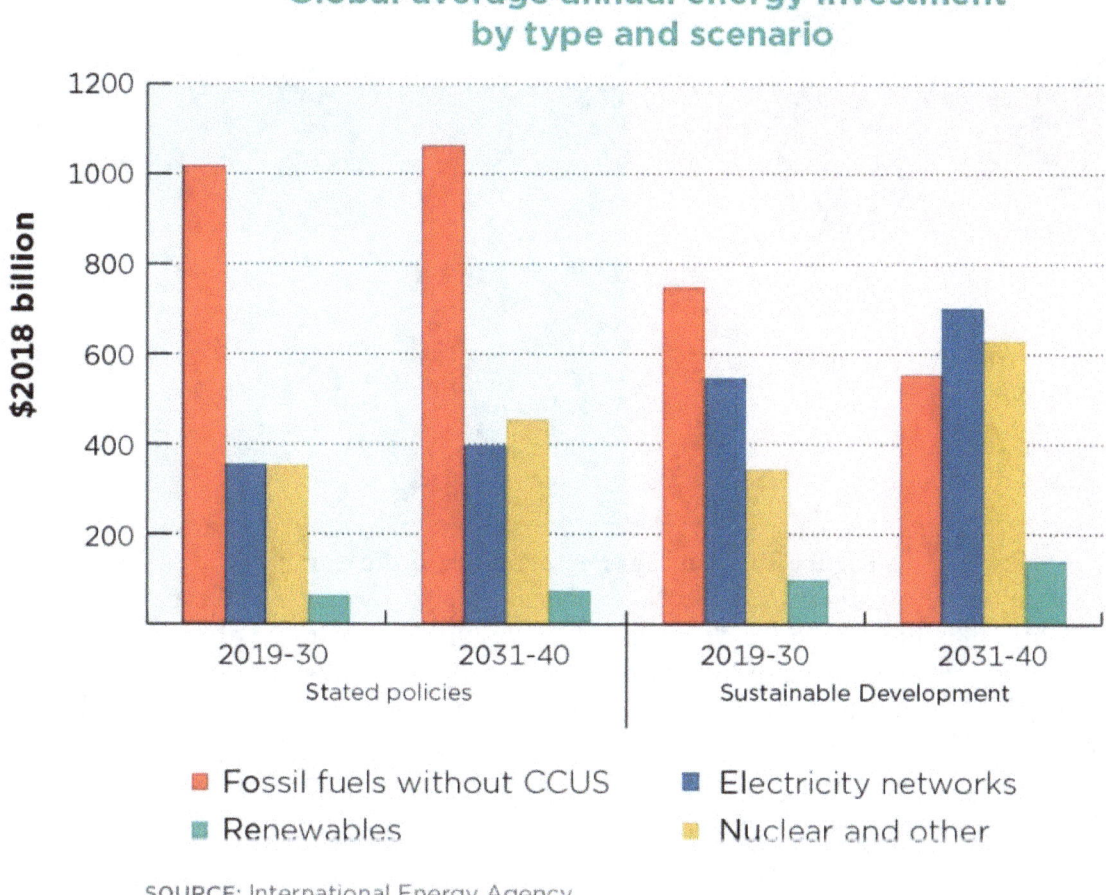

Figure 35: New Areas of Intervention for Energy Companies[lxxxi]

The above figure highlights that in the context of sustainable development, the reliance on fossil fuels will be reduced significantly during 2031-40. However, there will be a sharp increase in the demand of electricity networks, renewables, and nuclear energy. Therefore, oil and gas companies should also focus on these areas of energy management so that their business remains resilient and sustainable in the new national priorities set by the UAE leaders.

3.3. Emerging Sectors of the Economy – Tourism

Tourism is one area where it was comparatively easy for the UAE leaders to boost the sector as part of the economic diversification. It is because various visitors were already attracted to visiting the UAE for their personal and business reasons. Various international tournaments and exhibitions are also held in the UAE that enable the inflow of a large number of foreign tourists in the UAE.

According to the official website of the UAE Ministry related to the economy, the tourism sector contributed AED 167 billion to the GDP in 2022 that makes the contribution of this sector 9%. However, the contribution of the sector was also 9% in 2020 that shows that the tourism sector should further be developed as part of the agenda of economic diversification. The key indicators of the tourism sector in the UAE for the past year (2022) are shown in Figure 36 below:

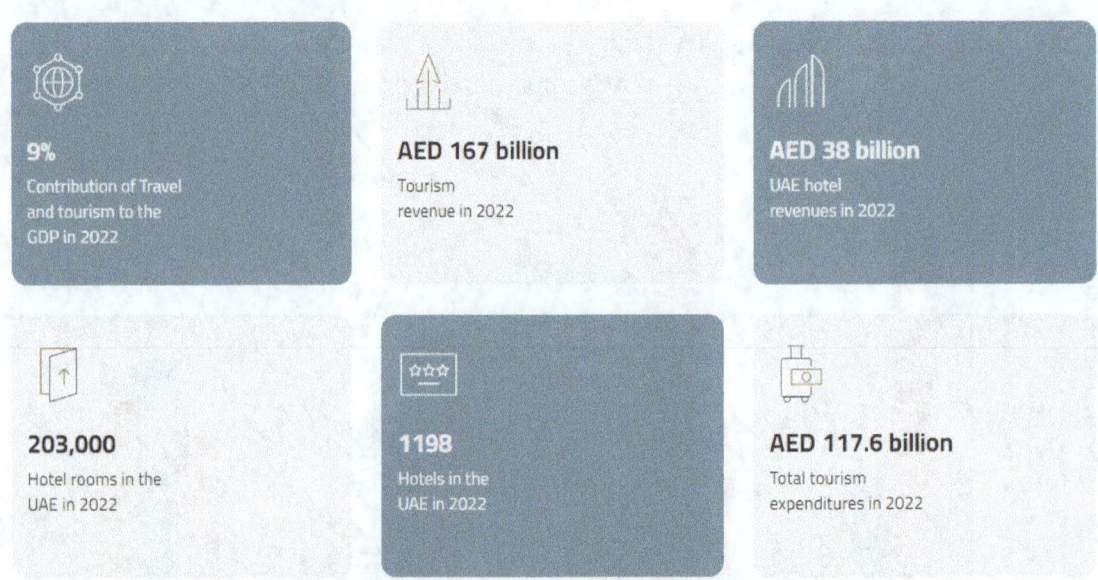

Figure 36: Tourism Performance Indicators[lxxxii]

The figure above highlights that the UAE hotels are also earning significant revenues and earned AED 38 billion in 2022. If this sector observes further growth, the revenues of the hotels will also grow and more employment opportunities will be generated in the hospitality sector. It should also be noted that a total of AED 117.6 billion were spent as tourism expenditures. It shows a commitment of the government to boost this sector and strengthen its contribution in the GDP. The UAE still ranks 25 in the tourism development index as shown in Figure 37 below:

Tourism Sector Indicators in 2020

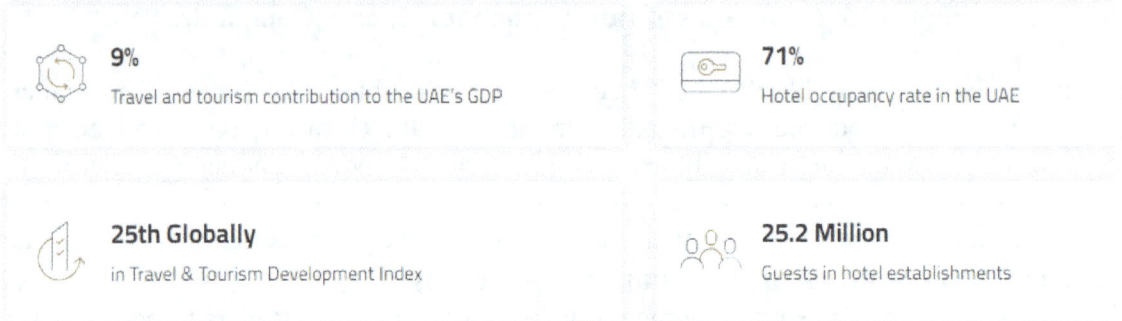

Figure 37: Indicators of the Tourism Sector[lxxxiii]

The above figure shows that there is still a lot of improvement needed in the tourism sector because the 25th rank does not match the standards of the UAE where the country has acquired key rankings in the other areas and the key national indicators ask to secure top 10 positions in various new and emerging domains.

3.4. Emerging Sectors of the Economy – Finance

Various key initiatives and institutions have been developed by the UAE leaders to strengthen the role of the financial sector and increase its contribution in the total GDP of the country. The banking systems and policies are regulated by the Central Bank. The UAE leaders believe in the principles of a free market economy and three stock markets are operational in the country including the Nasdaq, Abu Dhabi Exchange, and Financial Market.[lxxxiv]

The government-owned investment institutions offer various instruments and investment opportunities to the citizens. A summarized view of the current financial strategies of the government is shown in Figure 38 below:

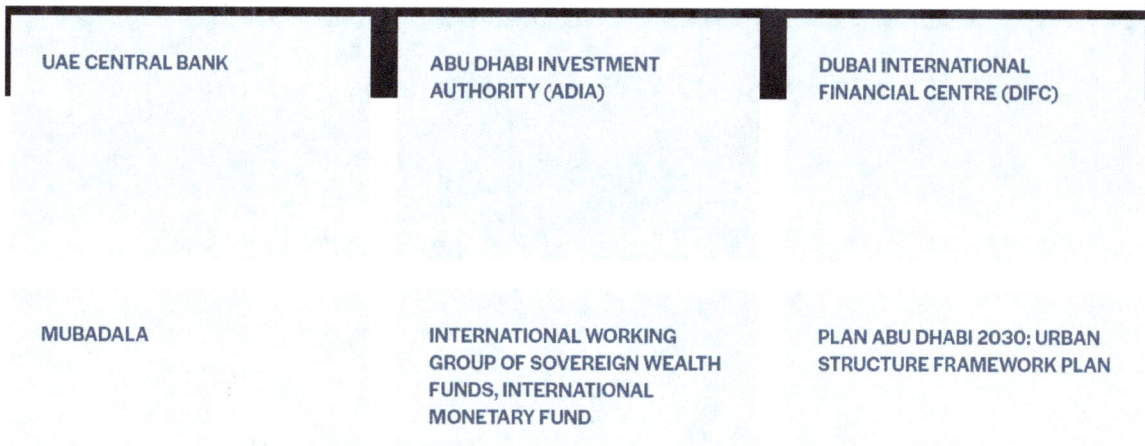

UAE CENTRAL BANK	ABU DHABI INVESTMENT AUTHORITY (ADIA)	DUBAI INTERNATIONAL FINANCIAL CENTRE (DIFC)
MUBADALA	INTERNATIONAL WORKING GROUP OF SOVEREIGN WEALTH FUNDS, INTERNATIONAL MONETARY FUND	PLAN ABU DHABI 2030: URBAN STRUCTURE FRAMEWORK PLAN

Figure 38: Key Financial Players and Instruments[lxxxv]

The above figure highlights that ADIA is an investment authority that invests the funds of their clients for a long-term value creation.[lxxxvi] DIFC was introduced in 2004, and it is regarded as a free zone for financial transactions. The investors get various incentives and tax benefits in this tax regime of the UAE. Mubadala performs as a sovereign investor in the UAE and manages the assets of the clients in the UAE and also outside the UAE.[lxxxvii] There is also an urban structural framework plan developed for the Abu Dhabi Emirate.

The contribution of the financial sector should also be further increased. The banking sector should provide loans to the new investors and startups on attractive rates to increase the investment in other sectors of the economy. The incubation centers and startup funding should also be increased at the levels of the government and the private sector.

3.5. Emerging Sectors of the Economy – Renewable Energy

The renewable energy is one sector that should particularly be focused by the UAE government. As I explained earlier, the revenues of oil and gas companies in the Arab countries may decline because the economic activities will be directed in other areas. Therefore, it will be prudent for oil and gas companies in the UAE to focus on those areas that will remain profitable even in the new scenario. The renewable energy is definitely one of those sectors that can be tapped by the companies dealing in the energy sector.

As part of the strategic directions of the economic diversification, the UAE leaders established the Abu Dhabi Future Energy Company Masdar way back in 2006. Masdar was also announced as the first city with carbon-neutral status.[lxxxviii] Other initiatives were also launched by the UAE leaders including the acceptance of the UAE in 2016 to sign the Paris agreement.[lxxxix]

It has been estimated by the UAE trade ministry that the renewable energy sector will observe an average growth of 16.7% for the period 2021-2030.[xc] If this growth target is achieved, then it will be even a larger contribution than the tourism sector whose current contribution in the GDP is 9%. According to the renewables report of the UAE, the country will increase the consumption of green hydrogen and solar energy to enable further growth of the renewables sector.

UAE 2050 energy goals

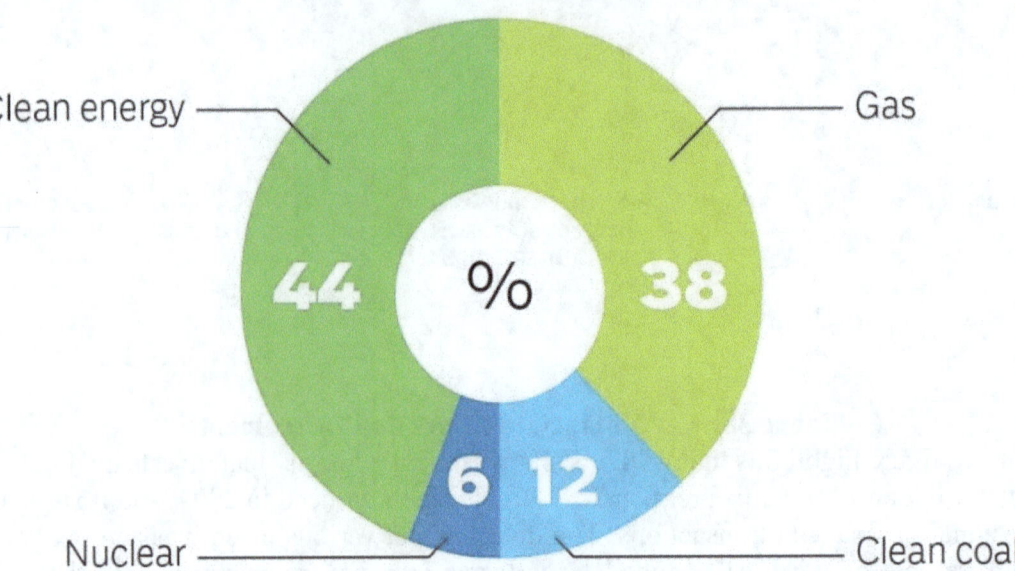

Clean energy — 44 % — Gas 38

Nuclear — 6 — 12 — Clean coal

Figure 39: Future Energy Goals of the UAE[xci]

The future energy goals of the UAE have been mentioned in a 2050 strategy document as shown in Figure 39 above. According to this strategy, the UAE leaders aim to create an energy mix for the UAE where the contribution of the clean energy sources will be increased in the overall energy consumption. It will account for 44% of the total energy use. The next energy leader will be gas with a contribution of 38%. The use of coal and nuclear sources will be reduced.

The strategy also sets targets for the economic strengthening and development of the renewable sector. According to these targets, new green jobs to the count of 50,000 will be introduced in the UAE by 2030. The capacity of the renewable energy will be increased by three times. The contribution of the clean energy will be raised by 30%. The UAE has been set to achieve the status of a carbon-neutral country by 2050.[xcii]

Another landmark initiative launched by the UAE leaders in the context of renewable energy is the establishment of Barakah Nuclear Energy Plant as shown in Figure 40 below:

Figure 40: Barakah Energy Plant[xciii]

The agreement regarding the above nuclear plant is popularly known as 123 agreement. This agreement was made in March 2021. One unit of this nuclear plant has already been made operational. The plan provides clean energy to the residents of the UAE round the clock. Unit two and three of this plan were also linked to the national grid of the UAE in 2022. When all four units of this plant operate at the commercial level, the plan will meet 25% of the electricity requirements of the UAE residents.[xciv]

These initiatives highlight that the UAE leaders have acknowledged the significance of clean and renewable energy. The contribution of this sector is expected to increase sharply in the coming years and it will be consistent with the visionary approach and strategic directions of the UAE leaders. The increased contribution will facilitate the goal of economic diversification of the UAE.

3.6. Emerging Sectors of the Economy – HealthCare

The ministry of economy has highlighted that there is a significant growth potential in the healthcare sector of the UAE as shown in Figure 41 below. The government entities and the private sector should tap these opportunities to strengthen the businesses and promote the agenda of economic diversification in the UAE.

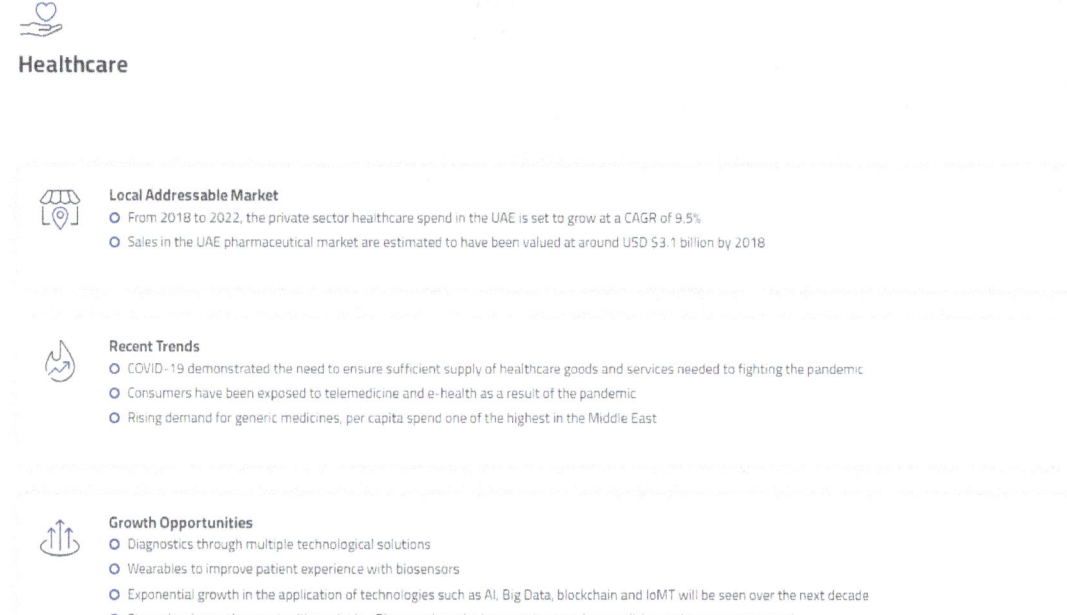

Figure 41: Indicators of Healthcare Sector[xcv]

The above figure indicates that there is a significant spending by the private sector on the provision of healthcare facilities and a growth rate of 9.5% was observed for 2018-22. The pharmaceutical market also has a significant growth potential and the market was valued at $3.1 billion in 2018.

The covid-19 pandemic also increased the demand for healthcare goods and accessories. The individuals and care providers realized that the essential supplies should be readily available because it has become a matter of life and death. The telemedicine and e-health initiatives were also welcomed by the customers in large numbers due to the requirement of social distancing. The demand for generic medicines also increased during the pandemic.

According to the healthcare ministry, these recent trends offer various growth opportunities for the companies in the UAE. The healthcare providers should offer diagnostics through various mechanisms by making use of the advanced technological tools. The technological gadgets such as wearables should be used to enrich the experience of the patients. The AI tools and technologies should be used in the healthcare sector for improving the provision of care. There are also various local growth opportunities in the UAE in the domain of ecommerce and epharma.

By tapping all these growth opportunities, the growth of healthcare sector should also be enabled in the UAE to the extent that it becomes a major contributor in the UAE economy. The economic diversification can be achieved effectively by including the healthcare sector as a major enabler.

3.7. Increased Job Opportunities through Localization

The phenomenon of localization in the UAE context is known as Emiratisation. As per this conceptual framework, the first priority of the UAE leaders is to ensure the employment for the UAE citizens. In this regard, a council has been made by the UAE leaders that is called Nafis.[xcvi] The primary objective of this council is to increase the employment of UAE nationals in the private sector.

The population of the UAE is 9,973,449 (approximately 10 million) and the country ranks 92 in the world population index. The local Emiratis are only 11.6% of the total population. South Asians are the majority population of the UAE making up 59.4% of the total population. South Asians include Pakistanis, Indians, and Bangladeshis. Other ethnic groups include Egyptians and Filipinos. If even 11.6% of the local Emiratis do not get good employment opportunities, then it becomes an area of concern for the UAE leaders and Nafis has been developed for this purpose to increase the participation of the Emiratis in the workforce.

The target given to the Nafis is that at least 75,000 UAE citizens should be included in the workforce of the private sector in the next five years.[xcvii] Those private sector institutions that offer employment to the Emiratis will also be offered incentives by Nafis.

The emiratization is not just a guideline by Nafis but a mandatory requirement to be followed by all private sector companies. This requirement has been classified into two categories for the private sector. Those companies that employ 50 or more employees fall under the first category and the requirement for these companies is mentioned in Figure 42 and Figure 43.

Rate of Emiratisation - (Companies with 50 or more workers)

The Cabinet approved a decision to raise Emiratisation rates to 2 per cent annually for skilled jobs in private sector establishments with 50 or more employees and to achieve an overall rate of increase by 10 per cent by 2026. This is accompanied by granting incentives to institutions that perform qualitatively in the training and employment of citizens.

To support the commitment to achieve the above employment targets for nationals, non-compliant companies will have to pay an amount of AED 6,000 monthly, starting from January 2023, for every citizen who has not been employed. The amount will be paid through the digital systems of Ministry of Human Resources and Emiratisation (MoHRE), provided that the value of the monthly contributions increases by AED 1,000 annually until 2026. To monitor the implementation of these decisions in the labour market, MoHRE is working with the Cabinet Secretariat to measure the indicator of Emiratisation in the private sector.

Figure 42: Emiratisation – Category One[xcviii]

The above figure shows that for the category one, the count of Emiratis in the private sector workforce for the skilled jobs should be at least 2 percent. This rate should be increased by 10% by 2026. If the private sector companies fail to achieve this rate, they will have to face a penalty of AED 6,000 per month per unemployed UAE citizen.

Expansion of the Emiratisation targets - (Companies with 20 to 49 workers)

Starting in 2024, private sector companies with a workforce of 20 to 49 workers will be required to hire at least one UAE citizen and from 2025, they would be required to hire at least two Emirati citizens. Previously, this mandate applied only to companies with 50 or more employees.

This requirement is applicable to companies operating in the following 14 sectors:
1. information and communications
2. financial and insurance activities
3. real estate activities
4. professional, scientific and technical activities
5. administrative and support services
6. education
7. healthcare and social work activities
8. arts and entertainment
9. mining and quarrying industry
10. manufacturing
11. construction
12. wholesale and retail trade
13. transportation and warehousing
14. Hospitality services.

Companies with 20 to 49 workers that fail to employ at least one Emirati in 2024 will have to pay a financial contribution of AED 96,000 to the government. This contribution will increase to AED 108,000 for companies that have not employed two Emiratis by 2025.

Figure 43: Emiratisation – Category Two[xcix]

Earlier, the Emiratisation requirement was only applicable to the category one, i.e. the companies having 50 or more employees. However, with the growth of startup companies in the UAE, Nafis has expanded the scope of this requirement to the companies that employ 20 to 49 employees. This category two will come into effect from January 2024. These companies are required to hire one or two Emriatis in their workforce as a minimum requirement. If they fail to comply with this requirement, they will face a penalty of AED 96,000 in 2024 and the penalty will be enhanced to AED 108,000 in 2025.

In a recent development, an investment fund in Abu Dhabi, RedBird IMI, announced that it would take over the famous UK newspaper and media group Telegraph. According to Arab News, this deal was announced on November 20, 2023 and RedBird will pay $750 million for acquiring Telegraph Media Group.[c] The CEO of RedBird is Jeff Zucker as shown in Figure 44 below. He also worked in a leadership capacity at CNN. It is also a significant development in the context of localization and will provide new opportunities to the Emiratis to build their careers in media outlets and newsrooms.

Figure 44: Telegraph Deal by RedBird[ci]

The above deal also provides a way out for Telegraph because according to the New York Post, the Telegraph group had gone bankrupt due to the lower demand and severe economic conditions. The Telegraph group is owned by Barclay family and this deal will also enable them to repay their debts that are long due to Lloyd group. The deal also includes the acquisition of the magazine Spectator that is being published since 1828. The administration of RedBird has made it clear that the current editorial team will not be removed from their posts. However, when the business expansion is pursued by the group, there will definitely be new and attractive opportunities for the Emiratis because the Telegraph group has been acquired by an Abu-Dhabi-backed investment fund.

The above examples of the emerging sectors indicate that the UAE leaders have made every possible effort for the transition from oil-based economy to a diversified economy. Significant progress has been achieved already in various industries. However, there is still a lot of work to be done for creating a sustainable economic future of the UAE population. The future initiatives are expected to further improve the contributions of these sectors in the GDP of the UAE.

4. Technological Advancement and Technology Hub

The use of technology has now become a competitive advantage not only for the organizations and industries but also for the countries. The countries not embracing technology can never become leaders in any area or field. Therefore, the UAE leaders have always encouraged the initiatives related to the technological advancement and development. Dubai Expo is a leading example in this regard. It is one of the most famous exhibition featuring the state-of-the-art technologies, products, and services.

When the Arab Spring captured the Arab world, the UAE remained unaffected from this wave of revolution. It was possible due to the steadfastness and committed approach of the UAE leaders. The vulnerable communities had been empowered through technological tools and systems.

Another initiative that helped the UAE in achieving the remarkable progress is the Ghadan 21 reforms. Through this reform package, the ruler of the Abu Dhabi promoted business and ecotourism in the emirate. As per the reform package, a new licensing regime was introduced in the UAE. The technology developers can now apply for an instant license and they will be allowed to conduct technology-led businesses in the emirate and contribute to the technological advancement of the emirate. The technology infrastructure and projects of the UAE provide a global leadership to the UAE in the technological advancement.

The year 2021 was a landmark year in the history of the UAE when Sheikh Mohammed bin Rashid directed the government institutions and agencies to implement the 10 core principles of the UAE in all their plans and strategies. These 10 principles were named as Principles of the 50 because Sheikh Mohammed bin Rashid believes that these 10 principles will be applicable and relevant for the next 50 years. The seventh principle mentions that the future development of the UAE will be powered by the advanced tools and technologies. It shows the commitment and long-term orientation of the UAE leaders that technological advancement can be a game changer for the country.

The UAE leaders have adopted various leadership strategies that eventually shaped a modern UAE. All the UAE leaders have a futuristic approach and they envision how the UAE will look in the next 10 to 25 years. I have mentioned various leadership strategies adopted by the UAE leaders in the previous section that shaped a great country. One of these strategies pursued by the UAE leaders is a continued focus on innovation. They believe that the technological advancements will guide the outlook of the future cities. Therefore, significant investments have been made in the technology and infrastructure development projects. The current prime minister established the Dubai Internet City, as part of this leadership strategy, in October 1999. The establishment of Dubai Media City was also announced in 2000.

The UAE leaders have also encouraged the technology startups and technology projects even when other countries are fearful in taking risks in the projects based on emerging technologies. As an example, the UAE leaders permitted various projects based on blockchain technology and artificial intelligence. The Dubai Land Department also launched a project to convert the real estate systems of the Dubai into blockchain technologies.

The UAE leaders are committed that the innovation and technological advancement will be promoted at all levels and a global talent pool will be nurtured. The entrepreneurial activities and the role of the private sector will also be promoted in the UAE. The fourth pillar in the new vision document of the UAE is called forward ecosystem. Under this visionary approach, the UAE leaders will ensure that UAE is the safest, secure, and the most connected country of the entire globe. The smart technologies and surveillance systems will be used in all the government and private sector domains and systems. The judicial system of the country will also be technologically equipped to preserve the human rights and dignity in a technology-advanced and a connected world environment.

In the previous chapter, I also described the economic diversification agenda of the UAE and the emerging sectors that the UAE leaders have selected for increasing their contribution in the GPD of the UAE. These emerging sectors are manufacturing sector, tourism sector, logistics and warehousing, pharmaceutical sector, renewable energy sector, and the technology sector. The UAE leaders have made investments in all of these sectors to provide more opportunities of businesses to the local and international investors.

The technology-based implementations also pose challenges regarding the deficiencies and limitations in the existing infrastructure. The advanced technological systems are now based on AI-driven systems and Internet of Things concepts. These systems can only work when the underlying IT infrastructure provides a good level of connectivity and can process a large volume of data. Sensors may also be attached to the devices for predictive maintenance and identifying risks of failures. Therefore, infrastructure deficiencies can affect the initiatives of economic diversification. The UAE leaders are also striving to overcome these limitations and develop a robust IT infrastructure.

The UAE leaders also aim to integrate the healthcare sector with the advanced tools and technologies. The healthcare providers should offer diagnostics through various mechanisms by making use of the advanced technological tools. The technological gadgets such as wearables should be used to enrich the experience of the patients. The AI tools and technologies should be used in the healthcare sector for improving the provision of care. There are also various local growth opportunities in the UAE in the domain of ecommerce and epharma.

The initiatives of the UAE leaders present a promising technology outlook of the UAE where the country can provide leadership not only at the local level but also at the global level. Various dimensions, initiatives, and projects launched by the UAE leaders have been described in this chapter in various sections.

4.1. Focus on Innovation and Technology

The UAE leadership presented visions 2021 and 2031. These visions mentioned key pillars that will form the national priorities for the nation. In Vision 2021, one of the key pillars was United in Knowledge. Based on this visionary approach, the UAE leaders have always focused on the promotion of innovation and technology in the country. Various milestones have already been achieved in the UAE in the domain of innovation and technology as shown in Figure 45 below:

The UAE's key achievements in innovation include:

O Development of education and the introduction of computers and smart devices in schools

O Expanding the creation of higher eEducation institutions

O Establishing a number of complexes and research institutions and technical institutes to promote research, creativity and innovation, such as:

   O Abu Dhabi's Masdar City

   O Dubai Science Park

   O Mohammed bin Rashid Solar Park

   O Arab Institution for Science and Technology in Sharjah

   O Technology and Innovation Center in Ras Al Khaimah

   O The Centre of Excellence for Applied Research & Training (CERT)

O Spreading and providing information and communications technology to the public

O Encouraging the culture of eLearning in the governmental and non-governmental sectors

O Formation of the Supreme Committee of UAE Innovation from a number of federal agencies

O Executing a Collaborative Care Agreement between the Ministry of Presidential Affairs and the Telecommunications and Digital Government Regulatory Authority-TDRA within the Be'tha scholarship programme to provide the opportunity to study at the best international universities in the specialisations that serve the information and communications sector.

Figure 45: Achievement in Innovation and Technology[cii]

The above figure mentions that the UAE leaders introduced smart devices, computers, and notebooks even at the school level so that the students learn to use technological gadgets at the very beginning of their educational attainment. It also provides an opportunity for the parents to know the inclination and aptitude of their children. If they are interested in the technological transformation, they can be sent in the relevant colleges and universities for the higher education and skills development.

The UAE leaders also created online and distance learning institutes so that the students could also acquire education from the comfort of their homes. This initiative proved particularly significant and relevant during the covid-19 pandemic when the requirement of social distancing had compelled the government to close the physical classrooms and in-person instructions.

The UAE leaders have also developed various institutes and centers that promote the use of technology and the research on using the advanced technologies. One of these initiatives is the development of Masdar City in Abu Dhabi. In 2006, the UAE leaders built collaboration with a renewable energy giant Masdar to expand the potential of the UAE energy companies and lead the energy-related initiatives. The three leading companies that joined this collaboration are ADNOC, Mubadala, and TAQA as show in Figure 46 below:

Figure 46: Masdar – Renewable Energy Partnership[ciii]

Another key technology-related initiatives of the UAE leaders is Dubai Science Park. The science park is regarded as a free zone area that has become a central place for global encounters. Under this initiative, the residential community, retail outlets, fitness centers, healthcare facilities, hotels, and schools have been built using smart and state-of-the-art technologies as shown in Figure 47 below:

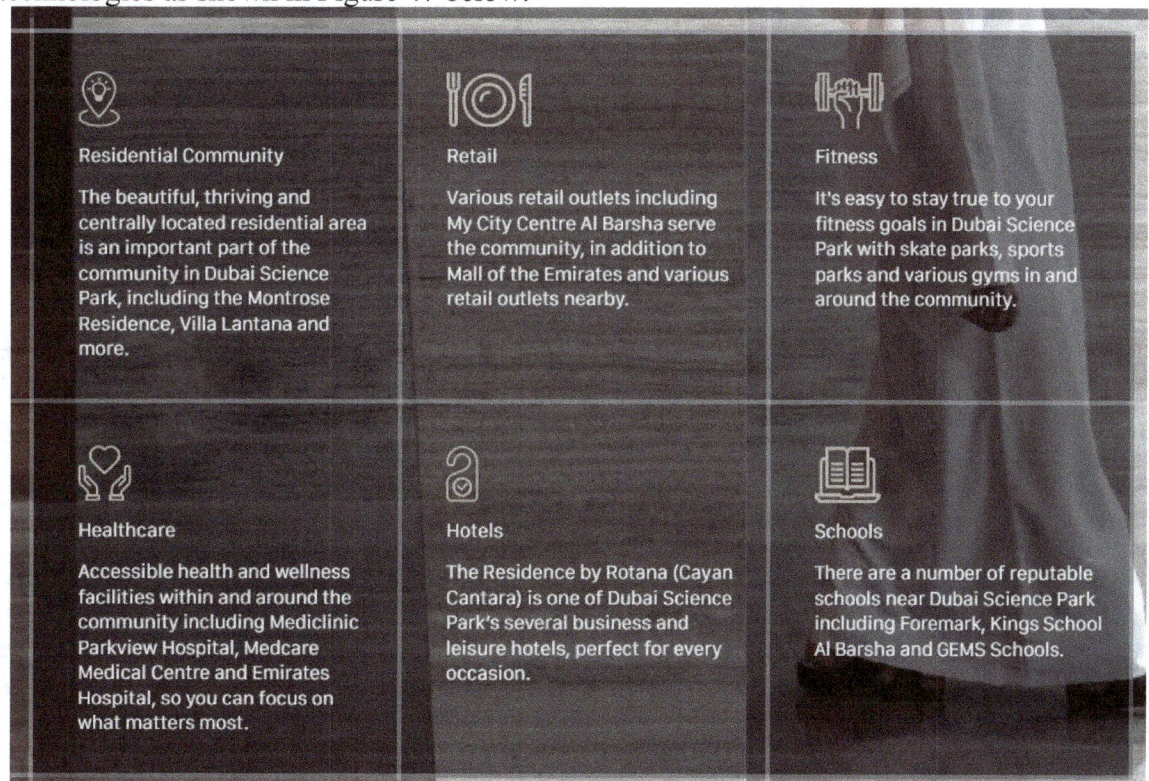

Figure 47: Amenities in Dubai Science Park[civ]

Another key initiative of the UAE leaders is Mohammed bin Rashid Al Maktoum Solar Park that was in line with the renewable energy adoption direction of the UAE. This solar park will be completed by DEWA. An investment amounting to 50 billion AED has been made by the prime minister in this project and the solar park will have a production capacity of 5000 megawatt by 2030.[cv] A model and blueprint of the solar park is shown in Figure 48 below:

Figure 48: Model of the Solar Park[cvi]

An innovation center has also been built in the emirate of Ras Al Khaimah by the UAE leaders. It is a research and development center where the experts focus on how sustainable energy sources could be utilized more in the daily life and routine of the UAE population.[cvii] The center acts as a connection point between the academic institutions and the industry leaders. The key services of the AURAK center are the delivery of weather data, conducting energy audit, testing the quality of water, performance testing concerning PV, and the testing of solar systems as shown in Figure 49 below:

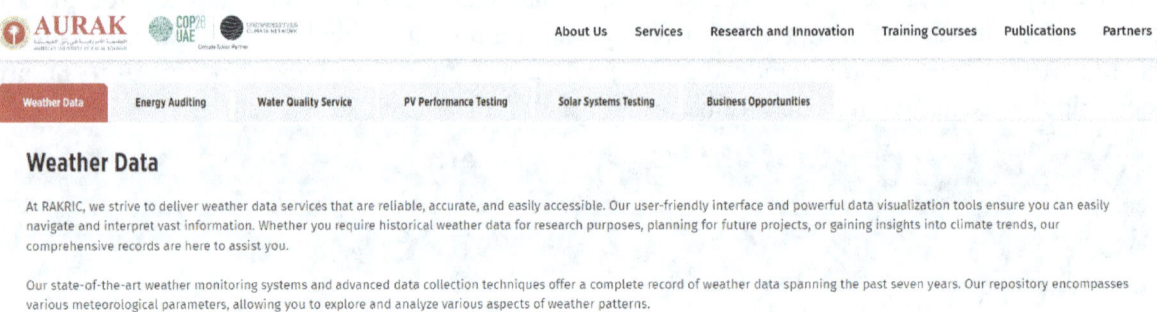

Figure 49: Services offered by AURAK[cviii]

4.2. Leadership Policies for Technological Advancement

Based on the vision document, the UAE leaders also developed a technology and innovation policy[cix] that facilitated in shaping a great country. This policy was presented by the second president Sheikh Khalifa. According to the innovation strategy of the UAE, an enabling environment for the development of innovation and technology will always be available in the UAE as shown in Figure 50 below. According to the innovation framework, priority sectors have been identified by the UAE leaders for the technological intervention. These include education, health, water, space, transportation, and renewable energy. The strategy outlines that innovation champions will also be highlighted and rewarded throughout the country. They may include individuals, corporations, and innovative governments. The UAE leaders have also developed the UAE regulatory framework so that the technology-based implementations follow the ethical guidelines and a level-playing field is available for the disruptive technologies. The framework also provides guidelines regarding the technology infrastructure, enabling services, investment climate, and incentives.

55

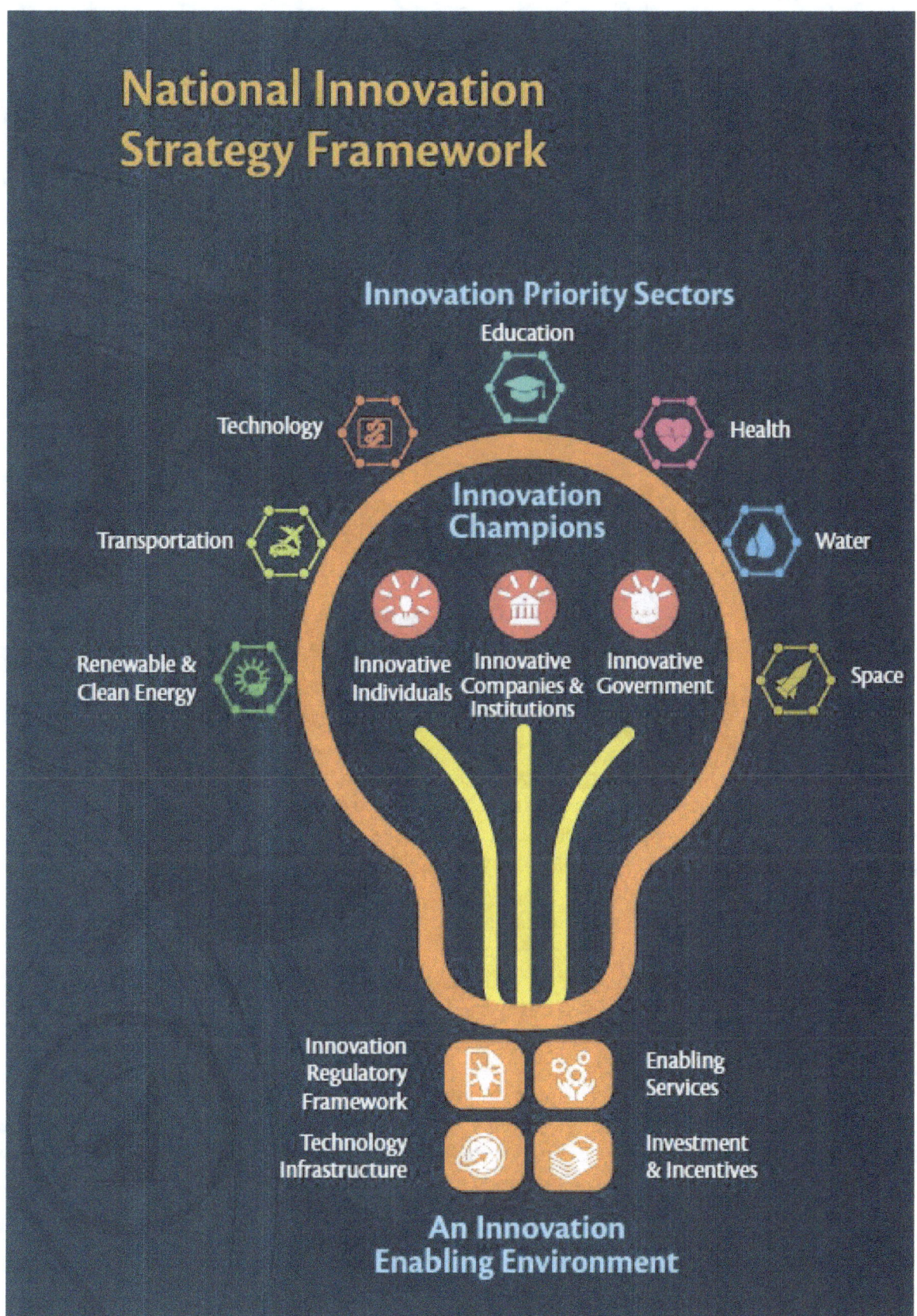

Figure 50: UAE Innovation Strategy[cx]

The technology framework of the UAE leaders classifies the technological interventions into three broader categories. These include science-based, technology-based, and business-based innovations as shown in Figure 51 below:

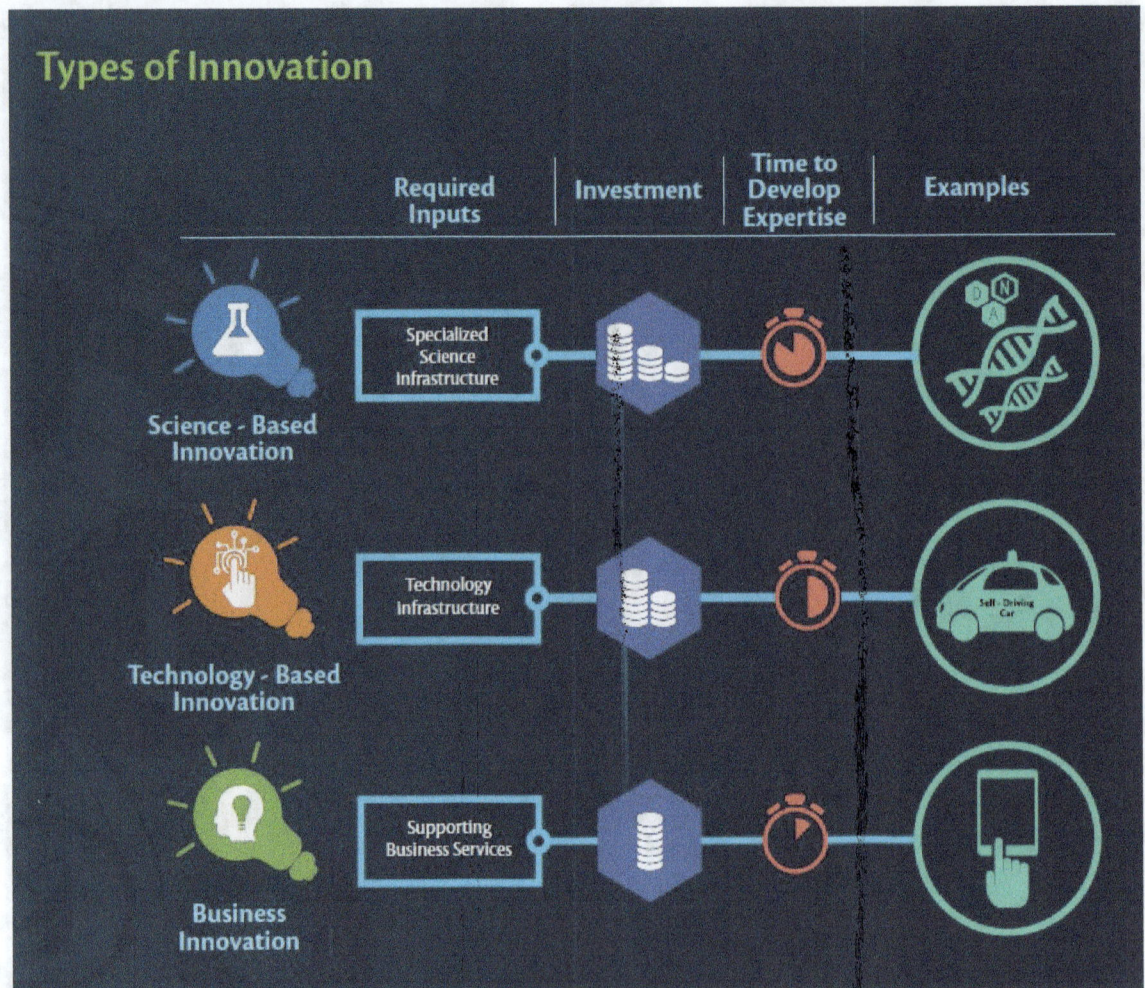

Figure 51: Innovation Categories[cxi]

As highlighted in the figure above, science-based innovations such as solar cells, biotechnology, and genomics are those innovations that require expensive laboratory facilities and equipment. There is a significantly higher return on investment in this category compared to the other two categories. A huge team of scientists and technology professionals is required for the development of science-based products.

Technology-based innovations such as virtual assistants and self-driving cars are those innovations that require specialized infrastructure and the involvement of subject matter experts. There is a good return on investment in this category as well. A huge team of software developers and AI developers is required for the development of technology-based products.

The third category is that of business innovation. Business-based innovations such as crowdfunding platforms and sharing economy applications are those innovations that become a platform for connecting the buyers and sellers. There is a low return on investment in this category compared to the other two categories. These innovations capitalize on the availability of existing tools and applications, and therefore, a higher level of technological and scientific expertise is not needed. Due to this factor, many startups have gained a huge success in business-based innovations.

The classification of the innovation in the above three broad categories by the UAE leaders have made it clear for the entrepreneurs and corporations in the UAE how their innovative models will be viewed and regarded at the national level. It is a great achievement of the leadership and the business leaders have acquired a clear direction for their future plans and budget planning in the UAE.

The UAE leaders have highlighted in the innovation strategy framework that the targets regarding science, technology, and business-based innovations can effectively be achieved regarding the focus areas, the enablers, and the ambitions as shown in Figure 52 below. Under the dimension of focus areas, it is crucial to select key areas of technological interventions that could provide maximum advantages to the UAE and the technology leaders are confident that the associated challenges will be overcome. Under the enablers dimensions, the UAE leaders have promised that a conducive environment will be provided to the technology companies and startups to ensure the implementation of sustainability initiatives and disruptive innovations. Under the ambition paradigm, the UAE leaders aim to develop an ambitious national policy so that the innovation framework is aligned with the global perspectives and practices.

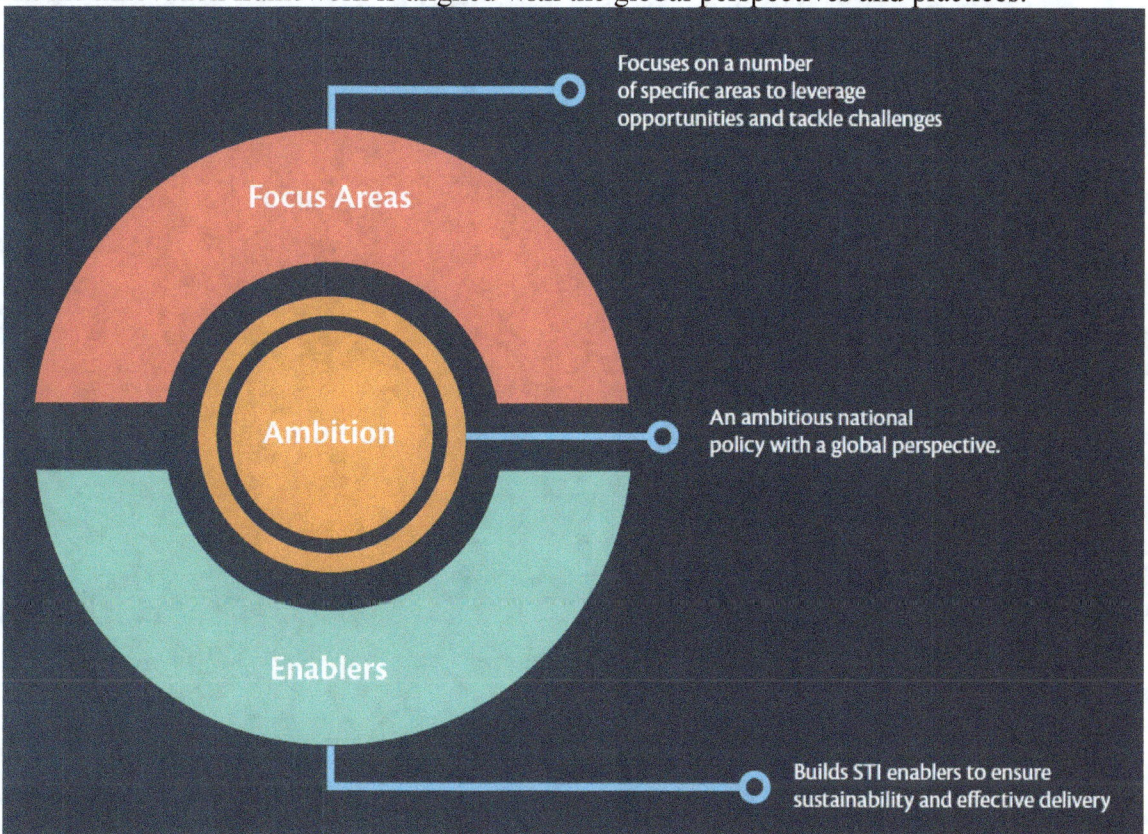

Figure 52: Key Dimensions of Innovation Framework[cxii]

The innovation framework has highlighted 24 areas where the technological interventions of the UAE should be focused and the skills of the UAE workforce should be utilized to gain a competitive advantage at the regional and global level. These 24 areas are education, health, wellness, genomics, water management, renewable energy, space science, nanosatellites, cybersecurity, semiconductor, robotics, smart cities, architecture, Arabic digital, financials, petroleum geosciences, Internet of Things, additive manufacturing, building and construction, food security, transportation, aerospace, driverless vehicles, and unmanned aerial vehicles. These focus areas are shown in Figure 53 below:

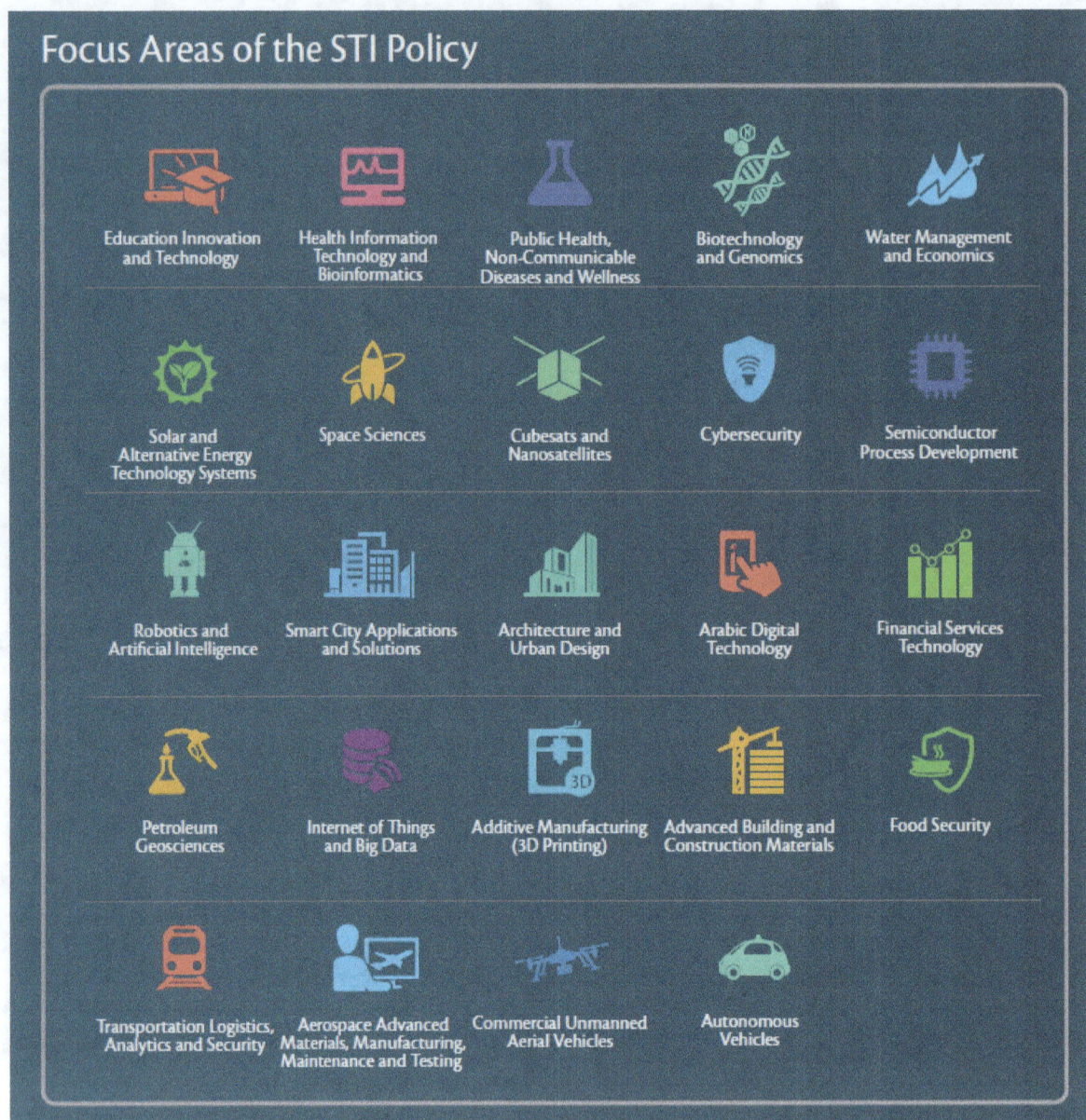

Figure 53: Focus Areas for Technology Interventions[cxiii]

A good level of development projects focusing on these technologies can make the UAE the leader in the Middle Eastern countries and at the global level. These technologies are going to shape the future of the nations, and the visionary approach of the UAE leaders have set an excellent directions for the UAE by focusing on the key areas beneficial for the UAE.

4.3. How Leadership made UAE a Global Trade Hub

The UAE also enjoys a geographical advantage that makes it an ideal location for the international visitors, businesses, and investors. The location of the UAE is at the crossroad of Asia, Africa, and Europe. Due to this strategic location, a significant number of international trades and businesses have made the UAE their business hub. The UAE leaders have also offered tax incentives and free trade zones to facilitate the foreign investors.

According to Visit Dubai, the interconnected setup offered by the UAE has made it a trade center where the investment and business amounting to trillion of dollars is conducted by the investors from Asia, Africa, Europe, and the Middle East.[cxiv] It has been made possible by the vision of the great leaders of the UAE who have capitalized on the strategic global location of the UAE. Moreover, they have developed a future-forward infrastructure and business-friendly policies for the regional and global investors. The strategic location of the UAE can be realized from the fact that approximately 2.5 billion people have access to Dubai with a four-hour flight.

Furthermore, approximately 5 billion people have access to Dubai with a flight up to eight hours.[cxv]

Several initiatives by the UAE leaders have enabled the leadership of the UAE as the global trade leader. Through the agenda of economic diversification, they have increased the volume of non-oil trade and the volume of non-oil trade has surpassed the volume of oil-based trade in most of the emirates of the UAE. The UAE leaders have also built trading partnerships with the global players and their top trading partners are China, India, USA, Saudi Arabia, and Switzerland.[cxvi]

The UAE leaders have also focused on optimizing the shipping and logistics operations at various ports and terminals. Due to this initiative, Dubai is now regarded as the fifth top shipping hub in the world.[cxvii]

In a recent development, the fifteen BRICS summit was held in August 2023 as shown in Figure 54 below:

Figure 54: 15th Session of BRICS[cxviii]

BRICS is a group and alliance of developing and emerging economies, and its current members are Russia, Brazil, China, India, and South Africa. In the fifteenth summit of BRICS, it was decided to include more emerging players and economic powers into the group. The invitations were sent to six countries that also included Saudi Arabia and the UAE. If these countries accept the membership, the countries will be part of BRICS from January 2024.

Al Arabia News has reported that the UAE leaders are desirous of joining BRICS and they believe that it will further expand the role of the UAE as a global trade hub.[cxix] The UAE leaders have also expressed their interests to inject more capital into the new development bank of BRICS.

Currently, the UAE compares its currency with dollar and has also allowed US forces to join its airbase.[cxx] Therefore, there were concerns that the UAE might not join an anti-US alliance such as BRICS. However, the UAE leaders have a forward-looking approach and they want to build cordial ties with all developing nations of the world. In 2022, the two biggest trade partners of the UAE were China and India. On the other hand, Japan and the US ranked third and four in the trading partnership.[cxxi] This move by the UAE leaders is being lauded across the globe because the energy producing countries are currently executing business transactions in dollars. When the BRICS alliance is strengthened by the entry of Saudi Arabia and the UAE, the BRICS bloc will have more ability and potential to enable energy trading in alternative currencies. The strategic directions of the UAE leadership have shaped UAE a great country, and this new strategy will be a game changer for increasing the role of the UAE as a global trade hub.

4.4. Integration of AI Tools and Systems in Public Services and Governance

The UAE leaders have always welcomed the technology initiatives. As highlighted in Figure 53, robotics and artificial intelligence is one of the key focus areas of the innovation policy of the UAE. The UAE leaders have made every possible effort to incorporate AI-based tools and systems in public services and governance. In this section, I am giving you examples of some of the latest implementations in this regard.

The UAE government has announced the Smart Dubai Strategy under which the city of Dubai will be developed as a technologically advanced and the happiest city in the world. The concepts of AI will be implemented in all focus areas including healthcare and public transportation. According to this strategy, Dubai will have a smart city governance and experience. The city will have the protocols for providing data insights and data exchange facilities. The city will demonstrate global leadership and smart city planning. The city will be characterized by emerging technologies and technology efficiency. A smart ecosystem will interconnect all the departments of Dubai. This smart Dubai strategy is shown in Figure 55 below:

Figure 55: Smart Dubai Strategy[cxxii]

The AI-based systems are also being used effectively in the healthcare sector of the UAE. The use of the AI-based tools has facilitated the care providers in making accurate predictions about the patient conditions. The medical care professionals have also been able to provide personalized healthcare plans.[cxxiii]

The AI-based systems are also being used by the law enforcement agencies in the UAE. These tools assist the police department in predicting the crime rates in a particular area and ensure surveillance through smart cameras.[cxxiv] Added force may also be deployed in those areas that are flagged by the AI-based systems as having the potential for criminal activities.

The UAE leaders have also presented the AI Strategy for the UAE that provides guidance for implementing AI with a forward-looking approach up to 2031. This strategy is developed under the National Program for Artificial Intelligence as shown in Figure 56 below. In the AI strategy, the AI ministry has projected that the implementation of AI-based tools in different sectors of the UAE will increase the overall output by 335 billion dirhams as shown in Figure 57 below. The largest increase in output is expected in the four industries of financial services, mining, construction, and retail.

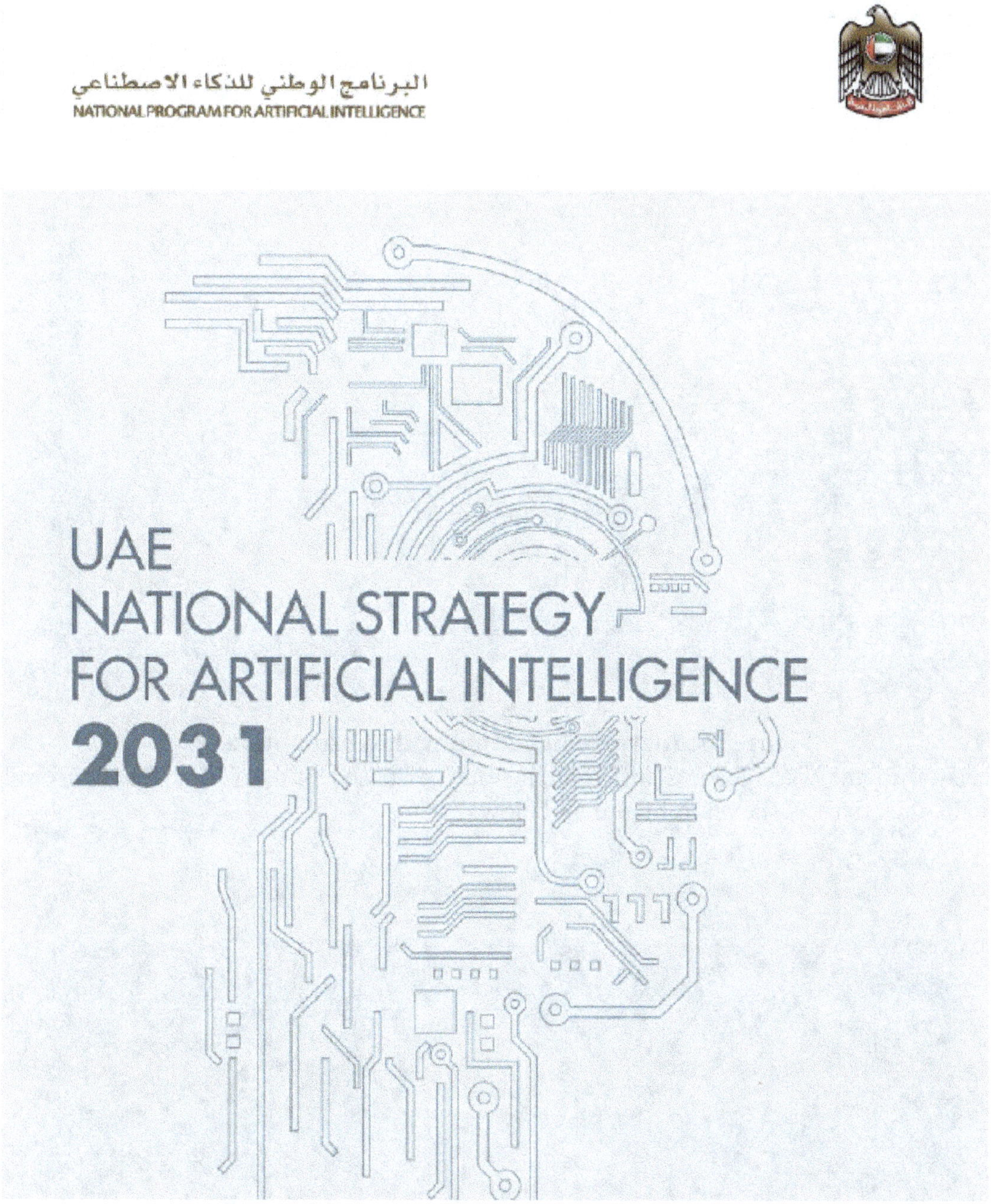

البرنامج الوطني للذكاء الاصطناعي
NATIONAL PROGRAM FOR ARTIFICIAL INTELLIGENCE

Figure 56: UAE AI Strategy[cxxv]

62

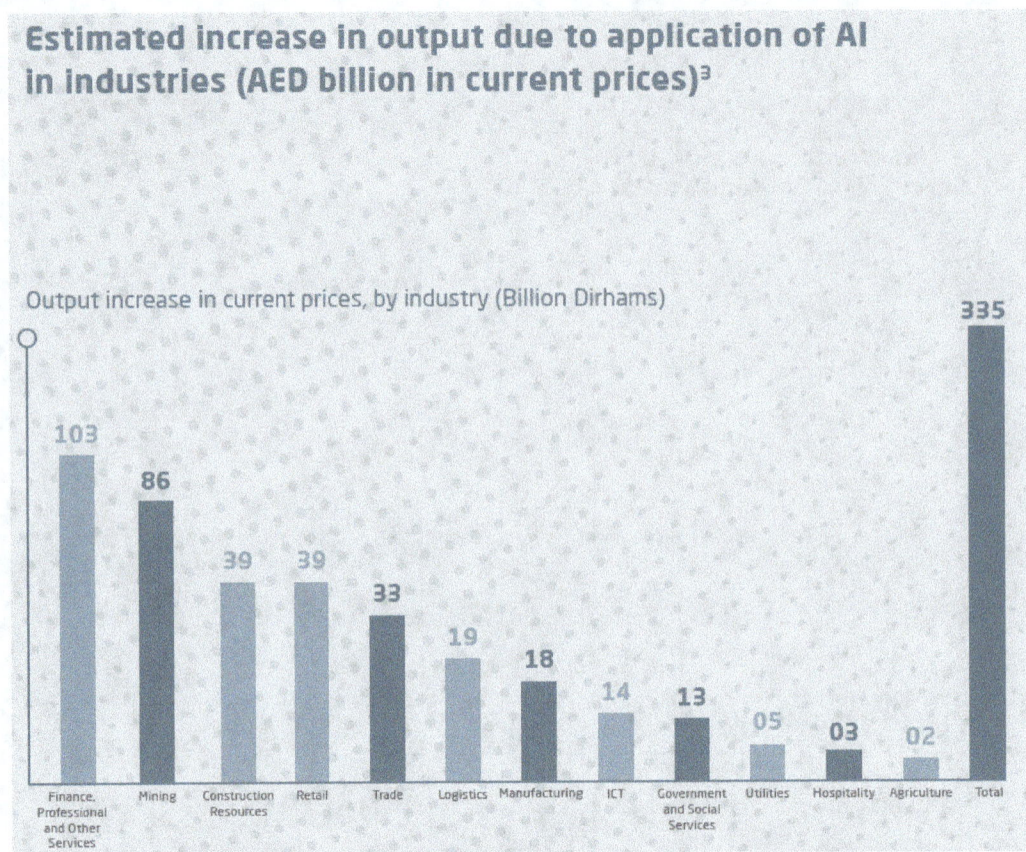

Figure 57: Increase in Output with AI Adoption[cxxvi]

The vision of the UAE leaders for implementing AI-based initiatives is founded on eight strategic objectives as shown in Figure 58 below.

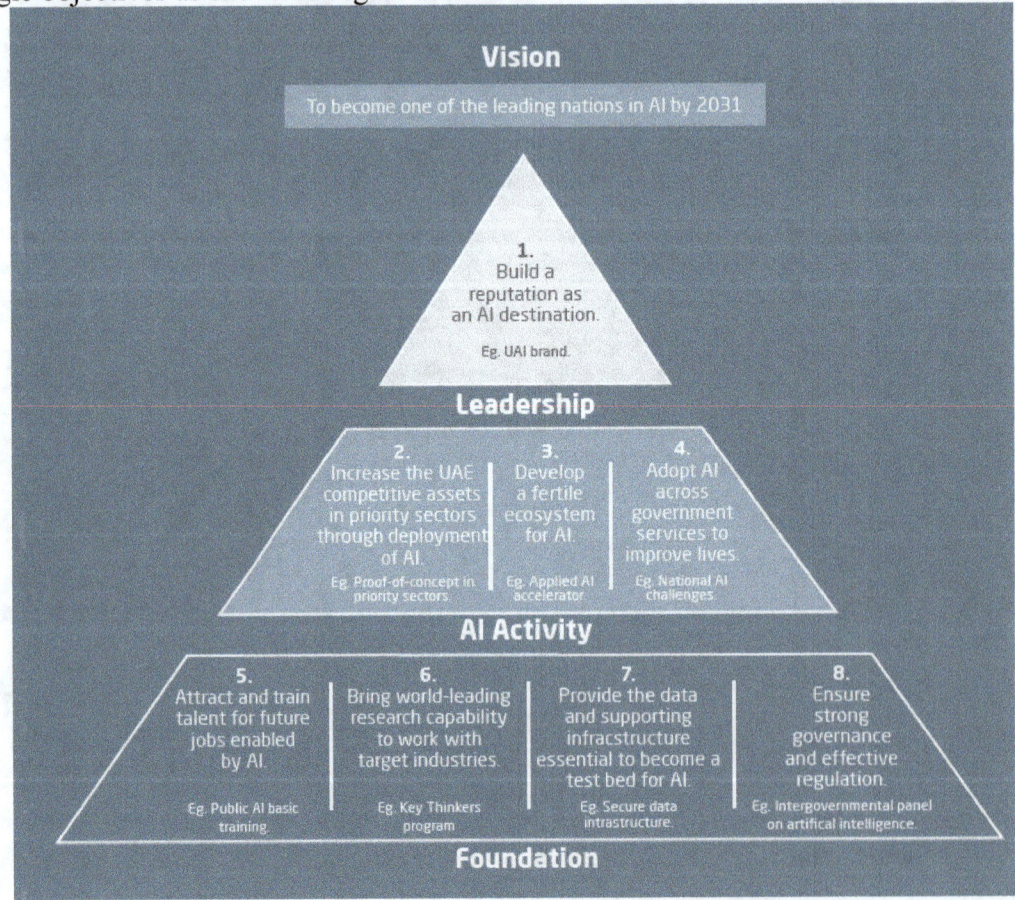

Figure 58: Strategic Objectives in AI Strategy[cxxvii]

The strategy document above shows that the UAE leaders aim to make UAE a leader in AI-based implementations by 2031. As per the first strategic objective, the UAE should become a preferred destination for implementing and replicating the AI-based initiatives in the world. As per the second objective, the skillsets of the UAE students and workforce should be expanded to the priority sectors where the AI-based implementations are being anticipated by the UAE leaders. The third objective requires the development of an ecosystem for AI that could provide a fertile environment for the investors and technology professionals.

As per the fourth objective, the AI tools and technologies should be used in all government services of the UAE. The fifth objective asks to attract the quality human resources in the AI implementation sectors so that high-quality deliverables could be produced in a timely manner. The six objective asks to improve the research and development facilities for the AI-based systems. The seventh objective asks to facilitate the AI-based systems and algorithms with the required data because the power of AI-based systems is based on the processing of a huge dataset, learning from the training dataset, and then producing results and recommendations. The quality of data plays a pivotal role in developing robust, AI-based applications. The eight strategic objective is the governance and regulation of the AI-based systems because they can also be used for ill motives and may fetch data from the systems without the explicit consent of the users and the data owners.

These eight strategic objectives provide leadership and foundation for implementing AI-based systems in the UAE. The AI activities in the UAE should adhere to these objectives so that the activities are consistent with the overall mission and objectives of the country.

The UAE prime minister launched advanced sciences agenda in April 2018 such that the agenda items are expected to be accomplished by 2031 as shown in Figure 59 below. The primary objective of this agenda is to utilize the modern tools of science and technology for developing solutions that are consistent with the visionary approach of the leaders and the centennial plan of the country. According to the agenda, four enablers of technology should be incorporated and promoted in the country.[cxxviii] The first enabler is the technology services related to economic information. The second enabler is a technology that is supportive and user-friendly. The third enabler is the development of a connected scientific community. The fourth enabler is the promotion of entrepreneurship in the domain of science and technology.

Figure 59: Agenda for Scientific Advancement 2031[cxxix]

4.5. Dubai Expo

The UAE leaders have developed Expo City Dubai where national and international events and occasions are celebrated with state-of-the-art facilities and an interconnected environment. This city has been developed with the intent of making it the city of the future as shown in Figure 60 below. The key features of this city are that the city is ideally connected to various locations through road, rail, and air transports. Moreover, the city considers the sustainability aspects in all its construction and event management. One of the most attractive facilities in the city is the Exhibition Center. The center provides an excellent level of connectivity to people from all over the world. It is a state-of-the-art venue for holding conferences, concerts, and other entertainment and infotainment events as shown in Figure 61 below. The center is conveniently located close to the metro station. The center also provides a magnificent view of Al Wasl Plaza. There is a customizable event space of 45,000 square meters in the center. The center has 14 multi-use halls and exhibition halls. The best audio-visual resources are available to the attendees along with the on-site catering services.

Figure 60: Dubai ECD^{cxxx}

Figure 61: Exhibition Center at ECD[cxxxi]

4.6. The Unique Role of the Ministry of Artificial Intelligence

As I highlighted in Figure 53, artificial intelligence and robotics have been declared as key focus areas in the innovation framework of the UAE. The UAE leaders believe that the AI-based tools and systems will play a dominant role in the future leadership role of the UAE in the Middle East and the world.

The visionary approach of the UAE leaders regarding technological advancement can be seen from the fact that UAE is the only country in the world that has an exclusive ministry of artificial intelligence.[cxxxii] Due to this fact, the Time Magazine included Omar Al Olama among the most influential people in the AI domain in 2023. His Excellency Omar Sultan Al Olama was not appointed recently as AI minister, but the UAE leaders with their long-term orientation appointed him way back in October 2017, when the AI based systems were just being introduced in different industries and sectors. As shown in Figure 62 below, he is not only appointed as AI minister but also the minister for remote work applications and digital economy. He was given these additional roles by the UAE leaders in July 2020.[cxxxiii]

The AI ministry in the UAE optimizes the performance of the government departments by introducing latest technologies and AI-based systems. The current minister aims to position the UAE as a world leader in the context of digital economy. He also presented AI national strategy for the country up to 2031 as shown in Figure 56. It is also part of the economic diversification agenda of the UAE to increase the contribution of other sectors such as digital economy in the GDP. For the World Government Summit, the current minister also holds the position of the managing director. He has also been given the membership of Dubai Chamber so that he could introduce projects by considering the interests of all stakeholders and business leaders.

H.E.Omar Sultan Al Olama
Minister of State for Artificial Intelligence, Digital Economy and Remote Work Applications

Figure 62: AI Ministry in UAE[cxxxiv]

With the description of the unique role of AI ministry in UAE, the discussion on the technological advancement and making the UAE a technological hub concluded. You must have appreciated that the UAE leadership has not only introduced projects in the current context but also developed vision and strategic directions for making the UAE a technological hub of the future. With these impressive efforts of the UAE leaders, the UAE is not only a great country now but it also has a sustainable and promising future. When the technological innovation and AI-based projects are fully implemented, its results will be seen in the UAE economy by a wider contribution of the technology sector in the GDP. As a result, the agenda of the UAE leaders to reduce the reliance on oil exports will be promoted. Moreover, it will also help in promoting the agenda of localization because new jobs and employment opportunities will be available to the Emiratis in the technology sector. The UAE has also developed world-class universities providing education in computer science, technology, and artificial intelligence. The local graduates from these universities will be a highly valuable resource for advancing the technology-based, science-based, and business-based innovations in the UAE.

5. Infrastructure Projects and Initiatives

In section 1.3, when I highlighted the remarkable transformation of the UAE from a desert to a global powerhouse, I mentioned that the UAE got independence in 1971, and in a short time, through the great efforts and contributions of the UAE leaders, the country has now become a global powerhouse. I also noted that if you had to visit Dubai in the decade of 50s, you would struggle finding a place to stay. There were no hotels developed at that time in Dubai. Dubai was just a fishing village in 1960.

The infrastructure projects and initiatives of the UAE leaders were one of the biggest reasons that shaped a great country. In section 1.3, I also gave you examples of various infrastructure projects such as Burj Al-Arab (1999), Palm Jumeriah (2007), Dubai Metro (2009), Burj Khalifa (2010), and Al Maktoum International Airport (2013). These were the examples in the historical context to give you an idea how the great leaders of UAE shaped a great country. These projects have improved the living conditions in the UAE and also optimized the global image of the country. Whenever the foreigners visit the UAE, they always go to these tourist attractions. In this chapter, I will describe the current and upcoming infrastructure projects introduced by the UAE leaders that will ensure that the UAE has smart cities, an impressive interconnectivity, and a technology-based, state-of-the-art infrastructure for the future generations.

5.1. Developments concerning Bridges, Roads, Airports, and Ports

The mega projects in the UAE are developed by considering the vision and directions of the UAE leaders. These projects are not only iconic architectural wonders but also adhere to the sustainability requirements. Through these projects, the UAE leaders have demonstrated that the nation is committed to the path of innovation and progress.

Figure 63: Burj Binghatti[cxxxv]

The first major infrastructure project in the UAE in the current context is Burj Binghatti that will be developed in the emirate of Dubai as shown in Figure 63 above. It has been claimed by the constructors that this burj will be the tallest residential tower of the globe. It will be established in the business bay of Dubai. It will be a symbol of luxury and comfortable living. The upscale apartments will also provide a magnificent city view. This project is currently in-progress and its expected completion date is December 2026.[cxxxvi] The total project value of this project is $80 million.[cxxxvii]

Figure 64: Palm Jebel Ali^{cxxxviii}

Another mega project in the UAE in the current context is Palm Jebel Ali as shown in Figure 64 above. This project will expand the marvels of the iconic Palm Jumeirah. It is described by the constructors as a human-made island. Through the visionary approach of the UAE leaders, the island will offer various areas including the residential and commercial developments, hotels, villas, entertainment avenues, and retail outlets. The construction of this palm is currently in-progress, and the expected completion date is December 2025.[cxxxix] The overall cost of the project is $500 million.[cxl]

Figure 65: Agri Hub[cxli]

Another mega project currently in-progress is Agri Hub. It is established by URB and it is an urban farming project that will be launched in Abu Dhabi. The virtual farming techniques will be utilized in this agri hub. The constructors claim that it will make a paradigm shift in the agricultural techniques currently utilized in urban setting. A variety of crops will be grown in this hub by using advanced technologies. Through the implementation of a controlled environment, sustainable annual production of different crops will be ensured. This project is expected to be completed by December 2026.[cxlii] The total estimated value of this project is $500 million.[cxliii] The agri hub will also have leisure, wellness, educational, and medical facilities. The project will create 10,000 jobs and all the infrastructure of the project will utilize renewable energy sources.[cxliv]

Figure 66: Urban Tech District[cxlv]

Another mega project undergoing in the UAE is Urban Tech District as shown in Figure 66 above. It is also being developed by URB, and it will be launched in Dubai. This project aims to promote startups and entrepreneurs in the UAE in the technology sector. This project will be developed on the concept of a smart city. It will have collaborative spaces, technology infrastructure, and research facilities for the graduates and the business professionals. This project will further optimize the position of the UAE as a global technology hub. This project is expected to be completed by December 2028.[cxlvi] The total project cost is estimated to be $500 million.[cxlvii] The project will create 4,000 jobs and employment opportunities.[cxlviii] The project will also have seminar rooms, conference facilities, dedicated offices, and shared desk spaces.

Figure 67: Uptown Tower[cxlix]

Another recent mega project in the UAE is the Uptown Tower District. It is regarded as a mixed-use development and it will be established in Dubai. There will be commercial, residential, and entertainment spaces available in this district. The luxury apartments and the trendy restaurants will create a vibrant, community environment and it will be a great place for meaningful interactions and socialization. The project is expected to be completed by December 2023 and the total project cost has been estimated to be $150 million.[cl] The targeted energy label of this infrastructure is LEED Gold.[cli]

Figure 68: National Museum[clii]

Another monumental project in the UAE is Zaid National Museum that has been dedicated to the founding father of the country. This museum highlights the timeline and achievement of the great UAE leader for shaping a great country. The history, culture, and values of the UAE are reflected throughout the museum. The museum will also become a center of research and education as per the directions and vision of the founding father. The project was completed at the last quarter of 2023 and the total project cost has been estimated to be $1,000 million.[cliii]

Figure 69: Midfield Terminal[cliv]

Another mega project in the UAE is the Midfield Terminal project as shown in Figure 69 above. Similar to the UAE vision document, the emirate of Abu Dhabi has also developed an Emirate level vision document known as Abu Dhabi's 2030 vision.[clv] This aviation project aims to support this visionary approach for promoting tourism. After the development of this project, the number of passengers arriving at the Abu Dhabi can be doubled on the annual basis.[clvi] This project is being supervised by AECOM. With this project, Abu Dhabi International Airport will have world-class facilities for a comfortable passenger journey. The spacious facility will be able to accommodate millions of passengers. The passengers will also receive the facilities of premium lounges, dining options, and retail stores. With this project, the UAE leaders aim to make the UAE a global aviation hub. The project is expected to be completed by October 2025, and the total project cost has been estimated to be $2,942 million.[clvii]

Hindu Temple[clviii]

The UAE leaders not only promote the principles and teachings of Islam but also have a great regard and respect for other communities of interpretations. The religious tolerance of the UAE leaders is manifested by the establishment of a Hindu Temple in Abu Dhabi. The UAE is one of the largest host of immigrants in the world. The immigrants account for 87.9% of the total population. The local Emiratis are only 11.6% of the total population. South Asians are the majority population of the UAE making up 59.4% of the total population. South Asians include Pakistanis, Indians, and Bangladeshis. Other ethnic groups include Egyptians and Filipinos. The UAE is a Middle Eastern country with majority Muslim population. The Muslims are 76% of the total population. People with other religious communities include Hindus, Christians, Buddhist, Parsi, Sikh, and Jews. Therefore, a Hindu Temple is being built to facilitate the occasions, ceremonies, and prayers of other communities.

The temple will not only include prayer halls but also architectural monuments and intricate carvings. It will be a place of worship for Hindus as well as a place for community gathering and cultural celebrations. The project is expected to be completed by February 2024 and the total project cost has been estimated to be $109 million.[clix]

There are also 40 churches established in the UAE.[clx] The UAE also has 700 Christian ministries that have a flexible administrative structure compared to churches, but they are all operated according to the principles of Christianity.[clxi] Another great example of the religious tolerance of the UAE leaders is that the leaders partnered with UNESCO in 2019 and participated in the restoration of Christian churches in Iraq.[clxii] These churches had been destroyed by ISIS during the fight with Iraq.

The UAE has also developed a Sikh Temple because Sikhs are an active community in the

UAE and their count in the UAE has reached to approximately 50,000 as shown in Figure 70 below:

Figure 70: Presence of the Sikh Communityclxiii

The Sikh Temple was opened for the community in Dubai in January 2012, and it covers a spacious area of 25,000 square feet. Within the Sikh community, this prayer hall is termed as gurdwara. A view of this gurdwara is shown in Figure 71 below. These initiatives highlight that the UAE leaders have always believed in an inclusive approach and their leadership approaches are dominated by pragmatism. They believe in pluralism and diversity, and the hardline ideologies never affect their decision-making approaches.

Figure 71: Prayer House for Sikh Communityclxiv

Figure 72: Falcon Island^{clxv}

Falcon Island is a luxury development in the emirate of Ras Al Khaimah. The project will have residential spaces as well as turquoise waters and pristine beaches. There will be well-designed villas supported with state-of-the-art amenities. The project will also provide a magnificent view of the Arabia Gulf. The project is designed to provide a peaceful environment to the residents away from the noisy city life. The natural beauty, tranquility, and privacy are the key aspects of the project. The project is expected to be completed by the third quarter of 2025 and the project cost is estimated to be $1,000 million.[clxvi]

In the above section, I have given you examples of the mega projects in the UAE that will be completed at the end of 2023 or afterward. From these examples, you will appreciate that the UAE leaders have introduced infrastructure projects in various domains and industries. They have promoted the transportation, aviation, built environment, agriculture, heritage, and religious tolerance. There are also other mega projects such as Ciel Dubai, Al Jurf, Jubail Island, History Museum, Guggenheim, Louvre Residences, SeaWorld, Sharjah Forest, Reem Island, World Islands, and Hatta.[clxvii] All these projects are extremely important for improving the living conditions of the UAE residents and optimizing the image of the UAE in the world community.

5.2. Role of Infrastructure in attracting Investment

You might be surprised why there is a significant level of focus in the UAE in the infrastructure projects. These projects actually bring several unique advantages to the country and the UAE leaders have foreseen these benefits for the population.

The biggest advantage is that numerous job opportunities are created in this project because these are mega projects whose cost is in millions of dollars. As per the policy of localization, the construction companies are also bound to hire a certain percent of Emiratis in the projects. Therefore, attractive employment opportunities are made available to the local population.

The second advantage is that these projects provide a competitive advantage to the UAE. For example, a ministry of AI is established in the UAE and the UAE is leader in this initiative because no other country has such minister in their cabinets. Under the ministry of AI, the technology-based projects are being initiated that are powered by AI. When these projects are implemented, the workforce implementing this project gets a valuable skill in their portfolios because the AI-based developments are only a recent phenomenon and the AI experts are available in limited numbers across the globe. Working in the mega, technology-driven projects improve the skills of the local workforce and provide them with an opportunity to apply their knowledge in the real-world projects.

The third advantage from the infrastructure projects is the transformation of the UAE. The remarkable transformation of the UAE from a fishing village to a modern metropolis has been possible by a variety of factors and infrastructure projects have been one of the major reasons. It is because for any new innovation and creative project, an enabling environment and a modern infrastructure is needed. I gave you an example of a mega project undergoing in the UAE, which is Urban Tech District It will be launched in Dubai. This project aims to promote startups and entrepreneurs in the UAE in the technology sector. This project will be developed on the concept of a smart city. It will have collaborative spaces, technology infrastructure, and research facilities for the graduates and the business professionals. This project will further optimize the position of the UAE as a global technology hub. Therefore, the infrastructure projects also create an enabling environment for implementing the economic diversification agenda of the UAE leaders.

Another benefit gained from the infrastructure projects is the reputation and the global image of the UAE. The tourists are highly attracted to visiting the new projects and facilities in the UAE. The tourism sector is one of the key sectors whose contribution will be increased in the UAE as part of the economic diversification. Therefore, infrastructure projects also increase the revenues of the tourism sector in the UAE and create a leading, successful example to be followed by other Middle Eastern countries.

6. Enabling Business Environment

The UAE has achieved the distinction of a business and technological hub through the efforts of the great leaders of UAE. This status of the UAE was possible because a conducive and enabling environment was provided for the business community locally and internationally. Traditionally, investors prefer those destinations where three are tax incentives and there is a continuity in the policies of the leadership. As I will highlight below, the UAE is an ideal business destination for the investors and they get a good return on their investment.

6.1. Enabling Environment for Foreign Investment through Leadership Initiatives

The UAE Ministry of Economy has published a guide for the foreign investors so that they know about the benefits and incentives of making investments in the UAE.[clxviii]

The first section of the guide mentions various benefits of making investments in the UAE. These include the strategic location of the UAE, the state-of-the-art infrastructure, political stability, social stability, protection of intellectual rights, ease of doing business, standard labor laws, economic stability, and a free economy. The guide also mentions various benefits available to the foreign investors when they make investments in the UAE as shown in Figure 73 below:

Figure 73: Facilities for the Foreign Investors[clxix]

The above figure highlights that the foreign investors get the opportunity of conducting their businesses in fully-furnished business centers. Various shopping centers and large malls are also present in the UAE. The UAE also showcases business towers for conducting business activities. The investors can also choose from different industrial zones. The zones also provide technology-related, media-related, and logistics-related facilities.

The investor's guide also mentions seven other benefits that can prove highly beneficial to the foreign investors. These seven benefits are highlighted in Figure 74 below:

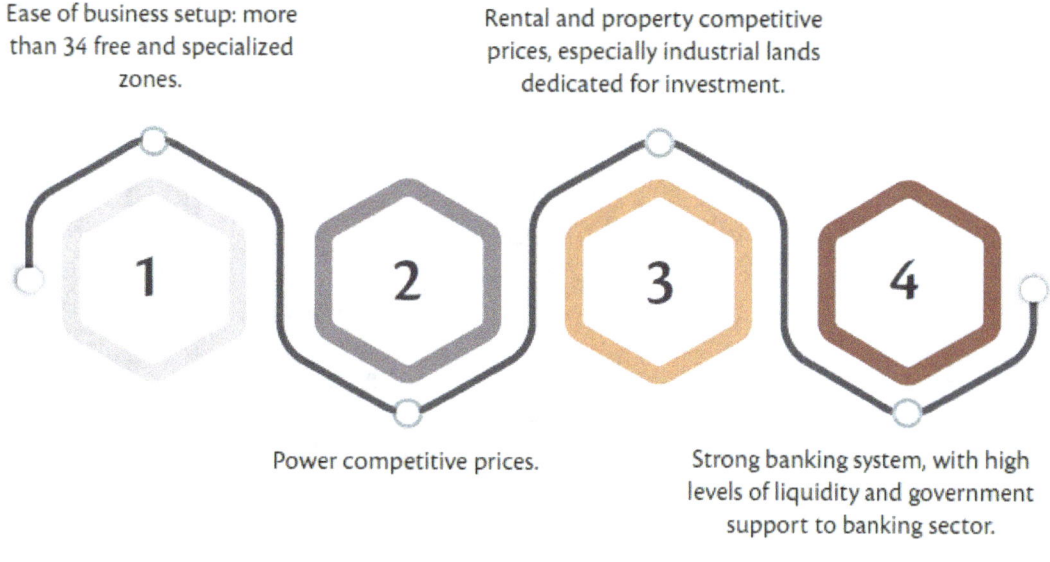

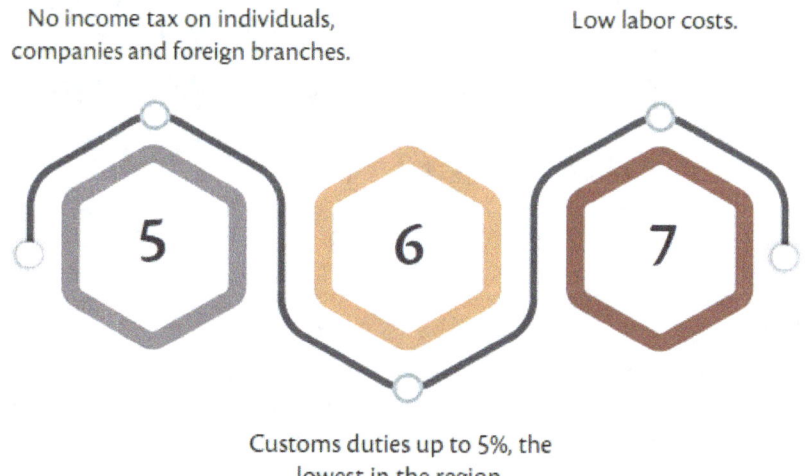

Figure 74: Benefits for Foreign Investors[clxx]

The above figure highlights that the first key benefit for businesses in the UAE is that the establishment of a business entity is very easy. The investors can choose from more than 34 specialized and free zones. The second advantage is that competitive prices are offered for the business activities. The rental and property prices are also highly competitive and can easily be offered by an average investor. The business transactions are supported by a strong banking system of the UAE. There is a high level of government support and liquidity in the banking sector of the UAE. When the foreign investors work in free trade zones, there is no income tax applied on individuals, corporations, and foreign branches. The customs duties have also been reduced to 5 percent, which is the lowest duty in the Middle Eastern region. As the country has a large population of immigrants, the foreign workforce also agrees to working at low labor costs.

The UAE leaders, with the objective of encouraging the foreign investment, have also permitted for the change of an existing companies in the UAE to a foreign direction investment (FDI) company. It can be accomplished in eight easy steps as shown in Figure 75 below:

Steps for the Change of an Existing Company to an FDI Company

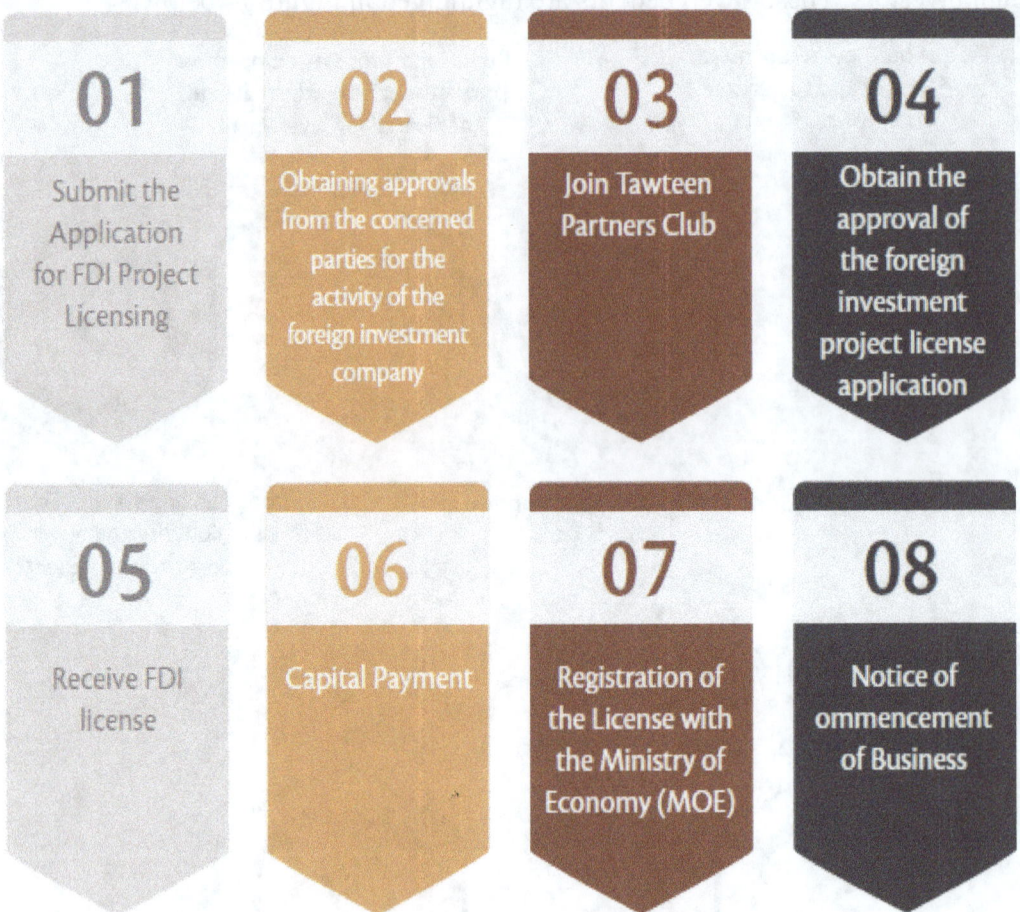

Figure 75: Existing Company to an FDI[clxxi]

As shown in the figure above, the existing company should first submit an application for the acquisition of a license for an FDI project. In the next step, the approvals should be sought from all the concerned parties. The existing company will then have to join Tawteen club. Then the foreign investment approval should be obtained for the concerned project. The requesting party will receive the FDI license in the next step. Then the capital payments should be made in the project. Afterward, the ministry of economy will register the license of the FDI Company. Then a notice should be issued by the FDI Company for the commencement of business. These eight steps make it evident that the establishment of an FDI company is a simple and easy process for the business professionals. It also highlights the commitment of the UAE leaders to provide an enabling environment to the foreign investors in the UAE.

The U.S. Department of State has presented several key indicators for different countries in the investment climate report of 2023. The key indicators and metrics have also been presented for the UAE.[clxxii] The first metrics presented in the investment climate report of the UAE is related to the corruption situation, position of innovation, FDI partnership, and gross national income (GNI) as shown in Figure 76 below:

Table 1: Key Metrics and Rankings

Measure	Year	Index/Rank	Website Address
TI Corruption Perceptions Index	2022	27 of 180	http://www.transparency.org/research/cpi/overview
Global Innovation Index	2022	31 out of 132	https://www.globalinnovationindex.org/analysis-indicator
U.S. FDI in partner country ($M USD, historical stock positions)	2021	$16.2	https://apps.bea.gov/international/factsheet/
World Bank GNI per capita	2020	41,770	http://data.worldbank.org/indicator/NY.GNP.PCAP.CD

Figure 76: Investment Climate Indicators of the UAE[clxxiii]

The above figure highlights that the UAE has a good ranking regarding the corruption perception (27); however, the country needs to move further up in this indicator. As shown in Figure 77, the UAE secured 67 points out of 100 in 2022, and it was two points down compared to the year 2021. There is a declining trend in the corruption perception since 2020, and the UAE should make improvements in this indicator.

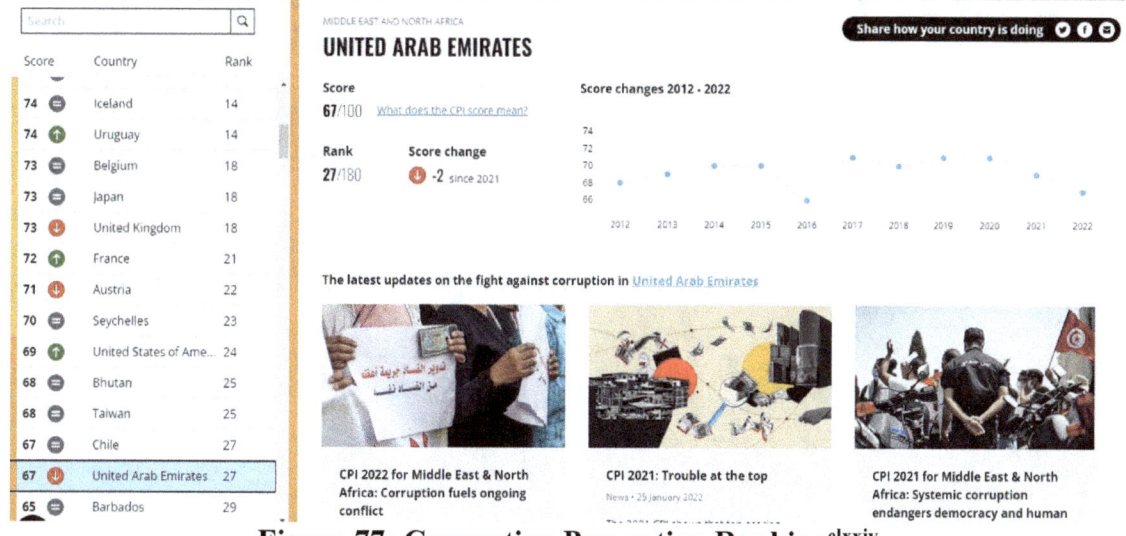

Figure 77: Corruption Perception Ranking[clxxiv]

Another indicator shown in Figure 76 is innovation index where the UAE has secured 31st rank. With the new innovation framework and AI strategy, it can be asserted with confidence that there will be a significant improvement of the UAE in the innovation index in the coming years.

The indicators in Figure 76 also highlight that the US FDI outward to the UAE stood at $16.2 billion in 2021 and it stood at $16.9 billion in 2022 as shown in Figure 78 below. The figure highlights that traditionally, the outward FDI were significantly more than inward FDI. However, the UAE lost this advantage since 2019 and now, the UAE FDI into the U.S is far more that the U.S. FDI into the UAE. The UAE should regain its competitive advantage in this regard.

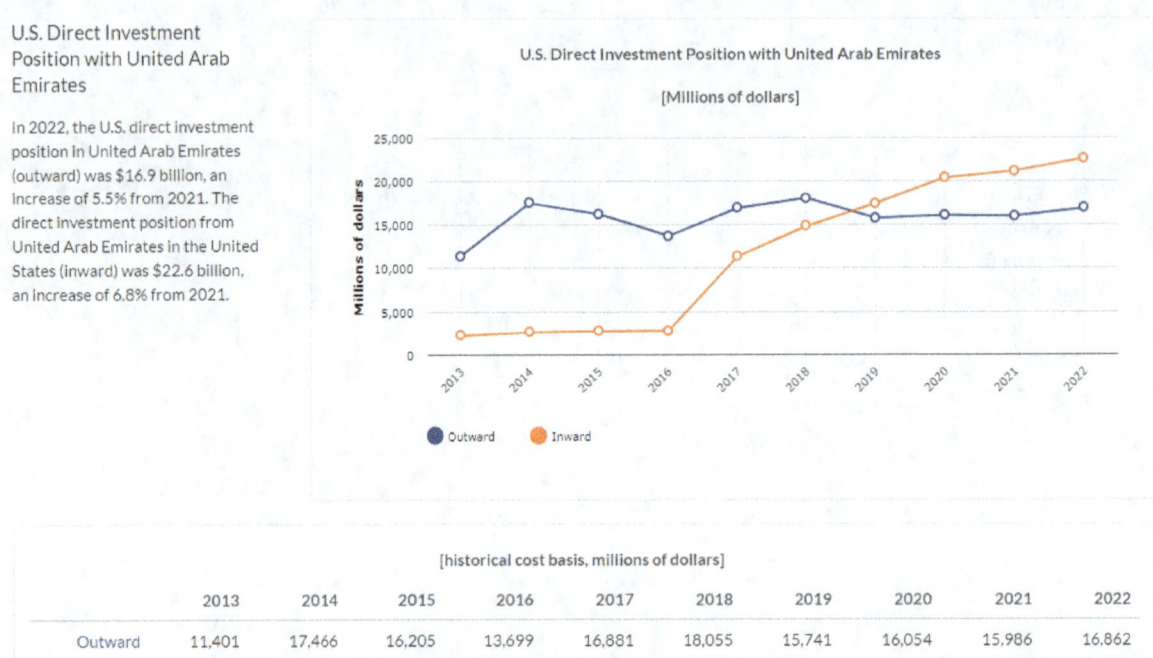

U.S. Direct Investment Position with United Arab Emirates

In 2022, the U.S. direct investment position in United Arab Emirates (outward) was $16.9 billion, an increase of 5.5% from 2021. The direct investment position from United Arab Emirates in the United States (inward) was $22.6 billion, an increase of 6.8% from 2021.

[historical cost basis, millions of dollars]

	2013	2014	2015	2016	2017	2018	2019	2020	2021	2022
Outward	11,401	17,466	16,205	13,699	16,881	18,055	15,741	16,054	15,986	16,862
Inward	2,245	2,618	2,752	2,796	11,341	14,795	17,426	20,409	21,181	22,625

Figure 78: US FDI – Inward and Outward[clxxv]

The last indicator in Figure 76 is Gross National Income (GNI), and the UAE has shown impressive performance in this indicator in 2022. The per capita GNI of UAE stood at $48,950 that is almost close to the UK as shown in Figure 79 below. However, when the GNI is compared with the U.S., there is still a huge difference ($76,370 versus $48,950) that shows the areas of improvement.

data.worldbank.org/indicator/NY.GNP.PCAP.CD

Tunisia	2022	3,840	
Turkiye	2022	10,590	
Turkmenistan	2019	7,080	
Turks and Caicos Islands	2022	24,160	
Tuvalu	2022	7,210	
Uganda	2022	930	
Ukraine	2022	4,270	
United Arab Emirates	2022	48,950	
United Kingdom	2022	48,890	
United States	2022	76,370	
Uruguay	2022	18,030	
Uzbekistan	2022	2,190	
Vanuatu	2022	3,560	
Venezuela, RB	2014	13,010	

Figure 79: Per Capita GNI of the UAE[clxxvi]

6.2. Free Trade Zones and Tax Incentives

The UAE has free trade zones in all seven emirates that offer special incentives and tax benefits for the foreign investors. Gulf News has published a list of 45 free zones that are available to the foreign investors in the seven emirates.[clxxvii]

There are various benefits available to the foreign investors in these free trade zones. The foreign nationals will get 100% ownership of the firm in the UAE. They will not be required to get the services of a local sponsor. The corporate taxes will be waived on the foreign investment. The personal taxes, import taxes, and export taxes will also be exempted. As a result, it will be possible for the foreign investors to have a 100% repatriation of their profits and revenues. Documentation process is reduced and simplified for the foreign investors.

The free trade zones also offer the option of long-term leasing that can be availed up to the extent of 25 years. Simplified and standard recruitment and selection policies can be implemented. The labor, housing, and legal services are easily available. The company incorporation process is faster compared to the incorporation process outside the free zone area. The transfer of funds can be made easily without the imposition of any additional charges.

These benefits make the free trade zones in the UAE an ideal place for the foreign investors and they can benefit from the conducive environment and tax incentives offered by the UAE leaders. The list of free zones is mentioned from Figure 80 to Figure 85 below. As is evident from the list, the highest number of free trade zones is in Dubai Emirate whereas Ajman and Umm Al Quwain Emirates have only one free trade zone. It is one of the reasons, the UAE people observe more business activities in Dubai than other emirates because the foreign investors are highly attracted to forming companies in free trade zones.

Dubai

Free Zones in Dubai

Dubai Airport Free Zone
Dubai Auto Zone
Dubai Cars and Automotive Zone
Dubai Design District
Dubai Flower Centre
Dubai Gold and Diamond Park
Dubai Healthcare City
Dubai Industrial City
Dubai International Academic City
Dubai International Financial Centre
Dubai Internet City
Dubai Knowledge Park
Dubai Logistics City
Dubai Maritime City Authority
Dubai Media City
Dubai Multi Commodities Centre
Dubai Outsource Zone
Dubai Science Park
Dubai Silicon Oasis
Dubai Studio City
Dubai Techno Park *(New name: National Industries Complex)*
Dubai Textile City
Energy and Environment Park
International Humanitarian City
Jebel Ali Free Zone Authority
Jumeirah Lakes Towers Free Zone
Dubai Production City

Figure 80: Free Zones in Dubai Emirate[clxxviii]

Abu Dhabi

Free Zones in Abu Dhabi

Abu Dhabi Airport Business City
Abu Dhabi Global Market
Abu Dhabi Ports Company
Higher corporation for specialized economic zones/ ZonesCorp
Industrial City of Abu Dhabi
Masdar City
TwoFour54

Figure 81: Free Zones in Abu Dhabi Emirate[clxxix]

Sharjah

Free Zones in Sharjah

Hamriya Free Zone Authority

Sharjah Airport Free Zone Authority

USA Regional Trade Center Free Zone

Figure 82: Free Zones in Sharjah Emirate[clxxx]

Fujairah

Free Zones in Fujairah

Creative City Fujairah

Fujairah Free Zone Authority

Figure 83: Free Zones in Fujairah Emirate[clxxxi]

Ras Al Khaimah

Free Zones in Ras Al Khaimah

RAK Investment Authority Free Zone

RAK Maritime City

Ras Al Khaimah Free Trade Zone

Ras Al Khaimah Media Free Zone

Figure 84: Free Zones in Ras Al Khaimah Emirate[clxxxii]

Ajman and Umm Al Quwain

These emirates have one free zone authority each; Ajman Free Zone Authority and Umm Al Quwain Free Zone Authority

Figure 85: Free Zones in Ajman and Umm Al Quwain Emirates[clxxxiii]

In addition to the above free trade zones, the UAE leaders are also developing further free zones to improve the corporate image of the UAE and attract foreign investment. For example, Dubai Maritime City is a mega project of UAE and it is also set to become one of the free trade zones of the UAE.[clxxxiv] Various other projects such as Technology Park, trucks zone, equipment zone, and auto parts city are set to become free trade zones in the UAE.

6.3. Attracting Foreign Investors

The UAE ranks first in attracting foreign direct investment in the Middle East. However, when a world comparison is made, the UAE still needs to improve its ranking. In 2022, FDI inflows in the UAE increased by 10% and reached the volume of $23 billion.[clxxxv] Among the six members of the GCC alliance, the UAE attracts 60% of the whole FDI attracted by the member states.[clxxxvi] The outward investments of the UAE have also increased significantly and reached the volume of $25 billion in 2022. This is an area where the UAE needs to make improvements. The inward investments should be significantly more than the outward investments. Currently, they are either matching or the outward investment surpasses the inward investment.

6.4. Supporting Startups and Entrepreneurs

According to the website of the ministry of economy, various accelerator programs have been introduced in the UAE to support the initiatives of the startups and entrepreneurs. The UAE leaders are highly confident that startups and entrepreneurs will contribute to the diversification and development agenda of the country and the contribution of these business entities will increase in the GDP. In this regard, an entrepreneurial national platform has been developed in the UAE.[clxxxvii]

In the UAE, it is not the responsibility of a single ministry to support the initiatives of the startups. Instead, a total of 8 ministries collaborate to ensure the success of startups and entrepreneurs as shown in Figure 86 below. These include ministries of enterprise development, Dubai SME, Sharjah SME, SME development, RAK SME, Sharjah Center, innovation fund, and development bank.

Government Entities Supporting Start-Ups

Figure 86: Eight Ministries for Startup Support[clxxxviii]

6.5. FinTech Hive and Dubai Future Accelerators

FinTech Hive is an innovation hub in Dubai. It is regarded as the largest innovation community of the Middle East. The innovation hub has hosted more than 500 tech firms and startups. The hub also includes digital labs, innovation companies and educational entities. As of December 2023, the performance of the innovation hub is mentioned in Figure 87 below. According to the statistics, the hub has been able to raise funding up to 530 million and it has a representation of more than 30 countries. More than 4000 companies have been registered in this innovation hub. A great achievement of the innovation hub is that more than 200 startups have joined the accelerator program in this hub.

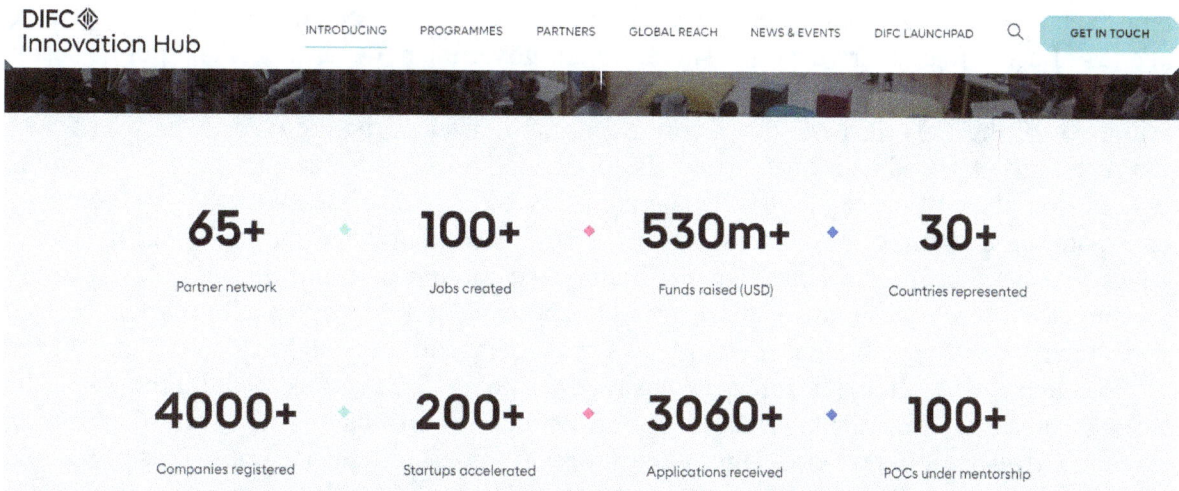

Figure 87: Performance of the Innovation Hub[clxxxix]

Dubai Future Accelerators (DFA) is also a unique initiative of the UAE leaders and its primary objective is to co-create the future of the local and international companies. The program facilitates the interactions between the private entities, startups, and the government institutions. The center provides all tools and infrastructure that can serve as a testbed for implementing innovative technologies.

The vision of the DFA mentioned by the crown prince of Dubai is shown in Figure 88 below. According to the vision of DFA, Dubai aims to become a leading city for the future generations. The mission highlights that the business leaders can achieve their goals and targets through collective wisdom, imagination, inspiration, and design.

Figure 88: Vision of DFA[cxc]

6.6. Streamlined Bureaucratic Process

The UAE governance system simulates a federation of monarchies. However, as I explained earlier, it is because of the tribal roots of the Arab culture. There are various examples where the UAE leaders have demonstrated exemplary leadership, and their visionary approach has made the UAE survive the tough economic conditions and the political uncertainties. The religious tolerance is also a strength of the UAE and people from different religious orientations are welcome in the UAE. I also gave you the example of the visit of Pop Francis, which was a good welcome gesture by the UAE leaders.

In the business domain as well, the UAE leaders believe that the bureaucratic hurdles and red-tapism can have a negative impact on promoting the foreign investment and implementing the agenda of economic diversification. Therefore, all government departments and public sector entities have been directed to facilitate the clients in their issues and queries. Through the initiatives of the UAE leaders, now every department has a corporate website as well where the customers can send their queries and also download forms. In some of the cases, the online portals are also available to the registered users to expedite the processes of company incorporation and filing the business details. I have also mentioned the list of all free trade zones that have been established for facilitating the foreign investors in the UAE. The tax incentives in these zones indicate the aggressive approach of the UAE leaders to attract foreign investment. A conservative leader would think that tax incentives would reduce the tax revenue in the country. But if a higher foreign investment is attracted, as is the case with the UAE, the overall returns are even higher through the economies of scale. Moreover, the foreign investment also provides good employment opportunities for the Emiratis. Therefore, the visionary approach of the UAE leaders has benefited both the local investors and the foreign investors in the UAE.

The UAE nation celebrated the national day on December 02, 2023. This day reminds the contribution of the great leaders for shaping a great country such that the UAE is a success story in both the Arab World and the Muslim World. The population of the UAE is 9,973,449 (approximately 10 million) and the country ranks 92 in the world population index. The local Emiratis are only 11.6% of the total population. Even with this comparatively small population and a lower percentage of the local Emiratis, the country has a strong influence on the business and political affairs of the world due to the visionary approach of the UAE leaders. The contribution of the UAE in the human development is more than even many countries that have a significantly large population. The national life of the UAE emirates began 52 years ago in the Arabian Desert by forming a union. Now these united emirates are regarded as the most modern, global technology leaders. UAE has secured the 10th rank in the Global Competitiveness Report of 2023.[cxci] This report is published by the World Economic Forum and the report highlights the competitive potential of a country at the global level.

The business strength of the UAE is complemented by its global reputation that is credited to the great UAE leaders. The UAE has also secured the first position in the recent passport power index as shown in Figure 89 below. If an individual is a UAE passport holder, the individual can travel 129 countries without a visa. The individual will have visa-on-arrival facility in 51 countries. There are only 18 countries where the individual will have to apply for the visa in advance, and this visa restriction of 18 countries is the lowest for any in the world and provides the first ranking to the UAE.

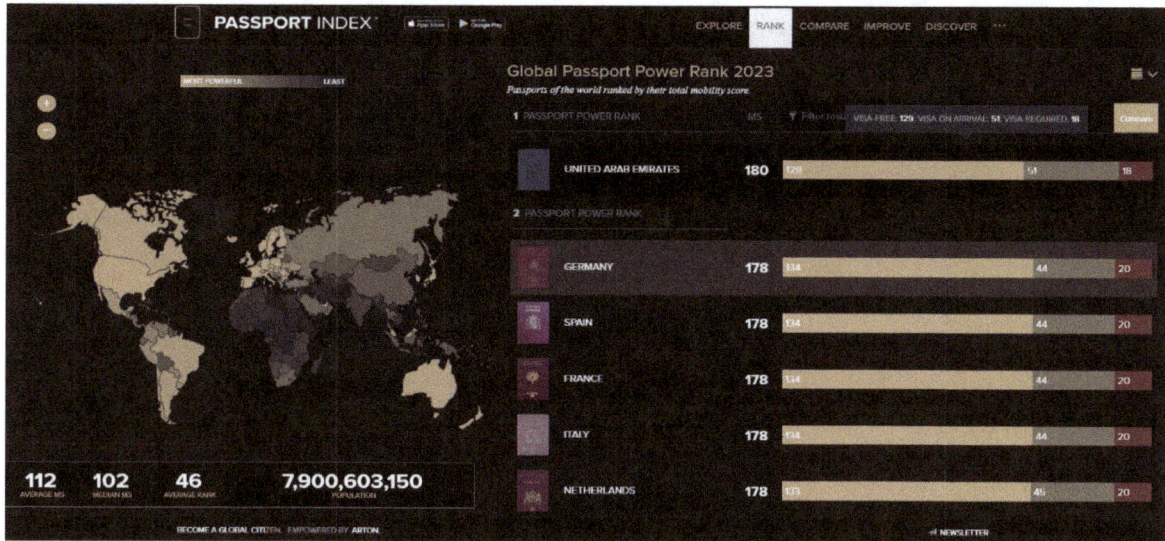

Figure 89: Passport Power[cxcii]

The UAE is also included in the list of 10 top donor countries that are providing financial assistance to under-developed countries or those countries where people are living in difficult circumstances.[cxciii] All these remarkable achievements of the UAE have not been made possible exclusively by the oil-based exports. The dreams of the nation were transformed into reality because all the UAE leaders adopted a balanced approach in leading the nation and their target was the development of a balanced, and modern nation.

When the UAE got independence in 1971, the founding father of the country, Sheikh Zayed made two important strategic decisions that led the country to the path of success and development. First, the country was made a unique blend of keeping the traditional roots and at the same time, embracing the contemporary ideas. The second decision was to promote a positive approach towards nationalism where the citizens of the country could work towards the shared inspirations. Due to this positive approach towards nationalism, there was no antagonistic approach adopted by the UAE leaders similar to other post-colonial states at that time. The UAE was not involved directly in any war among the Gulf States and maintained its peaceful existence throughout its history.

It will not be correct to say that the UAE did not have disputes with other countries at the time of independence. When the UK forces exited from the Trucial States, then its three islands were occupied by Iran. At that time, the UAE also had border disputes with Saudi Arabia and Oman. The UAE leaders were also attached with the Pan-Arab wave in the context of Palestinian Liberation. However, all three presidents of the UAE were never fixated into these issues and they did not let the situation escalate to a war-like situation. Their decision-making approaches were always dominated by pragmatism and Muslim brotherhood.

When the discovery of oil had earned huge revenues to the UAE, the UAE leaders used these financial resources for improving the living conditions and the quality of life of the UAE people. They developed world-class infrastructure, healthcare facilities, and academic institutions.

The UAE is a unique country where people from 190 countries work in different industries for better opportunities and improving their quality of life.[cxciv] This cosmopolitan outlook of the UAE has been possible by the guidelines, forward-looking approach, and an inclusive approach of the UAE leaders. UAE has always welcomed the great brains and skilled workforce from different parts of the world. According to an estimate, the foreign workers serving in different industries of the UAE send approximately $44 billion remittances annually to their countries of origin.[cxcv] These remittances are a huge source of relief to the relatives and the families at home. For example, the top five countries that receive remittances are Mexico, India, Philippines, China, and Egypt as shown in Figure 90 below. The UAE is also a major contributor in the remittance flows. Therefore, when the families of the low-income countries and middle-income countries receive the valuable foreign exchange, they can spend this amount for the betterment of their health and meeting the household and educational expenses.

Global Remittance Inflows

Remittance flows to low- and middle-income countries (LMICs) are estimated to have increased by 4.9% to reach USD 626 billion in 2022. The strong growth rate is coming after a surge of 10.2% in 2021 (according to revised official data). Globally, remittance flows are estimated to reach USD 794 billion in 2022. The top five recipient countries for remittances in 2021 were India, Mexico, China, the Philippines, and Egypt.

Growth Rate of Remittance Flows to LMICs

According to World Bank's Migration and Development Brief 37, several factors affected remittance flows to developing regions. Aside from migrants' determination to help their families back home, the continuous reopening of various industries in host countries' economies enhanced the income and employment situation of migrants.

2020 | **-0.8%**

Source: KNOMAD World Bank Migration and Development Brief 37 – Nov 2022

2021 | **10.2%**

Estimated Remittances

USD 794e bn

Remitted worldwide in 2022

2022 | **4.9%**
Estimated

Source: KNOMAD World Bank Migration and Development Brief 37 – Nov 2022

Source: KNOMAD World Bank Migration and Development Brief 37 – Nov 2022

Figure 90: Remittance Flows[cxcvi]

According to the global investment report published by the UN agency for the period 2017-2022, the FDI inflows to the UAE stood at $22.737 billion, which is larger than any other country in West Asia as shown in Figure 91 below. It highlights that the efforts of the UAE leaders have attracted the foreign investors in huge numbers and they want to establish their businesses in a safe and conducive environment of the UAE.

Figure 91 also highlights that FDI outflows from the UAE stood at $24.833 billion. It is because the UAE leaders also invest and support the business initiatives at the global level. The business leaders of the UAE have made international investments in sovereign wealth funds, investment corporations, and emirate-level business entities.

Annex table 1.	FDI flows, by region and economy, 2017–2022 (Continued)											

Region/economy	FDI inflows						FDI outflows					
	2017	2018	2019	2020	2021	2022	2017	2018	2019	2020	2021	2022
West Asia	33 183	34 989	37 147	35 429	55 911	48 268	41 599	49 019	42 053	37 920	55 015	27 487
Armenia	253	267	100	59	366	998	29	7	-133	-27	25	50
Azerbaijan	2 867	1 403	1 504	507	-1 708	-4 474	2 564	1 761	2 432	825	77	172
Bahrain	1 426	1 654	1 548	1 021	1 779	1 951	229	111	-197	-205	64	1 948
Georgia	1 991	1 352	1 352	590	1 242	2 000	269	340	282	23	322	348
Iraq	-5 032	-4 885	-3 508	-2 859	-2 637	-2 088	78	188	194	147	135	238
Jordan	2 030	955	730	760	622	1 137	7	-8	43	26	16	-16
Kuwait	348	204	351	240	567	758	9 013	3 715	-2 696	7 932	4 666	-25 603
Lebanon	2 522	2 658	1 905	1 607	605	458c	1 317	631	345	29	-1 366	99c
Oman	2 988	6 455	4 237	2 889	4 021	3 716c	2 424	718	-466	-697	-398	-520c
Qatar	986	-2 186	-2 813	-2 434	-1 093	76	1 695	4 450	4 450	2 730	160	2 384
Saudi Arabia	1 419	4 247	4 563	5 399	19 286	7 886	7 280	19 252	13 547	4 911	23 860	18 826
State of Palestine	188	252	132	80	353	233	3	31	56	59	-58	13
Syrian Arab Republic	..	..	..	..	..	..	..	..	..	..	..	..
Türkiye	11 113	12 511	9 543	7 686	11 840	12 881	2 626	3 666	2 966	3 230	4 966	4 715
United Arab Emirates	10 354	10 385	17 875	19 884	20 667	22 737	14 060	15 079	21 226	18 937	22 546	24 833
Yemen	-270c	-282c	-371c	..	..	..	6c	4c	3c	..	..	..

Figure 91: FDI Inflows and Outflows[cxcvii]

A recent example of the overseas investments of the UAE groups is the acquisition of a Pakistani Bank. A prominent investor of the UAE, Mr. Nasser Abdulla Hussain Lootah acquired Summit Bank of Pakistan by having a controlling stake in the bank. In April 2023, Lootah acquired new shares of Summit Bank to the volume of 3.98 billion. These shares were purchased at a share price of Rupees 2.51 per share. As a result, Lootah paid Rupees 10 billion for acquiring the new shares.[cxcviii] The purchase of shares to this large volume made him a majority equity stakeholder in the bank. Summit Bank issued a press release in July 2023 announcing the transition of the operation and the bank with a new name Bank Makramah as shown in Figure 92 below. The new owners aim to promote Islamic banking practices and financial instruments in the bank. It will also be ensured that all the new offered financial solutions are shariah-compliant.

Press Release

Summit Bank Limited Announces Name Change To Bank Makramah Limited

KARACHI, July 18, 2023: Summit Bank Limited is pleased to announce that the State Bank of Pakistan has granted its consent to change Summit Bank's name to Bank Makramah Limited (abbreviated as **BML**). This will become effective subject to other regulatory and corporate approvals. This name change follows the recent acquisition of a controlling stake in Summit Bank by prominent UAE investor, H.E. Nasser Abdulla Hussain Lootah.

H.E. Nasser Abdulla Hussain Lootah's vision for Bank Makramah Limited (**BML**) is to develop it into a leading Islamic bank, providing exceptional financial services and innovative products in line with Islamic principles. The name change from Summit Bank Limited to Bank Makramah Limited (**BML**) signifies the bank's commitment to embracing Islamic finance principles and delivering innovative and ethical financial services to its valued customers.

Bank Makramah Limited (**BML**) is in the process of developing a comprehensive plan to transition into a full-fledged Islamic bank. The bank's transformation will involve a complete overhaul of its operations, introduction of Shariah-compliant financial solutions, and adherence to Islamic banking practices. Bank Makramah Limited (**BML**) remains committed to serving its customers and ensuring a seamless transition throughout this transformative phase.

Bank Makramah Limited (**BML**) will continue to provide updates on its progress as it moves forward in its journey toward becoming a full-fledged Islamic bank.

---End---

For Media Queries:
Syntax Communications
Faisal Mushtaq: 0321-2431568
Sheeraz Mohiuddin: 0333-2235774

Figure 92: Acquisition of Bank by UAE Investor[cxcix]

The UAE leaders also emphasize that the business motives of the corporate entities should be balanced by their social responsibilities regarding sustainability and environmental protection. In this regard, the UAE leaders have introduced strategies for maintaining a balance between financial profits, environmental protection, and economic prosperity. This model has attracted even more foreign investors into the country. As of June 2023, the volume of the foreign trade of the UAE reached AED 1.239 trillion and it marks an increase of 14.4% on a year-on-year comparison.[cc]

In November 2021, the UAE opened a visa center in Karachi, Pakistan as shown in Figure 93 below. This visa center is regarded as the largest visa center by any country in Asia. It shows the love and affection of the UAE leaders for Pakistan because Pakistan was the first country that accepted the UAE after its independence. According to the UAE leaders, this visa center is a gift to the Pakistani nation. A unique aspect of this visa center is that a happiness desk has been established that is not found in any visa center of the world.[cci] The UAE leaders want to facilitate the Pakistani brothers in getting visa of the UAE. Happiness Desk also provides financial assistance if the visa requestors do not have sufficient funds for paying the visa fees.

The visa center also facilitates those visa requestors who want to go along with their children. They are made aware of the Wadeema's Law in the UAE.[ccii] This law makes them aware regarding the rights of the children while staying in the UAE. Through this law, the parents can take care of the health, education, and welfare of their children.

UAE Embassy PK ✔
@uaeembassyisb

H.E. Sheikh Nahyan bin Mubarak Al Nahyan, Minister of Tolerance and Coexistence, inaugurates the Visa and Cons. Services Center at Karachi in presence of H.E. Imran Ismail, Governor Sindh, H.E. Dr. Salem Al Dhanhani, Consul General of UAE and heads of consular missions in Karachi

9:06 PM · Nov 28, 2021

Figure 93: Largest Visa Center in Asia[cciii]

All these efforts of the UAE leaders make it evident that significant progress has been made in the UAE for streamlining the bureaucratic processes. An enabling business environment is being provided to the local investors as well as the international investors. The inflow of immigrants has enabled their families living in their countries of origin to live a quality life. The foreign investors are also benefiting from the free trade zone and other incentives of the UAE and turning their businesses into remarkable success stories.

7. Academic Initiatives

According to the vision of the founding father of the UAE, Sheikh Zayed, a good education is inevitable for a multidimensional and progressive society. After four years of independence, the adult literacy rate in the UAE was 58% in males and 38% in females. Through the efforts and strategic initiatives of the UAE leaders, the literacy rate is now 95% in both genders.[cciv]

7.1. Human Capital Development

The UAE leaders have always valued the human resources and invested massively in human capital development. The leaders believe that people-oriented approaches should be utilized in the organization and there should be a perfect alignment of the organizational goals and the personal goals of the employees. As shown in Figure 94 below, if there is a mismatch between the personal growth of the employee and the organizational goals, the complacency and stagnancy develops in the entire organizational lifecycle.

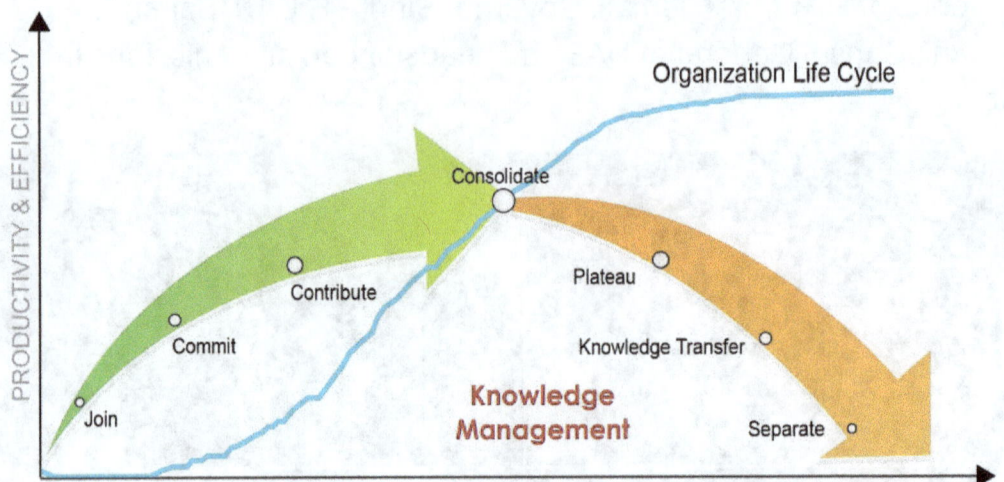

Figure 94: Match between Employee and Organization[ccv]

The UAE leaders have also focused on the challenges that are often faced in the human capital development. As highlighted in Figure 95 below, the six challenges may be faced by the organizational leaders and national leaders concerning human capital development. The first key challenge is the underutilization of the workforce. The UAE leaders have ensured that every UAE resident gets good employment opportunity that matches his/her qualification and the skill set. As a result, the employees are highly satisfied with their job and they are happily utilized by the senior management in key initiatives due to their outstanding performance and the commitment level.

Human Capital Challenges

Figure 95: Challenges in Human Capital Development[ccvi]

The second challenge is that the majority of the Emiratis might work in government organizations where they are easily recruited compared to the private sector. The UAE leaders have also addressed this issue by introducing the concept of localization where a certain percentage of Emiratis are required to be recruited by private sector organizations as well in the UAE.

The third challenge is the high level of unemployment among the recently passed-out graduates. This issue has also been addressed by introducing skills development programs by the UAE leaders. Moreover, the universities have been asked to collaborate with the corporate professionals so that the curriculum could be aligned with the latest demands of the corporate world. In the technology domain, a ministry of artificial intelligence has also been established so that the graduates are well-prepared for taking up the challenges in the corporate world.

The fourth challenge is the education and training of the recent graduates, and as I mentioned above, the UAE leaders have introduced impressive policies to improve the employability potential of the young graduates.

The fifth challenge is brain drain. It is a type of challenge in the human capital development that is not faced in the UAE context. The UAE is such an attractive industrial and technological hub that professionals from across the globe come to the UAE for better employment opportunities. Therefore, there is no risk that the local Emiratis will go abroad instead of working in their home land where good opportunities await them.

The sixth challenge is disparities in the acquisition of education. This issue has also been addressed effectively by the UAE leaders. There is a uniformity in educational opportunities and free education is available to the students up to the K-12 grade. Moreover, financial assistance is available to the students on need-cum-merit basis. The UAE also supports the inclusive education system and has also established separate schools for the people of determination.

As I highlighted in section 3.7, the UAE leaders have also introduced the concept of localization for better job opportunities for the Emiratis in the private sector. It has been made mandatory for the private sector companies and the fines and penalties have also been announced for non-compliance. The UAE is not the only country in the Arab world where the localization has been introduced. As highlighted in Figure 96 below, other Arab countries also felt that the nationalization policy is imperative for protecting the interests of the local citizens and following the agenda of economic diversification. Therefore, such policies were also introduced in Saudi Arabia, Kuwait, Qatar, Bahrain, and Oman.

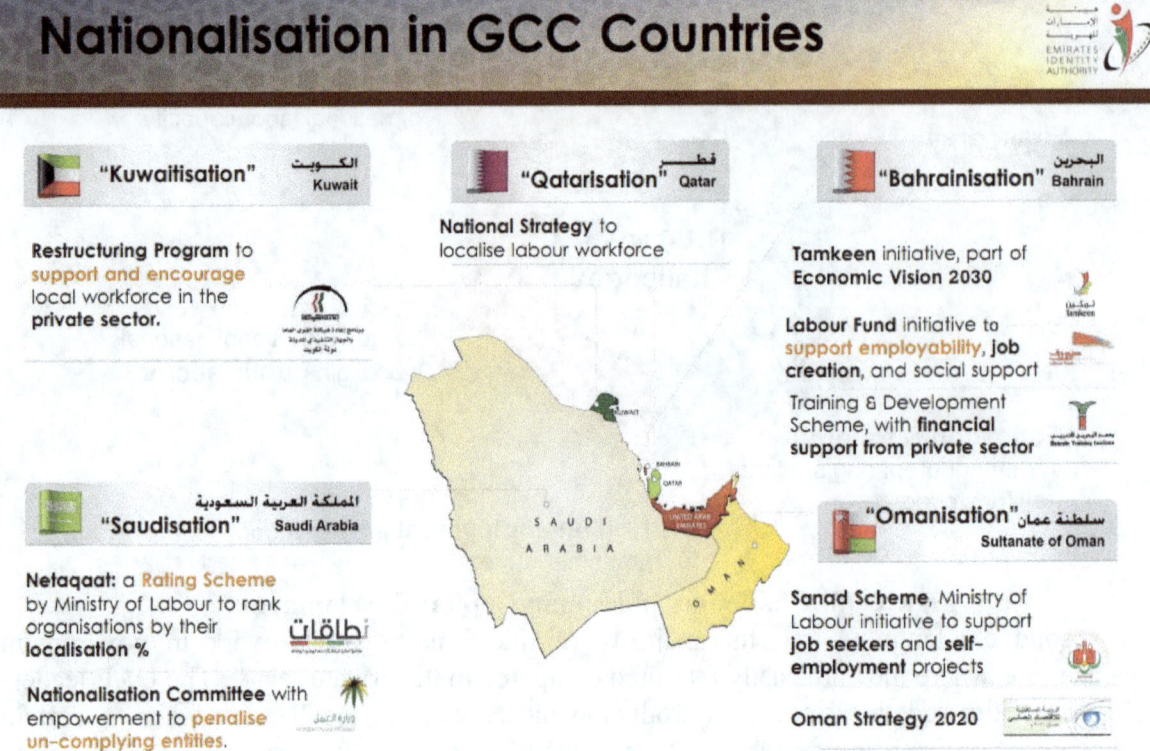

Figure 96: Localization in Arab Countries[ccvii]

The UAE leaders have introduced multiple programs for supporting localization and the mandatory requirement for recruiting Emiratis is just one part of this whole strategy. Other initiatives include the development of funds, foundations, and councils as shown in Figure 97 below:

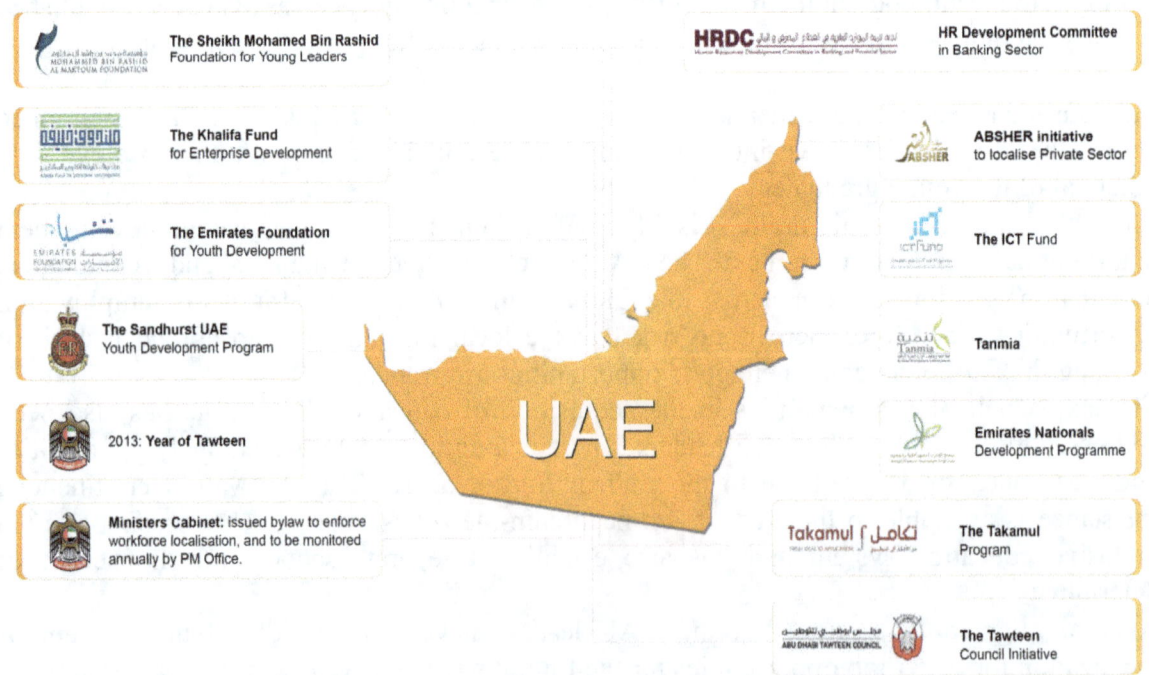

Figure 97: Initiatives to Promote Localization[ccviii]

7.2. Leadership Role in developing Research Centers, Universities, and Innovation Hubs

The efforts of the UAE leaders to promote investment in education and knowledge are being appreciated across the world. The academic leaders are foreseeing a competitive global market in the UAE and many renowned universities have established their programs and campuses in the UAE. It has proved to be highly beneficial for the local Emiratis and the population that was once residing in palm-frond houses have transformed them into highly educated citizens and the qualified graduates are working as experts with foreigners in different sectors and industrial establishments.

The education ministry of the UAE announced the national strategy in 2017 whose objectives are to be accomplished by 2030 in the context of higher education as shown in Figure 98 below.[ccix] The strategy aims to build the future leaders of the UAE by equipping them with the required technical and practical skills for contributing effectively to the economic growth of the UAE. The strategy highlights that the directions of the UAE leaders can be followed by focusing on the four main dimensions.

Figure 98: National Strategy for Higher Education[ccx]

The first pillar for the advancement in higher education is quality. The quality of higher education should be improved by adhering to the accreditation standards and giving incentives to the institutions to improve the skills of the faculty and the academic staff. The second pillar is efficiency. The higher education institutes should demonstrate optimal productivity by enhancing the completion rate of the graduates each year. The institutions should ensure that effective funding mechanisms are in place so that no student is left behind due to the lack of financial resources.

The third pillar is innovation. The universities should produce an academic environment that promotes scientific research and original, innovative research outputs are generated by the graduates of the universities. The fourth pillar is harmonization. The academic leaders and the management should also collaborate with the private sector to benefit from their expertise in curriculum design and teachers' training. The national strategy has identified 33 academic initiatives so that the implementation phase produces tangible outcomes.

The UAE leaders have also acknowledged that quality education is one of the key agenda items of the 2030 agenda of the UN. As highlighted in Figure 99 below, the fourth goal of the UN's agenda is quality education that should be accessible to all so that each individual could exercise his/her right for a better living condition, and no one is left behind.

The UN's 2030 Agenda

Sustainable Development Goals (SDGs) also known as Global Goals are a set of 17 goals that aim to provide better living conditions to all. The SDGs are based on the United Nations' Millennium Development Goals. The SDGs are part of 2030 Agenda for Sustainable Development. This section highlights the UAE's efforts to achieve the SDGs at home and abroad. Read the UAE's efforts to achieve the SDGs in this publication - UAE and the 2030 Agenda for Sustainable Development (PDF).

The UAE and the SDGs	1. No poverty	2. Zero hunger	3. Good health and well-being
4. Quality education	5. Gender equality	6. Clean water and sanitation	7. Affordable and clean energy
8. Decent work and economic growth	9. Industry, innovation and infrastructure	10. Reduced inequalities	11. Sustainable cities and communities
12. Responsible consumption and production	13. Climate action	14. Life below water	15. Life on land
16. Peace, justice and strong institutions	17. Partnerships for the goals		

Figure 99: UN 17 Objectives[ccxi]

The UAE leaders have developed various strategies to improve the quality of education provided in the UAE at the levels of primary, secondary, and tertiary education. In this regard, a smart learning program was introduced by the prime minister in 2012. This program provides a technology-enabled educational environment in UAE schools where students will also receive tablet PCs besides teachers. The academic institutes will be connected by high-speed, 4G internet connections. The objectives of the smart learning program are also highlighted in Figure 100 below:

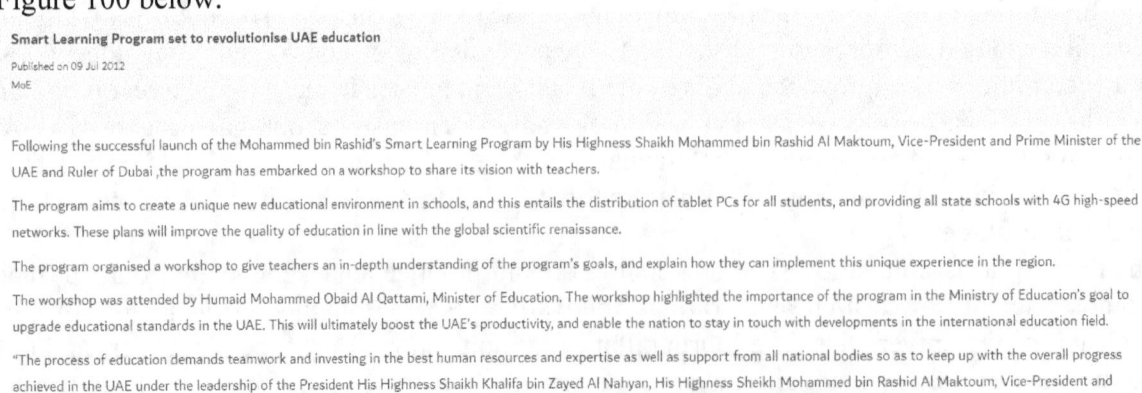

Smart Learning Program set to revolutionise UAE education

Published on 09 Jul 2012
MoE

Following the successful launch of the Mohammed bin Rashid's Smart Learning Program by His Highness Shaikh Mohammed bin Rashid Al Maktoum, Vice-President and Prime Minister of the UAE and Ruler of Dubai ,the program has embarked on a workshop to share its vision with teachers.

The program aims to create a unique new educational environment in schools, and this entails the distribution of tablet PCs for all students, and providing all state schools with 4G high-speed networks. These plans will improve the quality of education in line with the global scientific renaissance.

The program organised a workshop to give teachers an in-depth understanding of the program's goals, and explain how they can implement this unique experience in the region.

The workshop was attended by Humaid Mohammed Obaid Al Qattami, Minister of Education. The workshop highlighted the importance of the program in the Ministry of Education's goal to upgrade educational standards in the UAE. This will ultimately boost the UAE's productivity, and enable the nation to stay in touch with developments in the international education field.

"The process of education demands teamwork and investing in the best human resources and expertise as well as support from all national bodies so as to keep up with the overall progress achieved in the UAE under the leadership of the President His Highness Shaikh Khalifa bin Zayed Al Nahyan, His Highness Sheikh Mohammed bin Rashid Al Maktoum, Vice-President and Prime Minister of the UAE and Ruler of Dubai and Their Highnesses Members of the Supreme Council and Rulers of Emirates," Al Qattami said in a speech at the meeting.

Figure 100: Objectives of Smart Learning Program[ccxii]

The UAE leaders also believe in an inclusive education system in which differently-abled people could also participate in the mainstream education system. In this regard, the rights of the students with special needs are protected under law in the UAE. The concerned federal law in this case is known as law 29. In this law, the special people have been rightly termed as people of determination. In the context of education, article 12 is added in the law as shown in Figure 101 below:

Education
Article (12)

The country guarantees people of determination equal opportunities in education within all educational, vocational training, adult education and continuing education institutions in regular classes or special classes with the availability of curriculum in sign language or Braille and any other methods as appropriate.

Figure 101: Educational Rights of Differently-Abled People

As shown in article 12, the UAE leaders have provided equal opportunities to the differently-abled people and they can attend regular classes in all educational institutions and vocational institutes. Moreover, if they choose to get enrolled in special classes, it is the responsibility of the academic management to ensure the provision of curriculum in Braille or sign language.

The UAE government has also announced 2024 federal budget whose total volume is AED 64.060 billion. Out of this budget, a significant percentage 42% has been allocated to the social development sector that also includes education. The budget allocation for public education and university education programs is AED 10.2 billion that highlights the commitment of the UAE leaders to promote the academic initiatives in the country. The budget allocation for 2024 is shown in Figure 102 below:

Federal budget 2024

The federal budget for the year 2024 is AED 64.060 billion, 1.6 per cent more than the budget for the year 2023 (AED 63.066 billion). The federal budget for 2024 is allocated as follows:

O AED 26.7 billion (42 per cent of the total general budget) towards social development and social benefits sector, distributed as follows:

    O AED 10.2 billion (16 per cent of the total general budget) to public and university education programs

    O AED 5.2 billion (8 per cent of the total general budget) to healthcare and community protection

    O AED 3.6 billion (6 per cent of the total general budget) to social affairs

    O AED 6.1 billion (10 per cent of the total general budget) to pensions

    O AED 1.5 billion (2 per cent of the total general budget) to public services.

O AED 25.2 billion (39 per cent of the total general budget) allocated towards government affairs sector

O AED 2.6 billion (4 per cent of the total general budget) allocated towards infrastructure and economic resources

O AED 2.3 billion (4 per cent of the total general budget) allocated towards the financial investments sector, including AED 807.5 million allocated to federal investment projects

O AED 7.2 billion (11 per cent of the total general budget) allocated for other federal expenses.

Figure 102: UAE Budget for 2024[ccxiii]

The UAE leaders have also developed an Emirate-based assessment test to know the level of educational attainment of the students. This test is popularly known as EmSAT. The test is also used to evaluate the performance of the schools and the quality of education available to the students. The test also facilitates the students in selecting the best educational paths based on their skills set as shown in Figure 103 below:

The Emirates Standardized Test (EmSAT) Definition
The EmSAT is a national system of standardized computer-based tests, based on United Arab Emirates national standards.

Objectives
To ensure that students are equipped with the necessary knowledge and skills to effectively participate in the modern knowledge based global society.

Importance of EmSAT

• Assess the knowledge and skills of candidates in the transitional stages after the general education stage and the transition to the higher education stage.

• Used for university admission purposes

• Used for evaluating the effectiveness of schools' performance and the quality of the educational system and taking the necessary decisions for improvements

• Provide decision-makers information about the skills acquired by students in their different academic levels.

• Assembling accurate data about the knowledge and skills of students in the United Arab Emirates in academic subjects and across different academic cycles in accordance with national standards.

• Helping students determine the appropriate educational paths

• Determining the level of students' performance nationally and internationally.

Figure 103: Key Features of EmSAT[ccxiv]

EmSAT test has three levels and the Emirati students can appear in these tests at different stages of their academic life. As shown in Figure 104 below, the first test Baseline should be taken at Grade 1 when the students are enrolled in general education. The second test is Advantage in which students can appear at the grades of 4th, 6th, 8th, and 10th. The third test is Achieve in which students can appear at 12th grade. This test can also be taken when the students are interested in receiving scholarships or enrolling in master or doctoral level programs. This test is equally beneficial for the job candidates in the UAE.

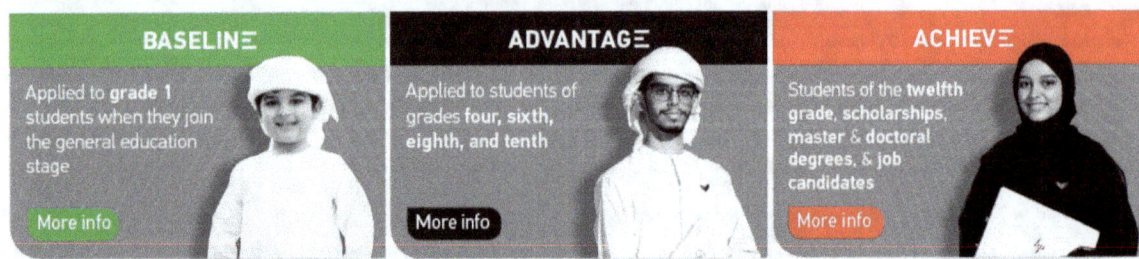

Figure 104: EmSAT Test Types[ccxv]

The UAE leaders have also introduced a licensing system for the teachers so that only qualified and trained teachers could teach in the esteemed institutions of the UAE. The new system was launched in 2017 and is popularly known as TELS UAE. Under the new licensing regime, a UAE teacher imparting education in the K-12 education system should at least have a 4-year bachelor's degree from a recognized university. The teacher should be medically fit and should not possess any criminal record as shown in the requirements in Figure 105 below:

Apply for a teacher's position in the UAE

In order to practise a teaching profession in the UAE, the applicant must have a minimum qualification of a bachelor's degree or a 4-year university degree or higher in the required field. This rule applies for public/government schools as well as private schools in the UAE. Other conditions include:

O   a criminal clearance record

O   a medical fitness report from the UAE

O   original of educational certificates

O   attested certificates in case the educator has graduated from a university outside the UAE; the certificate must be attested by Ministry of Foreign Affairs and International Cooperation and the country's embassy in the UAE.

If you want to apply to a private school, you have to approach the school administration itself. The school will then forward the necessary papers to Ministry of Education in the northern emirates or to KHDA in Dubai for tests required and final approval.

Figure 105: Teacher Licensing Requirements[ccxvi]

The UAE leaders have also developed a school inspection framework so that the quality of education at the school level could be monitored periodically by the inspectors. The inspectors evaluate the performance of the school in the light of the national agenda, innovation track record, the level of inclusiveness, and self-evaluation. After the inspection, the inspectors provide a rating to the schools based on a six level scale as shown in Figure 106 below. A school with the outstanding rating means that the inspector found the performance of the school exceeding the expectations as per the UAE standards. The rating of very weak means that the inspector found the performance of the school significantly below the expectation as per the UAE standards.

United Arab Emirates
School Inspection Framework

Inspectors will make judgements using a six-level scale.

The six levels of quality on the scale are defined as follows:

Outstanding	Quality of performance **substantially exceeds** the expectation of the UAE
Very Good	Quality of performance **exceeds** the expectation of the UAE
Good	Quality of performance **meets** the expectation of the UAE **(This is the expected level for every school in the UAE)**
Acceptable	Quality of performance **meets the minimum** level of quality required in the UAE **(This is the minimum level for every school in the UAE)**
Weak	Quality of performance is **below** the expectation of the UAE
Very Weak	Quality of performance is **significantly below** the expectation of the UAE

Figure 106: Rating Scale in the School Framework[ccxvii]

The UAE leaders have also developed a qualifications handbook under the mandate of the qualifications authority.[ccxviii] The book presents the opportunities for the planning and securing the certificates as part of the continuous learning. The book also provides information regarding all the training institutes and the professional bodies awarding certificates. According to the qualifications framework, a student has various opportunities of learning after completing the certificate 4, i.e. certificate of grade 12 or college education as shown in Figure 107 below. After completing the K-12 education, a student may opt for an associate degree or an advanced diploma that are termed as certificates 5 and 6. A higher level than the diploma holders is a Bachelor's degree that is classified as certificate 7. Then a student may opt for a post graduate diploma (certificate 8) or a master's degree (certificate 9). The highest level of academic achievement is the acquisition of a doctoral degree that is classified as the highest certificate 10.

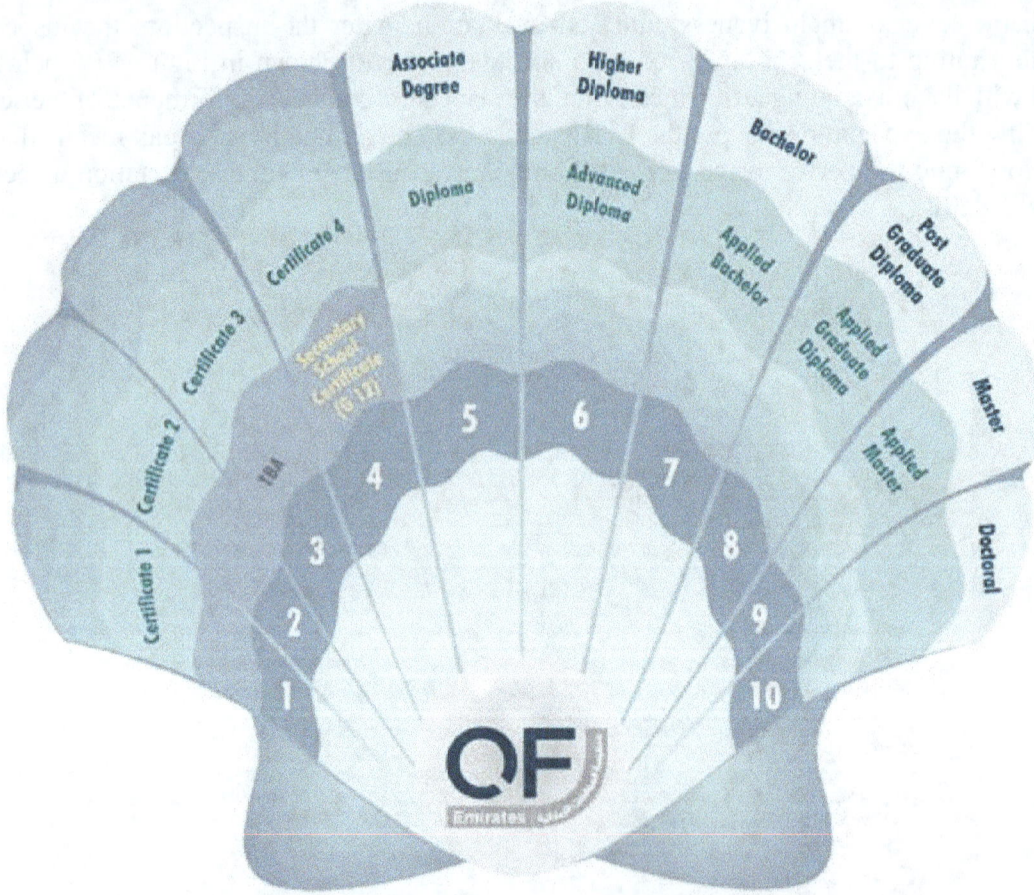

Figure 107: Higher Education Options[ccxix]

The handbook also mentions the equivalence of the Emirates qualifications framework with the European framework and Bologna framework (European Higher Education Framework). This equivalence is shown in Figure 108 below. The figure indicates that the tenth level of the framework equates with the eighth level of the European framework and third cycle of the Bologna framework.

QF*Emirates* level	EQF level	Bologna Framework
10	8	Third cycle
9	7	Second cycle
7,8	6	First cycle
6	5	Short cycle
5	4	
4	3	
3	2	
1,2	1	

Figure 108: Equivalence with Other Frameworks[ccxx]

The UAE leaders have made various achievements in line with the quality education target of the UN. As I highlighted earlier that the leadership approach of the UAE leaders is highly pragmatic and inclusive and they want to formulate policies that are consistent with the UN agenda and the sustainability goals. Some of the remarkable achievements are shown in Figure 109 below:

Key achievements towards 'Quality education'

- Dedicating nearly 20 per cent of the government's major spending for developing education system

- Providing free education to UAE citizens in public schools all the way until higher education

- Operating public and private education school system offering over 16 curricula to serve different nationalities living in the UAE

- Having a wide range of highly accredited universities, both public and private

- Having special facilities for adults learning, continuing education

- Dropping the illiteracy rate in the UAE to less than 1 per cent

- Signing an agreement with software company Microsoft to follow best practices in education to support smart education programmes

- Signing the UN's Convention on the Rights of Persons with Disabilities and Optional Protocol

- Adoption of the 'National Qualifications Framework Handbook 2012', for all educational tracks

- The existence of certified educational and training facilities to offer national professional qualifications

- Developing national professional qualifications in various economic fields according to the needs of the labour market.

Figure 109: Quality Education Achievements[ccxxi]

As shown in the above figure, the UAE has allocated almost 20% of the federal budget for the development of the education system. The primary and secondary level education is provided free of cost in the government schools. Different curricula have been developed to meet the diverse needs of the international students. Various renowned public and private sector universities have been developed in the UAE. The UAE also offers programs for continuous education and adult learning. The literacy rate of almost 99% has been achieved. The smart education programs have been introduced in collaboration with the renowned software vendor Microsoft. The UAE has also developed laws and adheres to the protocols and convention for the people of determination. The UAE has also developed qualifications frameworks and school inspection frameworks. The certifications and licensing systems have been introduced for the teachers of K-12 system.

7.3. Focus on Innovation and developing a Skilled Workforce

The UAE leaders have also presented a comprehensive innovation strategy that describes how a highly skilled and tech-savvy workforce can be developed in the UAE.[ccxxii] The strategy mentions human capital development, research, knowledge, and technology as innovation's key constituents as shown in Figure 110 below:

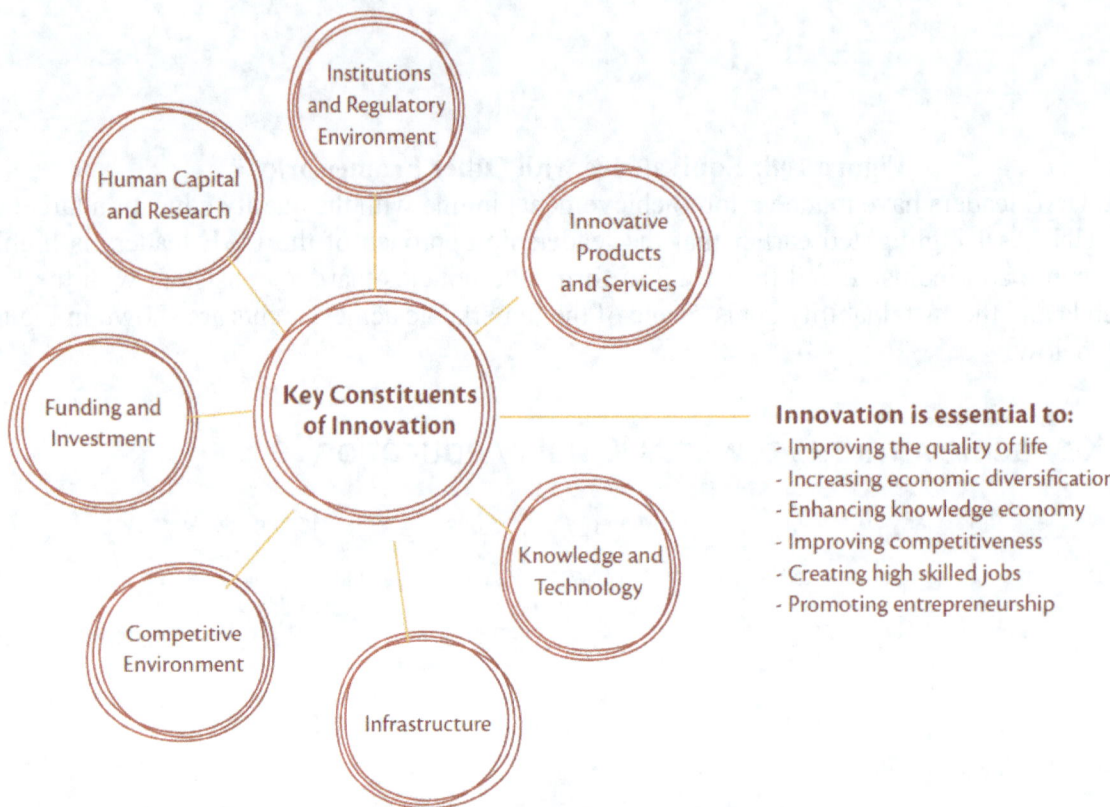

Figure 110: Innovation Constituents[ccxxiii]

The strategy also acknowledges that bringing innovation and advanced technologies in all areas will be quite challenging, and therefore, priority areas should be identified in the UAE for introducing innovation through advanced tools and technologies. The seven priority sectors identified in the strategy are transportation, renewable energy, education, technology, water, health, and space as shown in Figure 111 below:

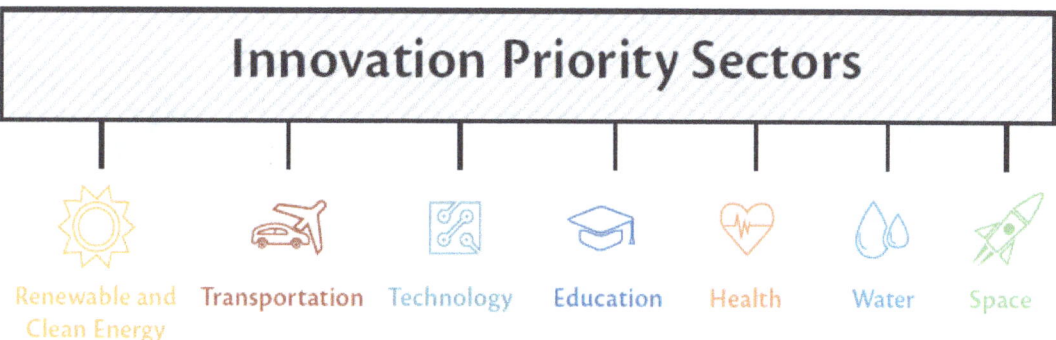

Figure 111: Key Sectors for Technology-based Innovation[ccxxiv]

The strategy also highlights what constitutes an enabling environment in the context of innovation. A disruptive innovation is possible when the required technology infrastructure is available, the implementation is compliant with the regulatory framework, the incentives are available to the technology startups, and the technology-enabling services are available in the country. These enablers are shown in Figure 112 below:

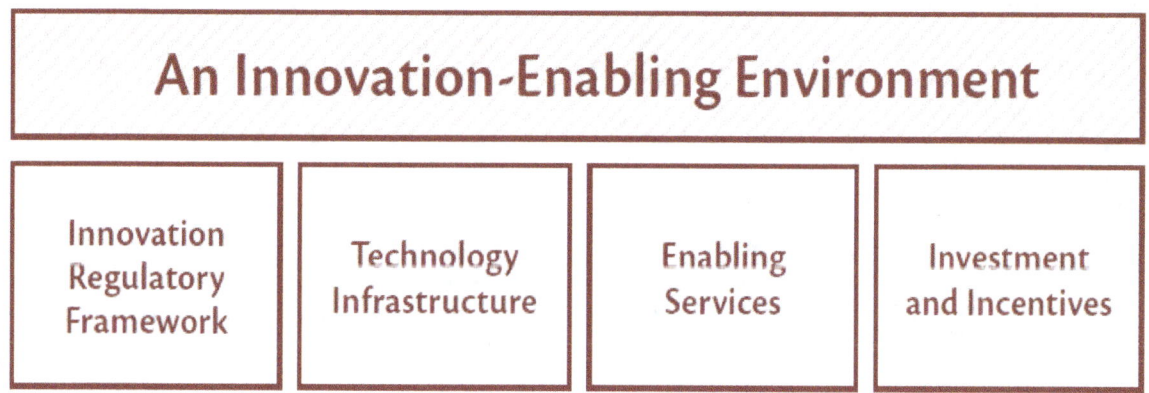

Figure 112: Innovation Enablers[ccxxv]

The UAE leaders have also aligned the innovation framework with the UN's agenda and goals where the innovation is marked as the ninth objective. The UAE also organizes an innovation festival each year known as UAE Innovates.[ccxxvi] This innovation festival is an annual festival in the UAE where the organizations and individuals can showcase their innovative projects and receive Innovates award from the UAE leaders. The next innovates festival will be held in February 2024. Seven award categories have been announced by the administrators of this award. These include the innovative digital, innovative community, innovative government, and other awards as shown in Figure 113 below:

Figure 113: Innovates Award Categories[ccxxvii]

The awards are distributed in Innovates Festival based on a well-defined criteria as shown in Figure 114 below:

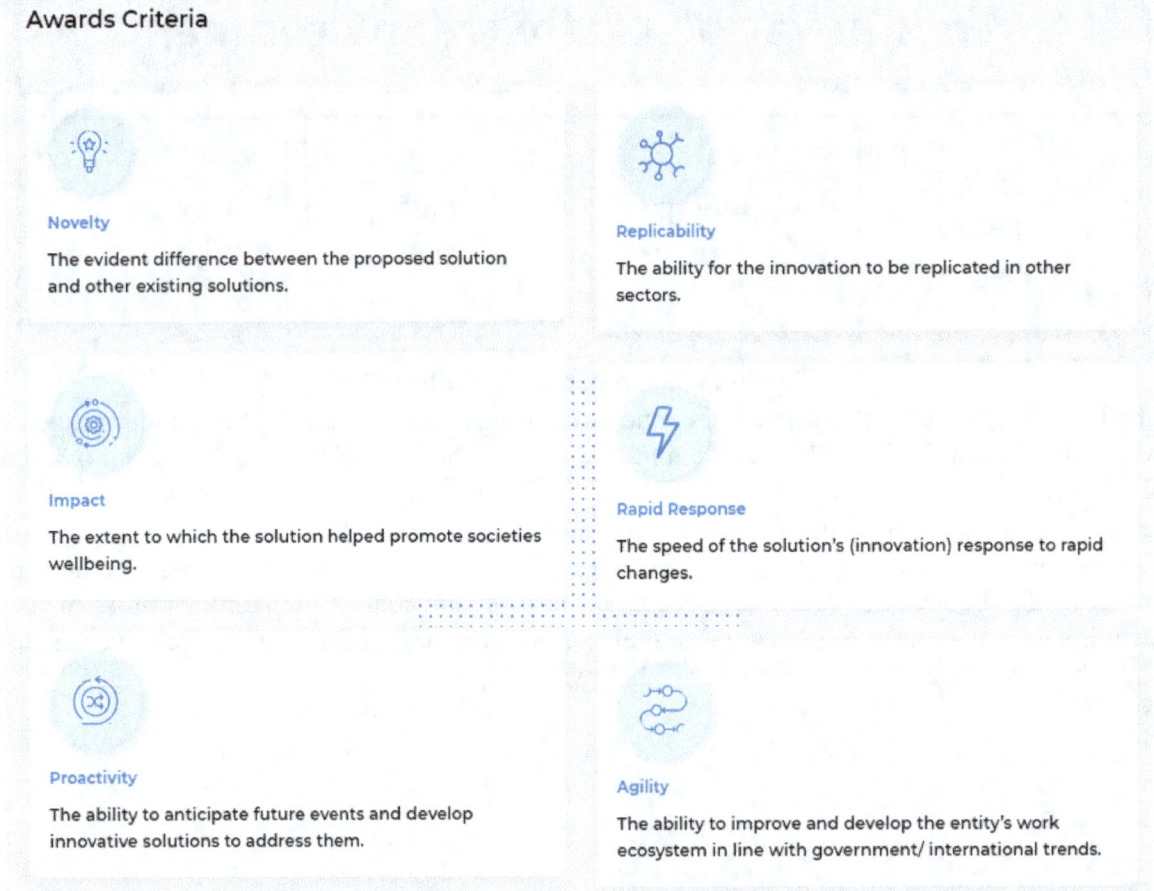

Figure 114: Award Criteria[ccxxviii]

As per the award criteria, there should be an element of novelty in the submitted project. The project should stand out among other similar technological solutions available in the market. The project should be replicable such that it is not limited to a specific location, industry, or domain. The concepts of the project should be replicable in other industries and projects as well.

There should also be a high impact factor of the project such that the project assists a wide range of communities and societies. The project should be responsive to the recent technological requirements in different industries. The project developers should demonstrate proactivity in the sense that the project was designed considering the future challenges and requirements. The project should be based on the agile framework such that there is a high level of flexibility and customization available in the project interface.

This chapter highlighted the academic initiatives of the UAE leaders. You will have appreciated that the efforts of the UAE leaders are not limited to the mega projects of infrastructure development. They have also assessed keenly the academic requirements of the current and future generations and introduced the academic initiatives accordingly. They have also invested heavily in the human capital development so that the skillset of the UAE workforce meets the global standards.

The UAE leaders have developed various institutions and research centers to ensure quality education at the levels of primary, secondary, and tertiary education. Through the innovation strategy, the key sectors have been identified and the innovation frameworks have been developed based on the tested models. These academic initiatives highlight the visionary approach of the UAE leaders that have shaped a great country.

8. Cultural Diversity and Pluralism
8.1. Leadership Commitment to Religious Tolerance and Cultural Exchange

As I highlighted in other sections of the book, the UAE leaders have demonstrated an exemplary level of religious tolerance and the appreciation for other cultures and communities. The religious tolerance can be seen by the fact that the UAE is also home to Hindu Temples, Sikh Temple, Churches, and Ministries. In this chapter, I will highlight more examples that indicate the commitment of the UAE leaders towards religious tolerance.

The website of the UAE embassy displays an old, memorable pic in which the tradition of inclusion of the UAE leaders has been highlighted. This picture is shown in Figure 115 below:

Figure 115: UAE Leaders travelling to Europe in 1951[ccxxix]

As is evident from the figure above, this picture was taken in 1951, much before the independence of the UAE. However, even at that time, the UAE leaders including Sheikh Zayed had a great respect for other religions and this tour was meant to learn about the religions and cultures practiced in the European countries. During the visit, the leaders also visited a Cathedral in Paris and the Vatican.

Another remarkable demonstration of religious tolerance was observed in the decade of 50s, when the Abu Dhabi ruler welcomed the oil and gas foreign workforce in the Arab world where all of these workers belonged to the Christian community. The welcome gesture of the Abu Dhabi ruler can be seen in Figure 116 below:

Figure 116: Welcome Gesture for the Christians[ccxxx]

At that time, the Abu Dhabi ruler also donated a vast portion of the land for the development of a church and a church was then opened for the Christian community in 1968 in Abu Dhabi. In the UAE, the followers of Judaism are also respected and they have been allowed to worship freely in their prayer halls. In this regard, a landmark Abraham Accords was signed in 2020. After this agreement, the Jewish community is continuously growing in the UAE. One Jewish worship place in the UAE is shown in Figure 117 below:

Figure 117: Jewish Prayer Place[ccxxxi]

The chief rabbi was also appointed in the UAE in 2019, and his name is Yehuda Sarna.[ccxxxii] Hindus also live in significant proportion in the UAE, and the UAE leaders have also developed Hindu Temples so that Hindus could practice their religion freely in the UAE. Dubai is now home to two Hindu Temples. Moreover, various cremation facilities have been established in the emirates of Dubai, Abu Dhabi, and Sharjah. The UAE leaders also coordinate and meet with the Hindu leaders to know their experiences of living in UAE as shown in Figure 118 below:

Figure 118: Interaction with the Hindu Community[ccxxxiii]

It is a surprising fact that Buddhists to the count of approximately 500,000 also reside in the UAE as shown in Figure 119 below. Most of them have originated from Sri Lanka. They also visit Dubai for viewing the monastery in Dubai and offering prayers. The Buddhist temple in the UAE is the only temple throughout the Arab world.

Buddhism

Roughly 500,000 Buddhists live in the UAE, most of them expatriates from Sri Lanka. Buddhists from around the UAE travel to the Mahamevnawa Buddhist Monastery in Dubai to practice their faith. The facility is the first Buddhist temple on the Arabian Peninsula.

Figure 119: Buddhists in the UAE

8.2. Multiculturalism and Acculturation

Dubai and London can be considered as two exemplary cities in the world that promote a cosmopolitan ethics. The foreigners in the UAE belong to numerous countries and all of them are welcome and greeted in this great country. The great leaders of UAE have always advocated diversity, pluralism, and tolerance. It can be seen from the fact that more than 85% of the population of the UAE is foreigners.[ccxxxiv] The visionary approach of the UAE leaders have also looked beyond the national borders and the UAE leaders make every effort to bring peace and harmony in the region and across the globe. The modern UAE has become a symbol of inclusion, social cohesion, and moderation.

The UAE also has an exclusive ministry of tolerance. According to an earlier minister of this portfolio, Shikha Lubna, the values of tolerance and inclusion promoted by the UAE leaders are deeply rooted in the Arab culture. The rulers of the great dynasties in this region have always been open to other cultures and civilizations. Its manifestations can be seen in the Baghdad dynasty, Andalusia, and Damascus dynasty.[ccxxxv]

The ministry of tolerance was introduced in the UAE in 2016 by the prime minister. In 2020, the tolerance ministry was further empowered and it was given the name Tolerance and Coexistence. The current minister of this portfolio is Sheikh Nahayan Mabarak Al Nahyan as shown in Figure 120 below:

Figure 120: Tolerance and Coexistence Minister[ccxxxvi]

UAE leaders have always promoted peace, harmony, and inclusiveness in the world. Due to this approach, the UAE is signatory to various international conventions and treaties. These conventions have a firm stance on diversity and pluralism and they renounce extremism, violence, and discrimination in the society. The UAE provides leadership in promoting peace and rapprochement across the globe because foreigners from numerous countries are present in the UAE and it has become a convergence point for the eastern and western civilizations. Considering the true spirit of tolerance, the UAE ministry promotes a holistic system of positive values as shown in Figure 121 below:

Figure 121: Positive Values for a Tolerant Society[ccxxxvii]

The above figure highlights that the UAE leaders, through the tolerance ministry, spread humane values. They respect other cultures and believe that every individual possesses unique talents and skills that should be regarded and utilized for the benefit of the country. The UAE has always been a peace-loving country and never gets involved in war and fighting with the neighboring countries. The extremism, in all its forms, is rejected by the UAE leaders and their decision-making is always based on a pragmatic and balanced approach. The UAE leaders also have acceptance and tolerance for other religions. Although the country's official religion is Islam, the temples, churches, and Sikh prayer halls have also been developed in the UAE in many places to facilitate the followers of these religions.

The UAE leaders believe in coexistence with other communities and groups who have different interpretations and worldview than the UAE leaders. They acknowledge that it is not possible that the whole world think it one direction and always agree to the decisions and initiatives of the UAE leaders. The difference of opinion and constructive criticism is a healthy culture in any society and the UAE leaders use these varied voices to make improvements in the overall governance system. The UAE leaders also aim to remove discrimination in the society. In the tribal Arab culture, the women had limited opportunities for professional growth and development. However, the UAE leaders have introduced women entrepreneurship program and also encourage them to work as employees in national and multinational organizations. The women have also been represented in government offices and key posts. In the next section, I will describe the role of ministry of happiness, which is a unique ministry in the UAE, and this post is currently held by a woman that shows the commitment of the UAE leaders to increase the participation of the women in all key domain and positions.

According to the tolerance ministry, a culture of tolerance and coexistence has been established in the UAE and core principles have been developed to be followed by all citizens. These principles are inspired by the teachings of Islam and provide a solid foundation for a sustainable development in the UAE as shown in Figure 122 below. The UAE citizens are expected to respect the culture and belief system of other communities. They need to develop a culture of knowledge sharing and openness in the society. The government and the people should resolve their conflicts with a spirit of love and a keen desire for peace.

A living embodiment of the teachings of true Islam

Living in peace with others, and respecting their beliefs and cultures

Developing knowledge and positive openness in all human beings

How to deal with conflicts, as well as spreading love and peace

An essential tool for achieving a comprehensive and sustainable development

Figure 122: Values of Tolerance[ccxxxviii]

The tolerance ministry has also introduced a Tolerance Program that is founded on the seven key pillars. According to the first dimension, the initiative regarding the promotion of a tolerant culture will be inspired by the true teachings of Islam. The next major source of inspiration will be the constitution of the UAE. The ministry will also consider the guidelines and the ethical principles described by the founding father of the UAE. The tolerance programs will also focus on the principles and guidelines mentioned in international conventions. Another source of inspiration will be the archaeology and history of the UAE. The programs will also consider the humanitarian aspect and the common values that should be adhered to as described in the human rights laws. These key pillars are focused on in all programs and initiatives of the ministry and they are highlighted in Figure 123 below:

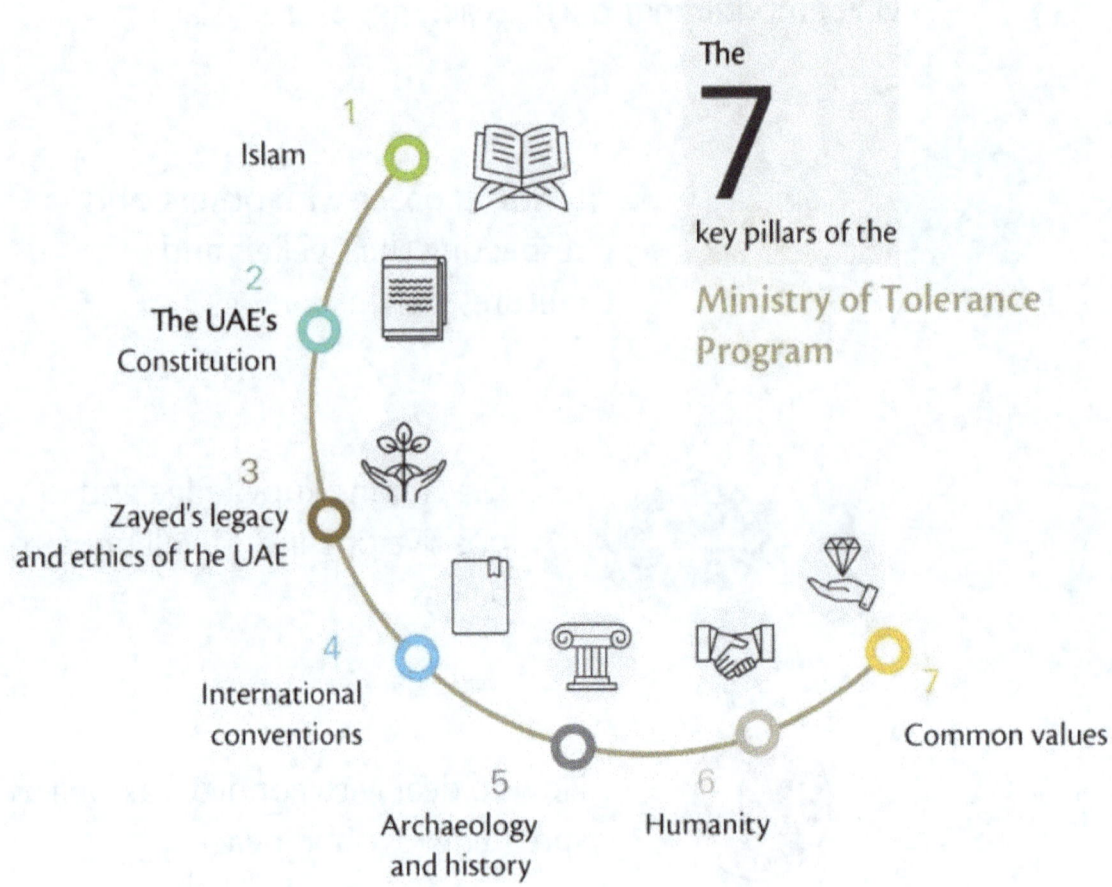

Figure 123: Key Pillars for the Tolerance Initiatives[ccxxxix]

Similar to technology and sustainability initiatives, the UAE leaders have also identified core areas of intervention for the tolerance ministry so that they are more focused in their work and tangible outcomes could be delivered within the stipulated time. The five core and priority areas are shown in Figure 124 below:

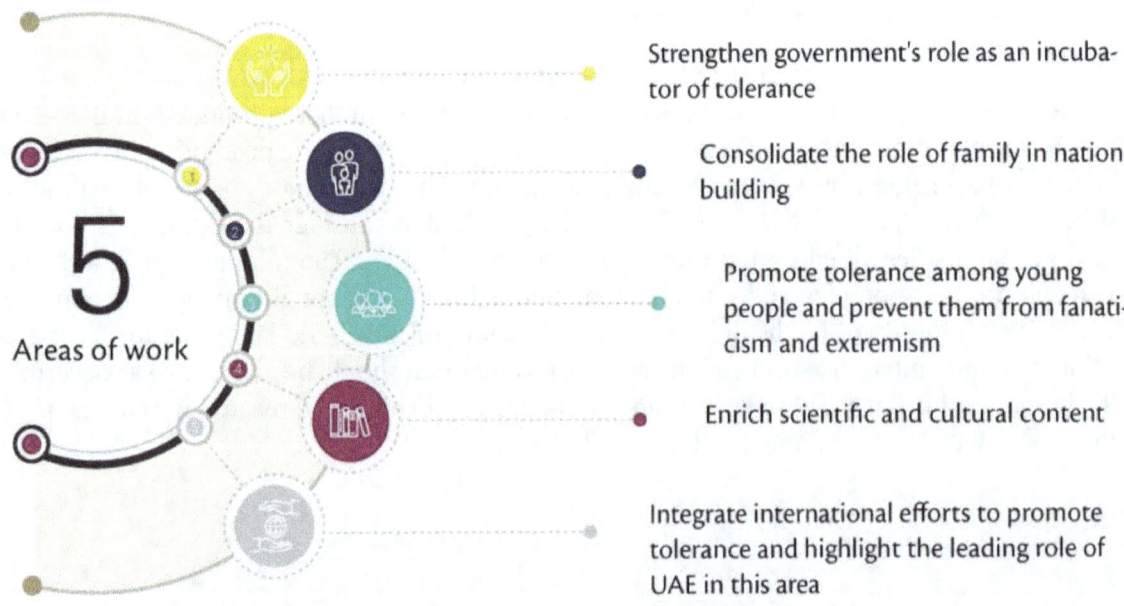

Figure 124: Core Areas for Tolerance-Related Interventions[ccxl]

The first area of intervention is to project the role of the government as a facilitator of tolerance. The UAE has its roots in the tribal culture, and therefore, the family unit can play a pivotal role in the nation building. The family head is a highly respected individual, and if the individual is made aware regarding the strategic directions of the UAE, the whole family can become productive and generate meaningful results.

The third area of intervention is related to youth because the UAE leaders believe that the transition from the adolescent age to the adulthood creates higher emotions and aggression among the individuals. If these energies are not routed to a positive direction, the issues and challenges may emerge. Therefore, the UAE leaders want the youth of the country to be tolerant and avoid the behavioral patterns of extremism and fanaticism. The UAE leaders have also emphasized that the academic literature on tolerance should be enriched with cultural content and scientific content so that the literature could attract the young generation and the old generation alike. The UAE also aims to support the international initiatives on tolerance.

The efforts of the tolerance ministry are not limited to presenting the framework and guidelines on tolerance. The ministry has also completed various programs successfully and announced 23 strategic initiatives as shown in Figure 125 below:

Figure 125: Strategic Initiatives for Promoting Tolerance[ccxli]

The above strategic initiatives have been consolidated into five categories of family, government, content, youth, and international efforts. Regarding the government initiatives, the ministry has established a community partnership forum. The ministry has also conducted various workshops and seminars so that the values of tolerance are understood and implemented in the workplace setting. The principles mentioned in the lighthouse of tolerance have also been integrated in the overall fabric of the UAE society.

Regarding the family initiatives, the UAE leaders organized national festivals for promoting human fraternity and tolerance. Conferences are also held for highlighting the role of the family unit. The government has also introduced tolerance initiatives that are beneficial exclusively for the people of determination.

The youth is also a key pillar of the tolerance-related initiatives, and the tolerance programs are also introduced at the school level in collaboration with the education ministry. The students are also motivated to become champions in tolerance initiatives. The government has also launched a new and innovative forum, Tolerance without Borders, to promote the values of tolerance at the international level by making use of the technology. The government conducts short workshops to highlight the concept of human fraternity. The significance of a legislative framework is also highlighted in ensuring a culture of tolerance.

Regarding the content-based initiatives, the tolerance ministry has launched the 1000 project where the projects for promoting tolerance are presented by the students and the professionals.

The creative writers are also encouraged to participate in the tolerance camps. The arts and literature contest are also held each year. The public and private sector educational institutes are also encouraged to include Arabic in their curriculum because it is the language of the Quran and the tolerance. A media campaign has also been started by the ministry under the caption Tolerance Path.

Regarding the participation in the international efforts, the UAE leaders are spreading the message of peaceful collaboration to integrate the international workforce into the UAE society. The Tolerance Cup is also organized for the UAE workers for the games of cricket and kabaddi. The participation of the community is also encouraged in the national festivals related to tolerance. The UAE is also part of the international efforts to build a global alliance on tolerance. Hay Festival is a popular literature festival that was initially organized in Wales, UK in 1988.[ccxlii] The UAE also arranged a literature festival on similar patterns in Abu Dhabi in 2020 and it gained a huge reputation from the scholarly community. The themes, related to tolerance and pluralism, were also promoted through this festival.

8.3. The Unique Role of the Ministry of Happiness

The United Nations has asked the member countries to consider happiness as a holistic theme where a person becomes happy when s/he is in a good physical, emotional, and spiritual state. Under these guidelines, the UAE leaders have also shown their keen desire to promote happiness in the country. The post for the Minister of State for Happiness was introduced in the UAE in 2016 as shown in Figure 126 below. When there was a realignment of the cabinet in 2017, the role of the happiness ministry was further expanded to include 'Happiness and Wellbeing'. In 2020, there was another cabinet realignment in the UAE during which the happiness portfolio was made part of a larger ministry of community development.

Minister of State for Happiness and Wellbeing

In February 2016, the UAE Government created the post of Minister of State for Happiness. Following the Cabinet reshuffle in 2017, another portfolio was added to the Minster of State for Happiness to become the Minster of State for Happiness and Wellbeing.

In the cabinet reshuffle in July 2020, the "Quality of Life and Happiness" portfolio was transferred to Ministry of Community Development. Read about the new structure of the UAE Government.

Figure 126: Happiness Ministry[ccxliii]

The current happiness minister is Ohood Al Roumi, and she is also known as community development minister under the new structure (Figure 127).[ccxliv]

Figure 127: Happiness Minister[ccxlv]

According to the state minister, the primary objective of this ministry is to develop an environment where people can grow freely and live up to their potential. The enabling environment of the UAE should be such that the whole population desires to be happy and reaches their true potential.[ccxlvi] The responsibilities of the ministry are to implement the government policies in a manner that results in maximum satisfaction and creates social good. In the World Happiness Report that was published for 2023, the UAE secured 26th rank out of the total 149 countries evaluated. The ranking was based on the average scores of the three years from 2020 to 2022 as shown in Figure 128 below. Although the rank of 26 is a good rank considering that the total number of countries evaluated is 149, yet from the UAE standards, much more work needs to be done to achieve top 10 ranking in the happiness index.

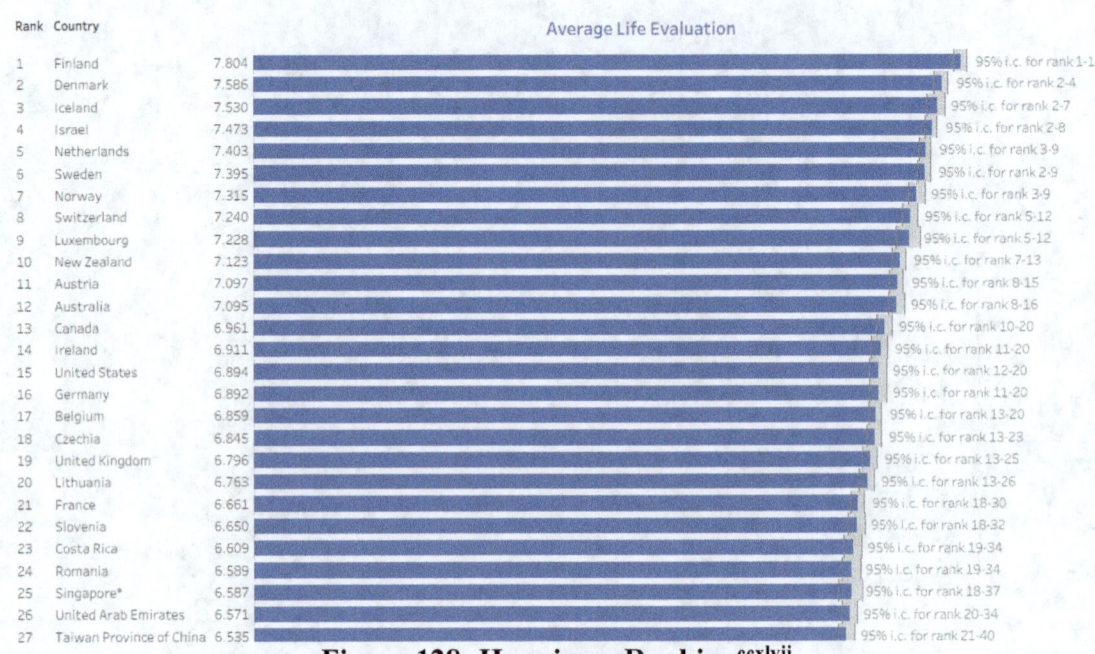

Figure 128: Happiness Ranking[ccxlvii]

To further improve the happiness ranking, the UAE leaders are focusing on all the determinants of the happiness as highlighted in the happiness report. The report has defined a total of six factors that together highlight the happiness level of a country.[ccxlviii]

The first factor is GDP per capita because it highlights the performance and size of the economy. If the country is not economically strong, there will be more poor people in the country and they will struggle to maintain their physical and mental wellbeing. The second factor is social support. Inequalities exist in all societies and countries and in the happiest countries, the people are always confident that if they get into trouble, they will get the required social support from friends, relatives, government agencies, and the institutions of the civil society.

The third factor is the expectancy regarding the healthy life. If the large segment of population possesses a good physical and mental wellbeing, only then longevity with good quality of life can be ensured. The fourth factor is the level of freedom available in a country for the individuals to make life choices.

The fifth factor is the level of generosity present in the society. If the rich people of a country are generous and donate the money for charitable activities, the lower and middle class can greatly benefit from this assistance and become happy. The sixth factor is the corruption perception. This index evaluates if the government entities are honest in the execution of their responsibilities or they follow corrupt practices. The same is also evaluated for the businesses and corporations. After considering all six factors, the happiness level of a country is ascertained.

8.4. Cultural Exchange Programs and Cultural Initiatives

The cultural initiatives of the UAE leaders are not restricted to the UAE, and they also participate and promote cultural initiatives across the globe. Various cultural programs of the global communities are also organized in the UAE due to the cosmopolitan outlook of the country. The UAE leaders also announced a strategy for the creative industries and the cultural industries in 2021.[ccxlix] According to the new strategy and as part of the agenda of economic diversification, the contribution of this sector in the national GDP of the UAE will be enhanced to 5%.

According to the new strategy, the scope of the cultural initiatives has been expanded to the creative sector as well, and a total of six industries are being focused by the cultural ministry as shown in Figure 129 below:

Figure 129: Sectors for Cultural Initiatives[ccl]

The figure above highlights that the key sectors for cultural initiatives identified in the UAE are books and press, conservation of national heritage, audiovisual and interactive tools, performing arts, design services, and visual arts services.

As I highlighted during the discussion on free trade zones, the UAE leaders have encouraged the trade and investment activities in the UAE by introducing free trade zones in the emirates. Among these zones, a significant number of zones also allow the operations of cultural and creative industries as shown in Figure 130 below. The free zones in all the emirates promote creative industries. As Dubai has the highest number of free zones, therefore, the count of free zones permitting creative industries is also the highest in the case of Dubai that is 12.

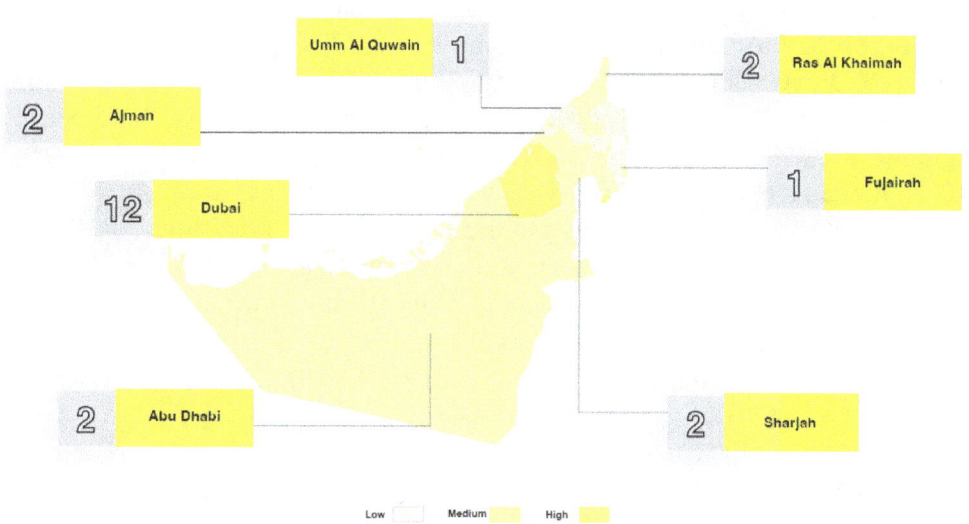

Figure 130: Free Zones Promoting Cultural Industries[ccli]

According to the new strategy framework, the cultural ministry has devised various initiatives in different domains. The count of these cultural initiatives is 40. As shown in Figure 131 below, there are 16 initiatives for supporting the creative professionals and their skillsets. Another 14 initiatives have been designed to create an enabling business environment for the creative industries. There are also 10 initiatives for developing a professional workforce in the creative industry.

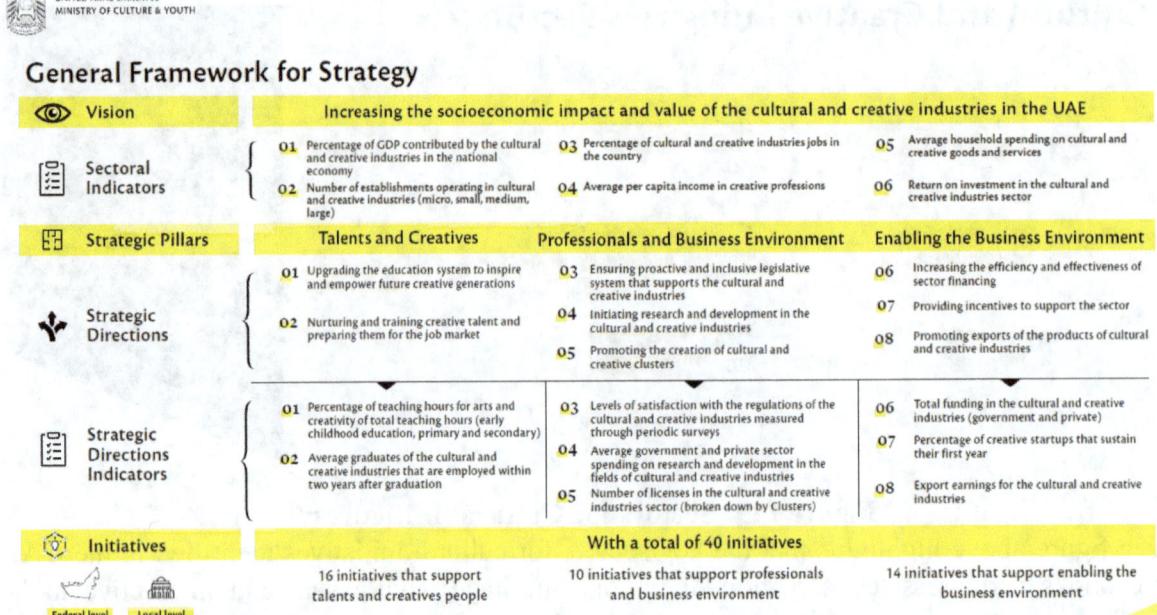

Figure 131: Strategy Framework for Creative Industries[cclii]

The discussion and elaboration in this chapter indicate that the UAE leaders have a great respect for the own culture and the culture of other communities of interpretation. They are also role models in the context of religious tolerance and strong believer of peaceful coexistence. Their cultural initiatives benefit both the local population and the global community. They encourage and promote the creative industries and aim to increase their contribution in the national GDP. The creative professionals find the UAE a highly attractive country for performing arts, human capital development, and an enabling business environment for the creative industries.

9. Tourism Development

The UAE leaders have realized that tourism can become a source of economic strength for the country due to the strategic location of the UAE. The UAE has a strategic location in the Middle East where its geographical boundaries are located between Asia and Europe. The strategic location of the UAE can be realized from the fact that approximately 2.5 billion people have access to Dubai with a four-hour flight. Furthermore, approximately 5 billion people have access to Dubai with a flight up to eight hours. In order to hold various international conferences, seminars, and sports events, the UAE has always been a preferred destination for the event managers.

In this chapter, I will introduce you to the various tourist attractions and how the UAE leaders have developed state-of-the-art hospitality services in the country. I will also elaborate on how the tourism sector can play a dominant role in the economic strengthening of the country.

9.1. Various Tourist Attractions

During my discussion on the historical evolution of the UAE and the mega projects, I have introduced to you various mega projects and historical places in the UAE. In this section, I will also mention to you other tourist attractions from the perspective of a tourist. It means that if a tourist visits the UAE for the first time, these are some of the must-see attractions in the UAE. These recommendations are based on the major attractions mentioned on the official website of the economy ministry.

In Dubai, the one destination, a tourist should never miss to see is Burj Al Arab. This destination has luxurious, seven-star hotels with fine restaurants. As shown in Figure 132 below, the destination also presents a beautiful view of the Arabian Gulf.

Figure 132: Burj Al Arab and the Outside View[ccliii]

Another famous attraction to view in Dubai is the global village where various cultures are represented in one place to represent the spirit of coexistence and tolerance. The tourists can explore handicrafts, vintage products, and the work of arts and craft from different countries. As highlighted in Figure 133 below, there is a festival-resembling environment in the facility and the destination outlook is also optimized by entertaining venues and restaurants.

Figure 133: Festival Environment in Global Village[ccliv]

In the case of Abu Dhabi, the place that attracts the tourist the most is the grand mosque. This mosque is named after the founding father Sheikh Zayed, and it is truly an architectural masterpiece in the world as shown in Figure 134 below. It is a unique blend of different architectural styles. The tourists can visit 82 domes in the mosque and the architecture symbolizes the concepts of peace, harmony, and coexistence based on the teachings of Islam.

Figure 134: Sheikh Zayed Grand Mosque[cclv]

Another destination in Abu Dhabi that attracts the tourists the most is Qasr Al Watan. This destination also has a captivating design and a marvelous architecture as shown in Figure 135 below. The destination is an integral component of the presidential palace. It has also been designated as a cultural landmark in the UAE .The tourists can appreciate the deep-rooted traditions of the UAE in this place and explore the historical evolution of the UAE that has shaped a great country. The rich history and culture of the UAE are showcased in Qasr Al Watan.

Figure 135: Qasr Al Watan showing History, Culture[cclvi]

In Sharjah, a great tourist attraction is Al Majaz Waterfront. This destination lies at the center of Sharjah and presents a beautiful view of Khalid Lake as shown in Figure 136 below. The visitors are mesmerized by the interconnecting gardens and green structures. The waterfront enriches the tourist experience by the availability of cafes, restaurants, and skyscrapers. The architecture of the facility combines the traditional outlook with the Islamic inspirations.

Figure 136: Waterfront and the View of Khalid Lakecclvii

In the case of Fujairah, a famous tourist destination is Fujairah Fort. It is a historical place in the country and this fort had a major role in protecting the whole region from the enemies throughout the history of the emirates. It was developed in the sixteenth century and the building structure was composed of one rectangular and three circular towers as shown in Figure 137 below. The fort has an elevation of 20 meters from the sea level. It is regarded as a captivating landmark in the emirate and an attractive destination for the tourists.

Figure 137: Fujairah Fort with Four Towerscclviii

In the case of Ras Al Khaimah, a famous destination that attracts the tourists is Jebel Jais. The mountains in this place are part of the larger Hajar Mountains. This mountainous place in the country is the highest peak level and the mountain has a height of 1,934 meters from the sea level as shown in Figure 138 below. It is a good attraction for those tourists who want to visit the mountain areas and rugged landscape and build memories of remarkable adventures.

Figure 138: Jebel Jais – Highest Peak[cclix]

9.2. Leadership Commitment to State-of-the-Art Hospitality Services

The UAE leaders also acknowledge the fact that when the foreigners from across the world visit the UAE, they expect outstanding level of hospitality services in the country. Their visit to the tourist attractions can be a memorable one only when they also have good facilities for comfort and passing the leisure time.

According to the reviews of the famous tourist information website tripadvisor, the best hotel in Dubai is Atlantis.[cclx] The rating is shown in Figure 139 below:

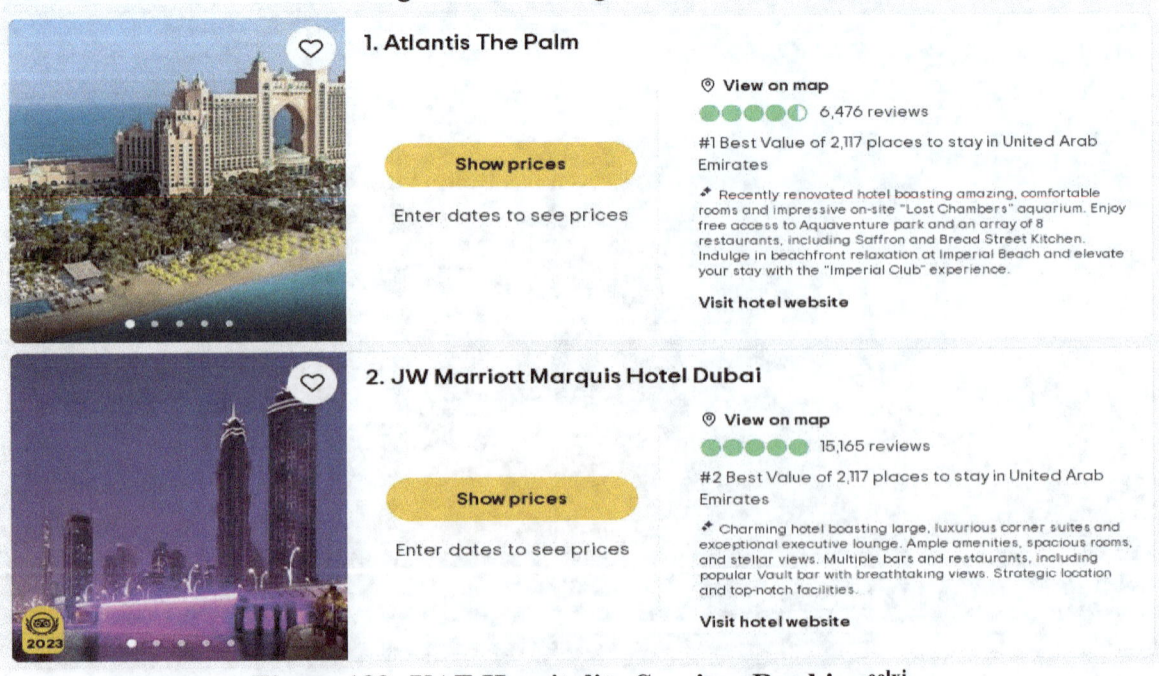

Figure 139: UAE Hospitality Services Ranking[cclxi]

This hospitality service is located in Dubai and it offers three unique experiences of The Royal, The Palm, and Aquaventure as shown in Figure 140 below:

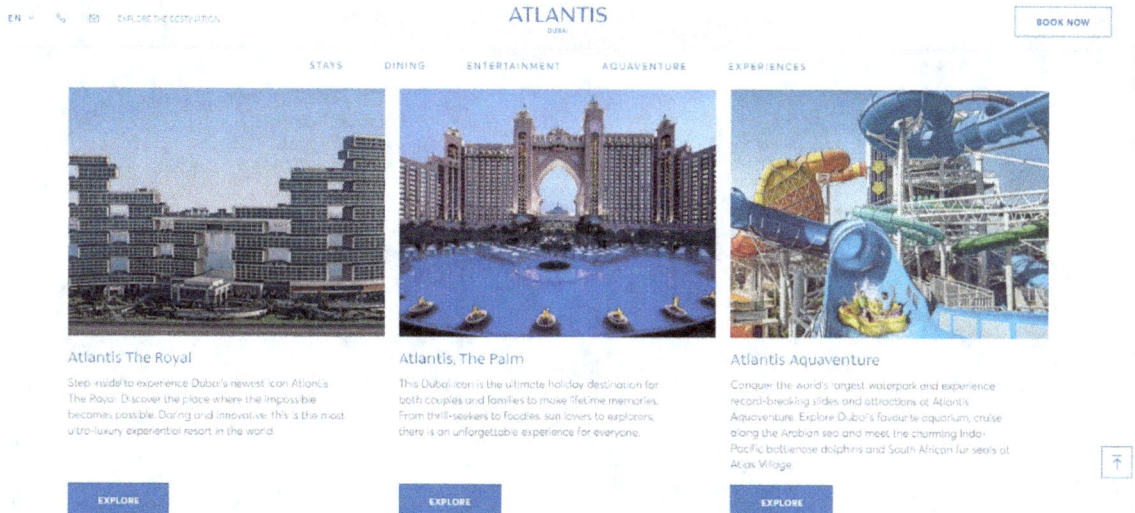

Figure 140: UAE Top Hospitality Service[cclxii]

Atlantis offers a luxurious stay at the royal and the palm and a unique dining experience. The dining facility has celebrity outlets, signature outlets, casual outlets, and the royal outlets. The hospitality service also has entertainment venues including bars, restaurants, and beaches. The aquaventure offers the attractions of waterpark, village, and aquarium. This facility has all the elements that can make the stay of a tourist a memorable one throughout the journey in the UAE.

9.3. Role of Tourism in Economic Development and Employment Opportunities

The UAE leaders want to increase the contribution of the tourism sector in the GDP so that the reliance on oil exports could be reduced. As part of the agenda of economic diversification, priority sectors were identified by the UAE leaders and the tourism is included in these priority sectors. The leaders want to capitalize on the strategic location advantage of the country and attract more investors and tourists into the country. The UAE is also a peaceful country and the crime rate is very low in the country. The tourists and investors also prefer this country because there is a good level of certainty in the political system. The president, the prime minister, and the individual emirate rulers are governing the country with a high level of commitment and a clear vision for the future. The investors are confident about the investment climate of the UAE and can make long-term investments with the expectations of a good return. The tourists also attract to various destinations to learn about the successful business models of the UAE. They are highly impressed by the great transformation of the UAE and they want to replicate these models in their home countries.

10. Sustainability and Environmental Protection

Although the UAE is a major oil-producing country, yet the country was among the first where the UAE leaders recognized the significance of renewable and environmental-friendly energy policies. The UAE presided the climate change conference of the UN that began in November 2023. This conference was held in Dubai and is known as COP28. The conference focuses on the challenges faced by the planet and the strategies are made to reduce the threats to the environment. For this purpose, the world leaders sit together in this conference and build a joint strategy. The leadership attending the conference is shown in Figure 141 below:

Figure 141: COPE 28[cclxiii]

In January 2023, the UAE president reiterated its commitment to the environmental sustainability and the president declared the whole year 2023 as the year of sustainability.[cclxiv] The UAE is committed to provide leadership in climate change initiatives by hosting the COP28 conference. The UAE has also set the target of achieving net zero carbon emissions throughout the country, and this target will be accomplished by 2050.[cclxv] The UAE has also partnered with the United States for the clean energy programs under the PACE agreement. Under this agreement, an investment worth of $100 billion will be made in environmental protection initiatives.[cclxvi] The projects and initiatives in this regard will be completed by 2035.

10.1. Leadership Focus on Renewable Energy and Sustainable Development

The UAE leaders have long been focusing on achieving the sustainable development goals in the country. The contribution of renewable energy is also being increased in all industrial sectors. Through the recent COP28 conference, the UAE leaders have also endeavored to develop actionable mechanisms so that more success could be achieved in the near future. The UAE leaders believe that climate change is one of the most crucial challenges in the contemporary context. The UAE has provided leadership in developing effective policies for dealing with the climate change issues. The leaders have focused on green economy and economic diversification. They have also established projects of clean and renewable energy. In all the future mega projects of the UAE, the focus is on sustainable urban planning, sustainable transportation, and energy efficiency.

10.2. Clean Energy Production Targets

In COP28 conference, 110 countries signed on an agreement that they will increase their capacity of renewable energy by 300% by 2030.[cclxvii] Moreover, 50 big companies working in the oil and gas development sector have announced in COP28 that they will become carbon neutral by 2050.[cclxviii] For this purpose, they will increase the use of solar, wind, and other sources of energy. Companies signatory to this agreement are from Saudi Arabia, UAE, and 29 other countries. They include Saudi Aramco and the UAE's ADNOC companies. These companies have also declared that they will reduce the emission of methane gas to 0%. The United States has also participated actively in COP28 and pledged $3 billion under the head of green climate fund.[cclxix]

The presidency of COP28 has emphasized that the future directions of the climate change initiatives should be based on four pillars.[cclxx] 1) There should be a transformation of the energy sector to a more equitable and responsible sector. 2) The global leaders should develop key mechanisms for climate change financing. 3) The focus of the world leaders should be on improving the livelihoods and quality of life of the citizens. 4) The previous four pillars of the conference should be supported and all stakeholders should be involved in the climate change initiatives.

The UAE leaders are striving to build sustainable energy systems and make significant reductions in carbon emissions to protect the environment. The key initiatives announced in COP28 include the increase in the production capacity of renewable energy by three times by 2030, increasing the production capacity of low-carbon hydrogen by twice by 2030, and the provision of sustainable cooling systems also by 2030.[cclxxi]

In COP28 conference, the global leaders reached an agreement on loss and damage due to climate change as shown in Figure 142 below. For example, Pakistan and Bangladesh recently affected badly by floods due to the climate change. It was also mentioned by King Charles in his keynote address. The rulers of these two countries argued that the environmental pollution caused by the developed countries resulted in the flood-like situation in their countries and therefore, the developed countries should contribute to the loss and damage. This argument was widely acknowledged in COP28 and more than $420 million were pledged by different countries to assist the countries severely affected by the climate change.

Figure 142: COP28 on Loss and Damage[cclxxii]

It was also mentioned by the participating countries that governments alone cannot fight the climate crisis due to the wide range of areas and sectors from which this crisis emerges. This key point of COP28 is illustrated in Figure 143. The governments should build collaborations with the private sector in this regard. The participating countries agreed to the idea of the UAE leaders that the developed nations should make investments in the sustainability initiatives in the developing countries.

Figure 143: Public Private Partnership[cclxxiii]

The UAE leaders were also convinced with the arguments of the developing countries that most of the industrial production is carried out in the developed and rich countries. However, the harmful effects of the climate change are being faced by the developing countries. The UAE leaders showed their support to this argument by pledging $100 million to the financial assistance fund for the countries affected by the climate change as shown in Figure 144 below. The fund will also provide financial assistance to those countries that have become high-risk areas due to climate change so that they can deal with the climate change challenges effectively. The amount will be utilized in the risk mitigation process and the recovery process.

COP28 PRESIDENCY UNITES THE WORLD ON LOSS AND DAMAGE

The UAE announced its commitment of $100 million to the Fund, which aims to provide financial assistance to countries at extreme risk from climate change, to support climate change mitigation and recovery.

→ Learn More

Figure 144: Fund for Countries at Risk[cclxxiv]

10.3. Investments in Quality of Life Indicators and Global Connectivity

The UAE leaders have also invested heavily in building a smart and connected technology infrastructure. This robust infrastructure is being used for improving the quality of life of the citizens. In the UAE, nearly all the population has access to a good quality internet connection. The residents can easily use the facilities and online portals of the government departments. The UAE leaders are also concerned about the confidentiality and privacy of the data and they have made serious efforts to host the data on the internet servers within the country. As shown in Figure 145 below, according to the figures of Statista, the internet penetration in the UAE reached a remarkable level of 98% as reported for the year 2023. The statistics also highlight a marked number of internet servers within the country whose count is now 14,690.

Digital & Connectivity Indicators - United Arab Emirates

United Arab Emirates

HIGHLIGHTS   MARKET DEFINITION   IN-SCOPE / OUT-OF-SCOPE   MARKET STRUCTURE   REPORTS   METHODOLOGY

- The internet penetration in the United Arab Emirates is forecast to amount to 98.00% in 2023.
- The estimated number of secure internet servers in the United Arab Emirates is 14.69k in 2023.

Figure 145: Connectivity Indicators[cclxxv]

The statista also projects that the number of internet servers will further grow in the UAE and reach the count of 17,200 by 2028 as shown in Figure 146 below:

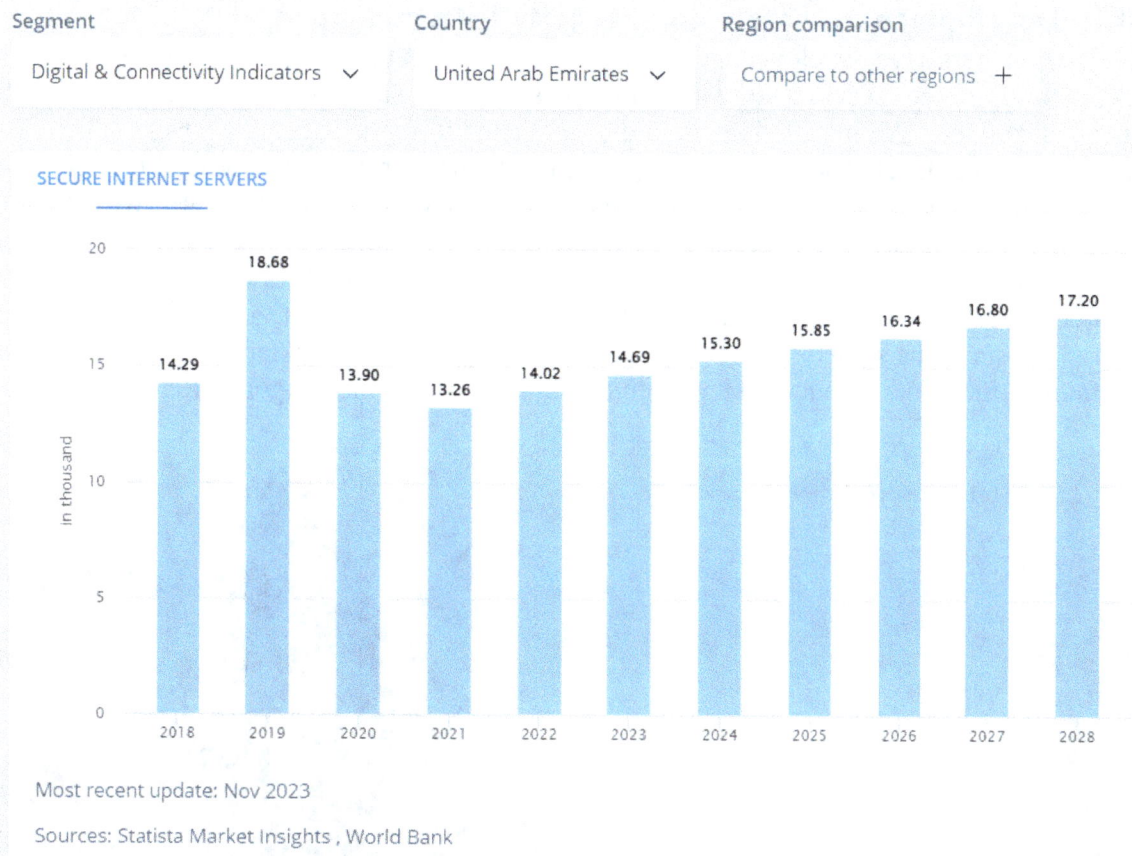

Most recent update: Nov 2023

Sources: Statista Market Insights , World Bank

Figure 146: Projected Growth in Internet Servers[cclxxvi]

Statista also predicts that the internet penetration will remain steady in the UAE and the UAE population will continue to receive high-quality internet services in the same proportion by 2028 as shown in Figure 147 below:

Most recent update: Nov 2023

Sources: Statista Market Insights , ITU - International Telecommunication Union

Figure 147: Projected Internet Penetration[cclxxvii]

10.4. Development of Safety and Security Infrastructure

The UAE leaders have developed an impressive, technology-based, smart infrastructure in the UAE. However, the leaders also realize that the safety and security of these facilities is also crucial and all the UAE installations should be protected from the adversary attacks at the local and international level. The war in the region such as the war between Iraq and Kuwait have highlighted that if the safety and security mechanisms are not in place, then it will become highly difficult for the border forces to prevent the entry of the enemy countries.

Considering all these aspects, the UAE leaders established Hedayah Centre in the country to counter the threats of extremism and terrorism. The aim of this center is to reduce extremism and radicalism in the society. The center achieves this goal through extensive research, global communications, and introducing innovative programs as shown in Figure 148 below:

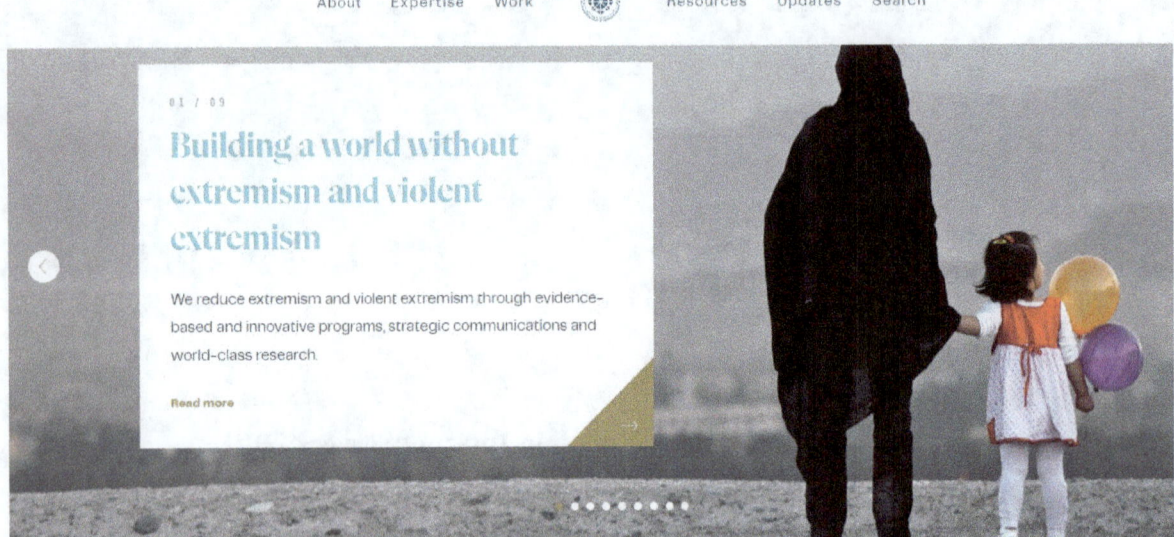

Figure 148: Hedayah Security Initiative[cclxxviii]

The UAE leaders have also established a digital platform, Sawab Center, to counter the propaganda of extremist and terrorist organizations and individuals. The center highlights that the extremist ideologies are based on a radical thinking as shown in Figure 149 below. Through extensive research and the achievements of the advocacy groups, Sawab Center highlights a unique perspective on the impact of radical thinking on individuals and communities. The center highlights that these belief systems are used for justifying terror and violence and making them a tool of achieving the political and financial objectives.

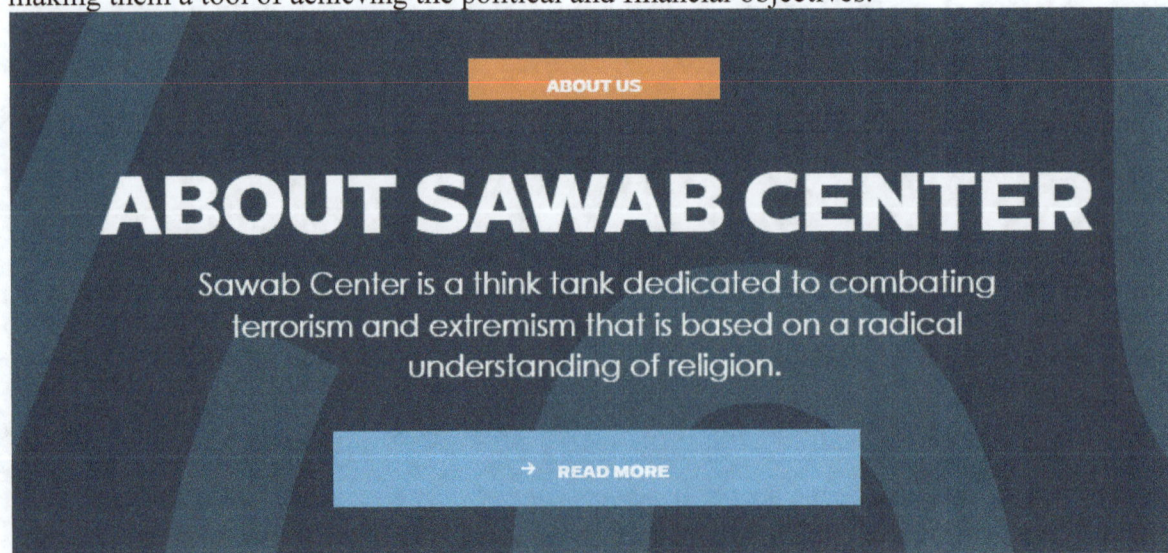

Figure 149: Center for Fighting Radicalism[cclxxix]

The UAE leaders have also strengthened the legal framework for combating the emerging security threats. In this regard, anti-terrorism, anti-hate, and anti-discrimination laws have been enacted through a federal decree.[cclxxx]

A training academy has also been established in the UAE to offer world-class education on the security parameters as shown in Figure 150 below. This academy is known as Rabdan Academy. The thematic areas covered in this academy are security, safety, emergency response, defense, and crisis management.[cclxxxi] The academy has a distinction of being the first academy in the world that is exclusively focused on the security parameters. Under the rating programs of the universities, the academy has achieved an impressive 5-star rating. The academy is situated in Abu Dhabi.

Figure 150: Security Training Academy[cclxxxii]

The sustainability and environmental protection is an area where the UAE leaders have provided leadership and encouragement to the whole world. The COP28 summit is a recent example of the commitment and efforts of the UAE for the accomplishment of sustainability goals. They have not only made the world realize the significance of a sustainable environment and business opportunities but also made significant investments in the project of energy-efficient products, green infrastructures, and clean energy production. The COP28 conference was an important forum where the world leaders have made specific targets for becoming carbon neutral at the country level and reducing the emissions of harmful gases in the environment. All these efforts highlight the visionary approach and the love for the environment and the planet by the UAE leaders. The UAE leaders have always emphasized that a sustainable future is a joint responsibility of the world community. The leaders actively participate in international initiatives on emission reduction and increasing the use of renewable energy. The local industries have also been provided incentives for building green structures and using energy-efficient products. These efforts indicate the vision of the UAE leaders to create a safe and sustainable environment for the future generations.

11. Conclusion

Now it's time to present the conclusion of this book. I have a mixed feeling at this stage of the book. On the one hand, I am extremely delighted that I have presented the transformation of the UAE as a great country through the committed and visionary approaches of the great leaders. I highlighted their contributions and achievements in multiple areas such as economic transformation, technological advancement, infrastructure development, enabling business environment, academic environment, cultural diversity, tourism development, sustainability, and environmental protection. However, on the other hand, I strongly believe that the contributions and achievements of the great leaders of the UAE have such a higher impact and a broader scope that even a book cannot summarize all of their efforts and determination. My focus in this book was to present to you a historical context of the evolution of the UAE and give you representative examples in every area pursued by the great leaders of the UAE. These representative examples will have given you a clear idea that the transformation of the UAE, the higher pace of development of the country than other countries in the region, and a peaceful transition to the modern UAE has been possible through the pragmatic and balanced approach of the UAE leaders. The leaders always believed in pluralism and diversity, and the hardline ideologies never affected their decision-making approaches. Through various strategic, conceptual, and visionary documents, I have also highlighted that the UAE leaders have a forward-looking approach and they plan for ten, twenty, or thirty years ahead. These type of roadmaps can be seen in the websites of every ministry of the UAE. Through the ideals of inclusiveness, coexistence, tolerance, and sustainability, it can be said with great confidence that the world will see further growth and development in the UAE in the years ahead due to the exemplary leadership approaches of the UAE leaders.

11.1. Summary of the Key Ideas

The Trucial States of the Persian Gulf surrendered the control of their defense to the United Kingdom. Six of these states merged in 1971 and formed a collected entity known as the UAE. The country got independence from the UK on December 02, 1971. Another state Ra's al Khaymah joined the federation in 1972. These seven states are now part of the UAE and each state is ruled by a separate ruler of the emirate. Most of the population of the UAE is concentrated on the three largest emirates Dubai, Abu Dhabi, and Sharjah. These three emirates are home to approximately 85% of the population. The UAE is one of the largest host of immigrants in the world. The immigrants account for 87.9% of the total population. The local Emiratis are only 11.6% of the total population. South Asians are the majority population of the UAE making up 59.4% of the total population. The UAE is a Middle Eastern country with majority Muslim population. The Muslims are 76% of the total population. People with other religious communities include Christians, Buddhist, Parsi, Sikh, and Jews.

The government system in the UAE is that of a federation of monarchies. The executive branch of the UAE is run by several key dignitaries. The current chief of state is President Muhammad Bin Zayid Al Nuhayyan. The head of government is Prime Minister Muhammad Bin Rashid Al Maktum. The cabinet of the UAE consists of the Council of Ministers. These ministers are appointed by the Prime Minister with the approval of the President. The president is elected by the Federal Supreme Council (FSC). The rulers of the seven emirates of the UAE are members of the FSC. The President is appointed for a 5-year term.

If you had to visit Dubai in the decade of 50s, you would struggle finding a place to stay. There were no hotels developed at that time in Dubai. Dubai was just a fishing village in 1960.

Today's UAE is a symbol of smart, connected, and resilient infrastructure, state-of-the-art hospitality services, and marvelous tourist attractions. At the time of independence, the economy of the country was dependent on pearl diving and fishing. However, after the discovery of oil and gas reserves, the country observed economic prosperity. The higher revenues and inflows made it possible for the UAE leaders to launch projects of infrastructure development as well that eventually shaped a great country and a modern UAE.

Besides oil and gas reserves and high-rise buildings, the UAE also enjoys a geographical advantage that makes it an ideal location for the international visitors, businesses, and investors. The location of the UAE is at the crossroad of Asia, Africa, and Europe. Due to this strategic location, a significant number of international trades and businesses have made the UAE their business hub. The UAE leaders have also offered tax incentives and free trade zones to facilitate the foreign investors. The airports and seaports of the UAE are well-connected and well-established and logistics and shipping operations can be carried out in a hassle-free manner through airport and maritime regions. The UAE leaders have also made the UAE a multicultural and cosmopolitan society and the UAE welcomes people from all backgrounds, ethnicities, and cultures. The respect for diversity and pluralism can be leveraged by the investors to tap into global markets and customer segments. Although the UAE government follows a conservative style of government rooted in its tradition, yet the country can be regarded as the most liberal country in the Arab world. There is a good level of tolerance for the differing beliefs, cultures, and religious communities.

The first chief of state of the UAE was His Highness Sheikh Zayed bin Sultan Al Nahyan. When the federation came into being, Sheikh Zayed was elected as the first UAE president by all emirate rulers. This post is for a five-year duration. However, the fellow rulers re-elected him after every five years till his death in November 2004. Sheikh Zayed is particularly remembered for his leadership philosophy and statesmanship. He believed that the resources of the UAE should be fully utilized and everyone should work for the betterment and the progress of the UAE. This philosophy of Sheikh Zayed also ensured women empowerment and gender equality. The UAE women got good opportunities of education, employment, and entrepreneurship.

In 1970, Sheikh Zayed had institutionalized the concept of majlis (council) and developed a National Consultative Council for Abu Dhabi. Main tribal leaders were made part of this council. When this initiative achieved a remarkable success, a similar council was developed for the entire UAE in 1971 and named the Federal National Council. This council was given the status of the parliament of the state. Council of Ministers is approved by the President and announced by the Prime Minister.

Despite being a majority Muslim country, Sheikh Zayed was a firm believer of religious tolerance and religious harmony. He enhanced cooperation with other countries to resolve the long-unresolved disputes. During the decade of 90s, Sheikh Zayed also encouraged the UAE armed forces to be part of the international peacekeeping forces. The UAE forces were part of the deterrent force to end the civil war in Lebanon. The forces also participated in the reconstruction program in Somalia. The UAE forces also took part in the aerial campaign that was aimed at stopping Serbia from the genocidal activities in Kosovo. Sheikh Zayed ruled the UAE from its foundation till his death in 2004. He died in his late eighties. All Emiratis know well the contributions and achievements of this great leader for shaping the modern UAE. He is truly regarded as the Father of the Nation.

After the death of Sheikh Zayed, his eldest son became the president, Sheikh Khalifa bin Zayed Al Nahyan. He continued the principles and policies of the founding father. While leading the country as the President, Sheikh Khalifa initiated major restructuring projects at the federal level and at the level of the emirate Abu Dhabi. Sheikh Khalifa made drastic changes in the current mode of government of the UAE for encouraging public-private collaborations and foreign investment. He believed that the government alone cannot meet the needs of all citizens, and the collaboration with the private sector and the civil society will be a prudent strategy. Sheikh Khalifa continued the policies of the previous chief of state to offer assistance to underdeveloped and vulnerable countries. In 2017, the UAE provided emergency assistance to Hurricane Irma that helped in the recovery process for the citizens of the US and the Caribbean. The relief efforts of the UAE were also offered during a major earthquake in Indonesia in 2018. In 2018, the Organization for Economic Cooperation and Development announced the UAE as the major donor of humanitarian assistance across the globe.

Sheikh Khalifa established a foundation for improving the accessibility of the utility services in the Northern Emirates. The foundation improved the accessibility in the areas of education, health, electricity, housing, water services, and transport services. In 2008, the UAE published a conceptual, policy document under the leadership of Sheikh Khalifa for the peaceful use of the nuclear power. Through this document, the UAE showed its strong commitment to safety, security, and transparency. The people of the UAE were highly inspired by the contributions and leadership of Sheikh Khalifa. As a symbol of their appreciation, in 2010, they renamed Burj Dubai to Burj Khalifa.

Sheikh Khalifa wanted that the local citizens also get good employment opportunities and do not lag behind in the competitive landscape of the UAE. Therefore, in 2012, he announced a new program known as Absher to increase the proportion of the Emiratis in the local workforce. Similar to other Middle Eastern countries, the phenomenon of localization is now a strategic direction employed by the UAE so that the local Emiratis also get good employment opportunities in the country. Under his leadership, the UAE had realized that relying on oil and gas export revenues will not be a good strategy, and the country should opt for the notion of economic diversification. With this strategic direction, in 2015, he marked the whole year as the Year of Innovation for the UAE. He continuously analyzed the needs of the UAE in the contemporary context and introduced those initiatives that can lead the UAE to the path of progress and development. Although, constitutionally, he was independent and autonomous in the decision-making for the UAE, however, he always consulted with the rulers of all the emirates before introducing new initiatives and programs.

The current chief of state and the president of the UAE is His Highness Sheikh Mohamed bin Zayed Al Nahyan. He is leading the country through a servant leadership model where the leaders are always available for the betterment of the people and improving their living conditions. He believes that the wellbeing of the UAE people is closely linked to the infrastructure development and regional security. He also believes in an inclusive and pluralistic society. He also believes that the gulf region today is highly threatened by external environment, and therefore, he encourages investments that are aimed at improving the military industries of the country such as Edge and Tawazun.

Another area of focus of Sheikh Mohamed is the development of a sustainable future. The UAE hosted COP28 in 2023 for highlighting the contributions of the UAE for the sustainable development and an inclusive climate. The conference also brought all the world leaders together and they made commitments regarding carbon neutrality in their countries and reducing the emission records. Sheikh Mohamed has also supported the industries in the UAE to invest in renewable energy, biotechnology, food security, water security, and robotics. The UAE has also appointed the first climate envoy so that the progress and development concerning net zero emissions could be tracked by the concerned authority.

Sheikh Mohamed is also credited to developing the first nuclear power plant of the UAE that is named Barakah. He supports the initiatives of arts and culture and preserves the local heritage for the inspiration of the future generations. He also believes in religious harmony, religious tolerance, and inter-faith dialogues. As part of this vision, he welcomed Pop Francis in the emirate of Abu Dhabi. It was the first ever visit of a Christian leader in the Arabian countries. A joint declaration of Human Fraternity was signed during the visit. The UAE also played an active role during the covid-19 pandemic and provided logistics support and medical supplies across the globe under the leadership directions of Sheikh Mohamed.

The current Prime Minister of the UAE is Sheikh Mohammed bin Rashid Al Maktoum and he took charge of the office in January 2006. He has introduced various revolutionary initiatives after assuming the office of the premiership. Under his leadership, the UAE government introduced UAE Vision 2021 and then the UAE Vision 2030. The vision sets the future journey of the UAE and provides strategic directions to all commercial and industrial establishments. He has also launched the UAE Centennial 2071 that provides the visionary directions for the UAE leaders for almost 5 decades.

The year 2021 was a landmark year in the history of the UAE when Sheikh Mohammed bin Rashid directed the government institutions and agencies to implement the 10 core principles of the UAE in all their plans and strategies. These 10 principles were named as Principles of the 50 because Sheikh Mohammed bin Rashid believes that these 10 principles will be applicable and relevant for the next 50 years.

The UAE leaders have adopted various leadership strategies that eventually shaped a modern UAE. All the UAE leaders have a futuristic approach and they envision how the UAE will look in the next 10 to 25 years. They also believe in the talent and skills of the UAE nation and do not hesitate to acquire the assistance of the foreign workforce if the project execution demands such expertise. The third strategy pursued by the UAE leaders is a continued focus on innovation. They believe that the technological advancements will guide the outlook of the future cities. The UAE leaders also believe in learning as a continued process. They have established higher institutions of learning with the great academic facilities to develop a highly knowledgeable and skilled workforce. The UAE leaders also believe in effective communication. The leaders have their presence on social media so that they could reach the wider audience through the social networking sites. The UAE government and all UAE ministries have their websites that provide up-to-date information regarding the government activities. Another leadership approach of the UAE leaders is their focus on unity. They are believers of teamwork and collaboration and have never tried to wage war against any neighbor country. The UAE leaders have also encouraged the technology startups and technology projects even when other countries are fearful in taking risks in the projects based on emerging technologies.

The UAE leaders presented the famous UAE Vision after considering several factors. Most of the countries in the Middle East were relying on oil exports for strengthening their economies. The decline in oil prices was a major source of concern for them. It was the leading reason that the Arab leaders realized that they need to change the strategic and economic directions of their countries and opt for economic diversification. Another area of consideration was the leading inflow of immigrants. It made it challenging for the local workforce to get good employment opportunities. The UAE leaders also encouraged and promoted the use of renewable sources of energy to clean the environment and improve the carbon footprints of the country. These three factors; the economic diversification, the localization, and sustainability initiatives made the UAE leaders realize that a new strategic directions of the country should be developed in the form of a vision statement and document. Therefore, a formal document known as 'UAE Vision 2021' was developed. Through the vision document, the UAE leaders set six key priorities for the UAE.

The targets of the UAE Vision 2021 were required to be accomplished by the golden jubilee of this great nation in 2021. After that, the UAE leaders felt that significant changes have occurred in the local and national outlook, and therefore, the strategic directions of the UAE should also be optimized accordingly. Therefore, a new vision document was developed that is known as 'We the UAE 2031' visionary approach. Similar to six national priorities presented in the 2021 document, this document highlights the four national priorities for the UAE. The first pillar is called forward society. The second pillar is called forward economy. The third pillar is called forward diplomacy. The fourth pillar is called forward ecosystem. According to the document, based on the four pillars, the vision document will be translated into a national agenda. The UAE leaders will guide the nation through this national agenda for the next 50 years. These factors highlight that the vision document is a highly significant document in the UAE context. Any individual who is interested in knowing how great leaders of UAE shaped a great country, and how they will lead the country over the next 50 years can get an idea from this vision document regarding the strategic directions of the UAE.

The economic experts have mentioned several areas where the economic activities can provide meaningful results to the UAE and other Middle Eastern countries. These emerging sectors are manufacturing sector, tourism sector, logistics and warehousing, pharmaceutical sector, renewable energy sector, and the technology sector. The UAE leaders have made investments in all of these sectors to provide more opportunities of businesses to the local and international investors. When the UAE leaders successfully achieve their agenda of economic diversification, the UAE will achieve various advantages and benefits. There will be more job opportunities for the Emiratis and foreign immigrants. There will be an increased resilience in the UAE economy where the economy will not be affected by sudden fluctuations in the oil prices or the reduced demand of the oil. The UAE will be able to develop a knowledge-based economy as per the key pillars of the vision. The UAE leaders will be able to ensure the long-term growth of the country. The standard of living and quality of life indicators will be improved and the UAE will be able to improve its ranking as set forth in the key national indicators based on the new vision document.

The initiatives of the UAE leaders present a promising technology outlook of the UAE where the country can provide leadership not only at the local level but also at the global level. The UAE leaders introduced smart devices, computers, and notebooks even at the school level so that the students learn to use technological gadgets at the very beginning of their educational attainment. The UAE leaders also created online and distance learning institutes so that the students could also acquire education from the comfort of their homes. This initiative proved particularly significant and relevant during the covid-19 pandemic when the requirement of social distancing had compelled the government to close the physical classrooms and in-person instructions.

Based on the vision document, the UAE leaders also developed a technology and innovation policy that facilitated in shaping a great country. This policy was presented by the second president Sheikh Khalifa. According to the innovation strategy of the UAE, an enabling environment for the development of innovation and technology will always be available in the UAE. According to the innovation framework, priority sectors have been identified by the UAE leaders for the technological intervention. These include education, health, water, space, transportation, and renewable energy. The technology framework of the UAE leaders classifies the technological interventions into three broader categories. These include science-based, technology-based, and business-based innovations. The UAE leaders have also presented the AI Strategy for the UAE that provides guidance for implementing AI with a forward-looking approach up to 2031. This strategy is developed under the National Program for Artificial Intelligence. In the AI strategy, the AI ministry has projected that the implementation of AI-based tools in different sectors of the UAE will increase the overall output by 335 billion dirhams. The UAE leaders have developed Expo City Dubai where national and international events and occasions are celebrated with state-of-the-art facilities and an interconnected environment. This city has been developed with the intent of making it the city of the future. The key features of this city are that the city is ideally connected to various locations through road, rail, and air transports. Moreover, the city considers the sustainability aspects in all its construction and event management.

The visionary approach of the UAE leaders regarding technological advancement can be seen from the fact that UAE is the only country in the world that has an exclusive ministry of artificial intelligence. Due to this fact, the Time Magazine included Omar Al Olama among the most influential people in the AI domain in 2023. The AI ministry in the UAE optimizes the performance of the government departments by introducing latest technologies and AI-based systems. The current minister aims to position the UAE as a world leader in the context of digital economy. He also presented AI national strategy for the country up to 2031. The UAE has also developed world-class universities providing education in computer science, technology, and artificial intelligence. The local graduates from these universities will be a highly valuable resource for advancing the technology-based, science-based, and business-based innovations in the UAE.

The infrastructure projects and initiatives of the UAE leaders were one of the biggest reasons that shaped a great country. Various infrastructure projects such as Burj Al-Arab (1999), Palm Jumeriah (2007), Dubai Metro (2009), Burj Khalifa (2010), and Al Maktoum International Airport (2013) facilitated the transition of the UAE from a fishing village to a global trade and technology hub. These projects have improved the living conditions in the UAE and also optimized the global image of the country. Whenever the foreigners visit the UAE, they always go to these tourist attractions. There are also current and upcoming infrastructure projects introduced by the UAE leaders that will ensure that the UAE has smart cities, an impressive interconnectivity, and a technology-based, state-of-the-art infrastructure for the future generations.

In the UAE, the foreign investors get the opportunity of conducting their businesses in fully-furnished business centers. Various shopping centers and large malls are also present in the UAE. The UAE also showcases business towers for conducting business activities. The investors can also choose from different industrial zones. The zones also provide technology-related, media-related, and logistics-related facilities.

There are 45 free zones that are available to the foreign investors in the seven emirates. There are various benefits available to the foreign investors in these free trade zones. The foreign nationals will get 100% ownership of the firm in the UAE. They will not be required to get the services of a local sponsor. The corporate taxes will be waived on the foreign investment. The personal taxes, import taxes, and export taxes will also be exempted. As a result, it will be possible for the foreign investors to have a 100% repatriation of their profits and revenues. Documentation process is reduced and simplified for the foreign investors.

According to the vision of the founding father of the UAE, Sheikh Zayed, a good education is inevitable for a multidimensional and progressive society. After four years of independence, the adult literacy rate in the UAE was 58% in males and 38% in females. Through the efforts and strategic initiatives of the UAE leaders, the literacy rate is now 95% in both genders. The UAE has allocated almost 20% of the federal budget for the development of the education system. The primary and secondary level education is provided free of cost in the government schools. Different curricula have been developed to meet the diverse needs of the international students. Various renowned public and private sector universities have been developed in the UAE. The UAE also offers programs for continuous education and adult learning. The smart education programs have been introduced in collaboration with the renowned software vendor Microsoft. The UAE has also developed laws and adheres to the protocols and convention for the people of determination. The UAE has also developed qualifications frameworks and school inspection frameworks. The certifications and licensing systems have been introduced for the teachers of K-12 system.

The UAE leaders have demonstrated an exemplary level of religious tolerance and the appreciation for other cultures and communities. The religious tolerance can be seen by the fact that the UAE is also home to Hindu Temples, Sikh Temple, Churches, and Ministries. The ministry of tolerance was introduced in the UAE in 2016 by the prime minister. In 2020, the tolerance ministry was further empowered and it was given the name Tolerance and Coexistence.

The United Nations has asked the member countries to consider happiness as a holistic theme where a person becomes happy when s/he is in a good physical, emotional, and spiritual state. Under these guidelines, the UAE leaders have also shown their keen desire to promote happiness in the country. The post for the Minister of State for Happiness was introduced in the UAE in 2016. In 2020, there was a cabinet realignment in the UAE during which the happiness portfolio was made part of a larger ministry of community development. According to the happiness minister, the primary objective of this ministry is to develop an environment where people can grow freely and live up to their potential. The enabling environment of the UAE should be such that the whole population desires to be happy and reaches their true potential. The responsibilities of the ministry are to implement the government policies in a manner that results in maximum satisfaction and creates social good.

The key sectors for cultural initiatives identified in the UAE are books and press, conservation of national heritage, audiovisual and interactive tools, performing arts, design services, and visual arts services. The UAE leaders have encouraged the trade and investment activities in the UAE by introducing free trade zones in the emirates. Among these zones, a significant number of zones also allow the operations of cultural and creative industries.

The UAE leaders have realized that tourism can become a source of economic strength for the country due to the strategic location of the UAE. The UAE has a strategic location in the Middle East where its geographical boundaries are located between Asia and Europe. The strategic location of the UAE can be realized from the fact that approximately 2.5 billion people have access to Dubai with a four-hour flight. Furthermore, approximately 5 billion people have access to Dubai with a flight up to eight hours. In order to hold various international conferences, seminars, and sports events, the UAE has always been a preferred destination for the event managers. The UAE has various tourist attractions such as Burj Al Arab, Global Village, Grand Mosque, Qasr Al Watan, Al Majaz Waterfront, Fujairah Fort, and Jebel Jais. The UAE leaders also acknowledge the fact that when the foreigners from across the world visit the UAE, they expect outstanding level of hospitality services in the country. The UAE has various world-class hospitality services including five-star and seven-star hotels.

The UAE leaders have developed an impressive, technology-based, smart infrastructure in the UAE. However, the leaders also realize that the safety and security of these facilities is also crucial and all the UAE installations should be protected from the adversary attacks at the local and international level. Considering all these aspects, the UAE leaders established Hedayah Centre in the country to counter the threats of extremism and terrorism. The aim of this center is to reduce extremism and radicalism in the society. The UAE leaders have also established a digital platform, Sawab Center, to counter the propaganda of extremist and terrorist organizations and individuals. The center highlights that the extremist ideologies are based on a radical thinking. In many NATO missions, the country UAE is often the only Arab country and the non-NATO state that actively takes part in the peacekeeping missions.

Although the UAE is a major oil-producing country, yet the country was among the first where the UAE leaders recognized the significance of renewable and environmental-friendly energy policies. The UAE presided the climate change conference of the UN that began in November 2023. This conference was held in Dubai and is known as COP28. The UAE has also set the target of achieving net zero carbon emissions throughout the country, and this target will be accomplished by 2050. In COP28 conference, 110 countries signed on an agreement that they will increase their capacity of renewable energy by 300% by 2030. Moreover, 50 big companies working in the oil and gas development sector have announced in COP28 that they will become carbon neutral by 2050. The UAE has also partnered with the United States for the clean energy programs under the PACE agreement. Under this agreement, an investment worth of $100 billion will be made in environmental protection initiatives. The key initiatives announced in COP28 include the increase in the production capacity of renewable energy by three times by 2030, increasing the production capacity of low-carbon hydrogen by twice by 2030, and the provision of sustainable cooling systems also by 2030.

11.2. Key Takeaways

The summary of the key ideas of this book has made it evident how great leaders of UAE shaped a great country. The summary also mentions the future directions and planning of the UAE leaders for making the UAE a leader in the region and the globe. One of the key takeaways from this book is that good leaders capitalize on the opportunities available in a geographic location instead of lamenting on the challenges and barriers. They turn the challenges into opportunities. The entire economy of the UAE was dependent on pearl diving and fishing in the earlier days. The emirates rulers exploited the potential of oil and gas reserves that brought prosperity in the country. When they observed a low demand of the oil exports, they introduced the agenda of economic diversification and increased the contribution of the identified priority sectors in the national GDP.

The second key takeaway is that a true leadership requires a lot of flexibility and a pragmatic approach. If hardline ideologies dominate the decision-making approaches, the development and progress of a nation is substantially affected. The UAE leaders have made continuous improvements in their strategies based on the changing regional and global scenarios. The targets of the UAE Vision 2021 were required to be accomplished by the golden jubilee of this great nation in 2021. After that, the UAE leaders felt that significant changes have occurred in the local and national outlook, and therefore, the strategic directions of the UAE should also be optimized accordingly. Therefore, a new vision document was developed that is known as 'We the UAE 2031' visionary approach.

The third key takeaway is that the UAE leaders have a strong focus on technological advancement and they believe that only technological advancement can provide the UAE a competitive advantage in the current circumstances. Therefore, the UAE is the only country in the world that has an exclusive ministry of artificial intelligence. In 2021, the UAE gained the distinction of being the first Arab and Muslim country to send its Hope spacecraft to the Mars mission. Dubai and other cities of the UAE are now popularly known as smart cities.

The fourth key takeaway is that the UAE is a Middle Eastern country with majority Muslim population. The Muslims are 76% of the total population. However, the UAE leaders still have a high level of respect and regard for other cultures and religions. Sheikh Mohamed also believes in religious harmony, religious tolerance, and inter-faith dialogues. As part of this vision, he welcomed Pop Francis in the emirate of Abu Dhabi. It was the first ever visit of a Christian leader in the Arabian countries. A joint declaration of Human Fraternity was signed during the visit. The UAE is also home to Hindu Temples, Sikh Temple, Churches, and Ministries. The UAE leaders have also introduced a dedicated ministry of tolerance.

11.3. The Enduring Impact of the Great Leaders

The UAE people are strongly attached to the guidelines and teachings of their great leaders. They value their contributions and efforts for shaping a great country. The people of the UAE were also highly inspired by the contributions and leadership of HH Sheikh Khalifa. As a symbol of their appreciation, in 2010, they renamed Burj Dubai to Burj Khalifa. In Abu Dhabi, the place that attracts the tourists the most is the grand mosque. This mosque is named after the founding father Sheikh Zayed, and it is truly an architectural masterpiece in the world. In Qasr Al Watan, the tourists can appreciate the deep-rooted traditions of the UAE and explore the historical evolution of the UAE that has shaped a great country. The rich history and culture of the UAE are showcased in Qasr Al Watan.

11.4. Role Model for Other Developing Countries

The UAE has provided leadership to the developing countries as to how they can become an advanced and a modern country within a short time of their history. The national day on December 2 was the 52nd national day, and within this time period, the country has achieved amazing and remarkable progress. It requires political certainty, peaceful relations with the neighboring countries, and motivating the whole nation to work for the development. The challenges of reduced oil exports, economic recession, and war-like situations in the Middle East were also faced by the UAE. The successful governance model of the UAE is an example to be followed by the other countries as how the great and visionary leaders face the challenges and turn them into opportunities for the future generations.

11.5. The Future Outlook of the UAE

The future outlook of the UAE is quite promising and the leadership is leading the country towards the path of economic, social, and technological developments. The quality of life of the people is improving and the contribution of the priority sectors other than oil and gas is also improving in the national GDP. The leadership initiatives are welcomed by the UAE people and they are happy and satisfied with the strategic directions set by the UAE leaders.

The UAE also plans to launch MBZ-SAT satellite in 2024. The launch of this satellite will be a significant contribution to the space research initiatives of the UAE. According to Economic Forum, Dubai has also established a target that by 2050, it will extract at least half of the energy requirements from the renewable sources. A new energy policy of the UAE was announced in 2021 in which the target of net zero emissions has been set for the entire country to be accomplished by 2050. The UAE government introduced UAE Vision 2021 and then the UAE Vision 2030. The vision sets the future journey of the UAE and provides strategic directions to all commercial and industrial establishments. The prime minister has also launched the UAE Centennial 2071 that provides the visionary directions for the UAE leaders for almost 5 decades.

The UAE government has also announced 2024 federal budget whose total volume is AED 64.060 billion. Out of this budget, a significant percentage 42% has been allocated to the social development sector that also includes education. The budget allocation for public education and university education programs is AED 10.2 billion that highlights the commitment of the UAE leaders to promote the academic initiatives in the country. The UAE leaders have also presented the AI Strategy for the UAE that provides guidance for implementing AI with a forward-looking approach up to 2031. UAE has secured the 10th rank in the Global Competitiveness Report of 2023. The report highlights the competitive potential of a country at the global level. With all these indicators, the UAE is one of the most attractive destinations in the world and people from across the world will continue to enter into this great country for better opportunities and a sound future of their families and future generations. This impressive outlook of the UAE is credited to none other than the great leaders of the UAE.

12. About the Author

The Author is a business professional and has worked in different industries and commercial sectors. The author has used all his knowledge, experience, and skill set, acquired by working in different sectors, for explaining different dimensions of UAE leaders' contribution in shaping a great country. In author's island home, the sea's love, sailing's legacy, and leadership's flame passed down through generations with pride and glory. He is a skilled navigator of words, charting a course through the vast ocean of knowledge. He believes in every word and section written in this book and all the content is the outcome of a critical analysis, intellectual discourses, and key debates concerning the historical evolution and a great transformation of the UAE. With his expertise and passion, he guides readers towards the core foundations and the visionary approaches of the UAE great leaders, unveiling the secrets of great leadership and economic success in concise and captivating prose.

References

[i] https://www.cia.gov/the-world-factbook/countries/united-arab-emirates
[ii] Ibid.
[iii] Ibid.
[iv] https://gisgeography.com/united-arab-emirates-map
[v] https://www.cia.gov/the-world-factbook/countries/united-arab-emirates
[vi] Ibid.
[vii] Ibid.
[viii] https://www.chathamhouse.org/2023/03/abraham-accords-and-israel-uae-normalization
[ix] https://www.cia.gov/the-world-factbook/countries/united-arab-emirates
[x] https://news.abplive.com/news/world/sheikh-mohamed-bin-zayed-al-nahyan-will-be-the-next-president-of-the-uae-1531561
[xi] https://www.bbc.com/news/world-middle-east-14703998
[xii] https://www.planetary.org/space-missions/uae-hope
[xiii] https://www.mbrsc.ae/portfolio/mbz-sat
[xiv] https://www.dubaiweek.ae/director-general-of-the-mohammed-bin-rashid-space-agency-mbz-sat-is-the-second-satellite-in-emiratis-hands
[xv] https://www.weforum.org/agenda/2019/11/dubai-uae-transformation
[xvi] Ibid.
[xvii] https://www.thenationalnews.com/uae/government/ghadan-21-abu-dhabi-to-boost-business-and-ecotourism-with-major-new-reforms-1.878805
[xviii] https://www.youtube.com/watch?v=udWs-YsvjNo
[xix] Ibid.
[xx] Ibid.
[xxi] Ibid.
[xxii] Ibid.
[xxiii] https://www.moca.gov.ae/en/area-of-focus/uae-government-leaders
[xxiv] Ibid.
[xxv] https://www.uaeglp.gov.ae/en
[xxvi] https://www.bbc.com/news/world-middle-east-14703998
[xxvii] https://www.uae-embassy.org/discover-uae/sheikh-zayed-bin-sultan-al-nahyan
[xxviii] Ibid.
[xxix] Ibid.
[xxx] Ibid.
[xxxi] Ibid.
[xxxii] Ibid.
[xxxiii] Ibid.
[xxxiv] https://www.uae-embassy.org/discover-uae/governance/about-sheikh-khalifa
[xxxv] Ibid.
[xxxvi] Ibid.
[xxxvii] Ibid.
[xxxviii] Ibid.
[xxxix] Ibid.
[xl] https://www.uae-embassy.org/discover-uae/governance/about-uae-president-sheikh-mohamed-bin-zayed
[xli] Ibid.
[xlii] Ibid.
[xliii] Ibid.
[xliv] Ibid.
[xlv] Ibid.
[xlvi] Ibid.
[xlvii] Ibid.
[xlviii] Ibid.
[xlix] Ibid.
[l] Ibid.
[li] https://sheikhmohammed.ae/en-us
[lii] Ibid.
[liii] https://uaecabinet.ae/en/biography
[liv] Ibid.
[lv] https://u.ae/en/about-the-uae/uae-in-the-future/initiatives-of-the-next-50/the-principles-of-the-50

lvi https://u.ae/-/media/Images-2021/Images-September-2021/Principles-of-the-50-En-01.ashx

lvii https://u.ae/-/media/Images-2021/Images-September-2021/Principles-of-the-50-En-02.ashx

lviii https://www.bbc.com/news/world-middle-east-47106204

lix https://www.vatican.va/content/francesco/en/travels/2019/outside/documents/papa-francesco_20190204_documento-fratellanza-umana.html

lx https://www.branex.ae/blog/leadership-traits-of-sheikh-mohammed-bin-rashid

lxi https://www.itu.int/net4/wsis/archive/stocktaking/Project/Details?projectId=1515496900

lxii https://www.vision2030.gov.sa/en

lxiii https://www.vision2021.ae/en

lxiv Ibid.

lxv Ibid.

lxvi https://u.ae/-/media/Documents-2nd-half-2023/We-the-UAE-2031-(2).pdf

lxvii Ibid.

lxviii Ibid.

lxix Ibid.

lxx Ibid.

lxxi Ibid.

lxxii Ibid.

lxxiii https://u.ae/en/about-the-uae/strategies-initiatives-and-awards/strategies-plans-and-visions/innovation-and-future-shaping/we-the-uae-2031-vision

lxxiv https://u.ae/en/information-and-services/public-holidays-and-religious-affairs/public-holidays/uae-national-day-celebrations

lxxv https://fastercapital.com/content/Economic-Diversification--Expanding-Industries-in-SEZs.html

lxxvi Ibid.

lxxvii Ibid.

lxxviii https://link.springer.com/chapter/10.1007/978-981-15-5728-6_5

lxxix https://www.sciencedirect.com/science/article/pii/S0921800922003421

lxxx https://www.atlanticcouncil.org/in-depth-research-reports/report/the-role-of-oil-and-gas-companies-in-the-energy-transition

lxxxi Ibid.

lxxxii https://www.moec.gov.ae/en/tourism-indicators

lxxxiii Ibid.

lxxxiv https://www.uae-embassy.org/business-trade/uae-real-estate-and-financial-sector

lxxxv Ibid.

lxxxvi https://www.adia.ae

lxxxvii https://www.mubadala.com

lxxxviii https://www.trade.gov/energy-resource-guide-united-arab-emirates-renewable-energy

lxxxix Ibid.

xc Ibid.

xci https://www.uae-embassy.org/discover-uae/climate-and-energy/uae-energy-diversification

xcii Ibid.

xciii Ibid.

xciv Ibid.

xcv https://www.moec.gov.ae/en/-/healthcare-en

xcvi https://u.ae/en/information-and-services/jobs/emiratis-employment-in-private-sector

xcvii Ibid.

xcviii Ibid.

xcix Ibid.

c https://www.arabnews.pk/node/2412191/media

ci https://nypost.com/2023/11/20/media/jeff-zuckers-redbird-imi-agrees-to-deal-with-telegraph-and-spectator-publications

cii https://u.ae/en/about-the-uae/the-uae-government/government-of-future/innovation-in-the-uae

ciii https://masdar.ae/en/our-company/about-masdar

civ https://dsp.ae/discover/about-us

cv https://www.dewa.gov.ae/en/about-us/strategic-initiatives/mbr-solar-park

cvi Ibid.

cvii https://aurak.ac.ae/research-centres/rak-research-innovation-center

cviii https://aurak.ac.ae/research-centres/rak-research-innovation-center/services

cix https://u.ae/-/media/Science-Technology-and-Innovation-Policy.ashx

cx Ibid.

cxi Ibid.

139

cxii Ibid.

cxiii Ibid.

cxiv https://www.visitdubai.com/en/invest-in-dubai/why-dubai/global-gateway

cxv Ibid.

cxvi Ibid.

cxvii Ibid.

cxviii https://edition.cnn.com/2023/08/24/business/saudi-arabia-brics-invitation-intl/index.html

cxix https://english.alarabiya.net/business/economy/2023/08/28/UAE-emphasizes-role-as-trade-hub-sees-ties-with-West-unbroken-after-BRICS-invite

cxx Ibid.

cxxi Ibid.

cxxii https://u.ae/en/about-the-uae/strategies-initiatives-and-awards/strategies-plans-and-visions/strategies-plans-and-visions-untill-2021/smart-dubai-2021-strategy

cxxiii https://www.linkedin.com/pulse/ai-tools-citizen-services-global-uae-perspective-alkaabi

cxxiv Ibid.

cxxv https://ai.gov.ae/wp-content/uploads/2021/07/UAE-National-Strategy-for-Artificial-Intelligence-2031.pdf

cxxvi Ibid.

cxxvii Ibid.

cxxviii https://u.ae/en/about-the-uae/strategies-initiatives-and-awards/strategies-plans-and-visions/industry-science-and-technology/national-advanced-sciences-agenda-2031

cxxix https://wam.ae/en/details/1395302678913

cxxx https://assets.ctfassets.net/r2cfrvo3y08m/vXGuANuaAEZ0FoQdRQUes/2d953fc304387a43c1d386a3458176a5/ECD_Brochure_EN.pdf

cxxxi Ibid.

cxxxii https://time.com/collection/time100-ai/6308957/omar-al-olama

cxxxiii https://ai.gov.ae/about_us

cxxxiv Ibid.

cxxxv https://provident.ae/binghatti

cxxxvi https://www.venturesonsite.com/content-hub/uae-megaprojects-unveiling-developments-shaping-the-future

cxxxvii Ibid.

cxxxviii https://jebelali-palm.com

cxxxix https://www.venturesonsite.com/content-hub/uae-megaprojects-unveiling-developments-shaping-the-future

cxl Ibid.

cxli https://urb.ae/projects/agrihub

cxlii https://www.venturesonsite.com/content-hub/uae-megaprojects-unveiling-developments-shaping-the-future

cxliii Ibid.

cxliv https://urb.ae/projects/agrihub

cxlv https://urb.ae/projects/urbantechdistrict

cxlvi https://www.venturesonsite.com/content-hub/uae-megaprojects-unveiling-developments-shaping-the-future

cxlvii Ibid.

cxlviii https://urb.ae/projects/urbantechdistrict

cxlix https://www.venturesonsite.com/content-hub/uae-megaprojects-unveiling-developments-shaping-the-future

cl Ibid.

cli https://www.skyscrapercenter.com/building/uptown-tower/31308

clii https://abudhabiculture.ae/en/experience/museums/zayed-national-museum

cliii https://www.venturesonsite.com/content-hub/uae-megaprojects-unveiling-developments-shaping-the-future

cliv https://aecom.com/projects/midfield-terminal

clv Ibid.

clvi Ibid.

clvii https://www.venturesonsite.com/content-hub/uae-megaprojects-unveiling-developments-shaping-the-future

clviii Ibid.

clix Ibid.

clx https://www.thenationalnews.com/opinion/comment/2023/12/02/the-uaes-rise-rests-on-two-critical-decisions-sheikh-zayed-made-in-1971

clxi Ibid.

clxii Ibid.

clxiii https://www.uae-embassy.org/discover-uae/society/religious-inclusion

clxiv https://www.gurudwaradubai.com/news/uaes-first-gurdwara-opens-in-dubai

clxv https://al-hamra-village.ae

clxvi https://www.venturesonsite.com/content-hub/uae-megaprojects-unveiling-developments-shaping-the-future

clxvii Ibid.
clxviii https://visituae.economy.ae/investment/en/old-en/Publications-En/New/200314BSA_Investor%20Guide_En%20V8_for%20browsing.pdf
clxix Ibid.
clxx Ibid.
clxxi Ibid.
clxxii https://www.state.gov/reports/2023-investment-climate-statements/uae
clxxiii Ibid.
clxxiv https://www.transparency.org/en/cpi/2022/index/are
clxxv https://apps.bea.gov/international/factsheet
clxxvi https://data.worldbank.org/indicator/NY.GNP.PCAP.CD
clxxvii https://gulfnews.com/lifestyle/community/45-free-zones-in-the-uae-find-the-right-one-for-your-new-business-1.1716197
clxxviii Ibid.
clxxix Ibid.
clxxx Ibid.
clxxxi Ibid.
clxxxii Ibid.
clxxxiii Ibid.
clxxxiv https://dubaimaritimecity.com/about
clxxxv https://www.reuters.com/markets/uae-attracts-record-23-bln-foreign-investment-2022-un-report-2023-07-05
clxxxvi Ibid.
clxxxvii https://www.moec.gov.ae/en/entrepreneurship-support-entities
clxxxviii Ibid.
clxxxix https://innovationhub.difc.ae/introducing
cxc https://www.dubaifuture.ae/about
cxci https://www.thenationalnews.com/opinion/comment/2023/12/02/the-uaes-rise-rests-on-two-critical-decisions-sheikh-zayed-made-in-1971
cxcii https://www.passportindex.org/byRank.php
cxciii https://www.thenationalnews.com/opinion/comment/2023/12/02/the-uaes-rise-rests-on-two-critical-decisions-sheikh-zayed-made-in-1971
cxciv https://www.thenationalnews.com/opinion/comment/2023/12/02/the-uaes-rise-rests-on-two-critical-decisions-sheikh-zayed-made-in-1971
cxcv https://www.thenationalnews.com/opinion/comment/2023/12/02/the-uaes-rise-rests-on-two-critical-decisions-sheikh-zayed-made-in-1971
cxcvi https://www.ferguae.org/themes/zircon/assets/pdf/annual-reports/FERG_Annual%20Report%20v19_Website.pdf
cxcvii https://unctad.org/system/files/official-document/wir2023-annex_tables-1_en.pdf
cxcviii https://www.brecorder.com/news/40273019/summit-bank-changes-name-to-bank-makramah-limited
cxcix https://summitbank.com.pk/wp-content/uploads/2023/07/Summit%20Bank%20Limited%20Announces%20Name%20Change%20to%20Bank%20Makramah%20Limited.pdf
cc https://www.thenews.com.pk/print/1134364-message
cci https://www.thenews.com.pk/print/1134365-consul-general-of-the-uae-confident-about-pakistan-s-progress-in-near-future
ccii https://www.khda.gov.ae/CMS/WebParts/TextEditor/Documents/Children_Law_English.pdf
cciii https://twitter.com/uaeembassyisb/status/1464988993704144896
cciv https://www.thenationalnews.com/opinion/comment/2023/12/02/the-uaes-rise-rests-on-two-critical-decisions-sheikh-zayed-made-in-1971
ccv https://icp.gov.ae/wp-content/uploads/2020/10/Human-Capital-Development-in-the-Arab-World.pdf
ccvi Ibid.
ccvii Ibid.
ccviii Ibid.
ccix https://wam.ae/en/details/1395302634891
ccx https://gulfnews.com/uae/education/uae-launches-national-strategy-for-higher-education-2030-1.2097191
ccxi https://u.ae/en/about-the-uae/leaving-no-one-behind
ccxii https://web.khda.gov.ae/en/About-Us/News/2012/Smart-Learning-Program-set-to-revolutionise-UAE-ed
ccxiii https://u.ae/en/information-and-services/finance-and-investment/federal-finance/federal-budget
ccxiv https://emsat.moe.gov.ae/emsat/EmSAT_About.aspx
ccxv https://emsat.moe.gov.ae/emsat/Default.aspx

ccxvi https://u.ae/en/information-and-services/education/school-education-k-12/joining-k-12-education/qualifications-to-be-a-teacher

ccxvii https://www.moe.gov.ae/Ar/ImportantLinks/Inspection/PublishingImages/frameworkbooken.pdf

ccxviii https://www.nqc.gov.ae/assets/download/4dc3b81c/qf-emirates-handbook.aspx

ccxix Ibid.

ccxx Ibid.

ccxxi https://u.ae/en/about-the-uae/leaving-no-one-behind/4qualityeducation

ccxxii https://www.moei.gov.ae/assets/download/1d2d6460/National%20Innovation%20Strategy.pdf.aspx

ccxxiii Ibid.

ccxxiv Ibid.

ccxxv Ibid.

ccxxvi https://uaeinnovates.gov.ae

ccxxvii https://uaeinnovates.gov.ae/2023-awards

ccxxviii Ibid.

ccxxix https://www.uae-embassy.org/discover-uae/society/religious-inclusion

ccxxx Ibid.

ccxxxi Ibid.

ccxxxii Ibid.

ccxxxiii Ibid.

ccxxxiv https://onlinelibrary.wiley.com/doi/full/10.1111/dome.12282

ccxxxv Ibid.

ccxxxvi https://www.tolerance.gov.ae/minister

ccxxxvii https://www.tolerance.gov.ae/uaetolerance

ccxxxviii Ibid.

ccxxxix Ibid.

ccxl Ibid.

ccxli Ibid.

ccxlii https://www.hayfestival.com

ccxliii https://u.ae/en/about-the-uae/the-uae-government/government-of-future/happiness

ccxliv https://wam.ae/en/details/1395302853277

ccxlv https://sdgs.un.org/panelists/he-ohood-bint-khalfan-al-roumi-30089

ccxlvi https://www.thenationalnews.com/uae/government/happiness-is-a-serious-job-uae-s-minister-of-happiness-embraces-new-role-1.201750

ccxlvii https://happiness-report.s3.amazonaws.com/2023/WHR+23.pdf

ccxlviii Ibid.

ccxlix https://u.ae/-/media/Documents-2023/Cultural-and-Creative-Industries-Eng.pdf

ccl Ibid.

ccli Ibid.

cclii Ibid.

ccliii https://www.moec.gov.ae/en/tourist-attractions?delta=40&emirate=101581

ccliv Ibid.

cclv https://www.moec.gov.ae/en/tourist-attractions?delta=40&emirate=101580

cclvi Ibid.

cclvii https://www.moec.gov.ae/en/tourist-attractions?delta=40&emirate=101582

cclviii https://www.moec.gov.ae/en/tourist-attractions?delta=40&emirate=101586

cclix https://www.moec.gov.ae/en/tourist-attractions?delta=40&emirate=101585

cclx https://www.tripadvisor.com/Hotels-g294012-United_Arab_Emirates-Hotels.html

cclxi Ibid.

cclxii https://www.atlantis.com/dubai

cclxiii https://www.consilium.europa.eu/en/meetings/international-summit/2023/12/01-02

cclxiv https://www.mofa.gov.ae/en/mediahub/news/2023/1/21/21-01-2023-uae

cclxv Ibid.

cclxvi Ibid.

cclxvii https://www.reuters.com/sustainability/climate-energy/over-110-countries-set-join-cop28-deal-triple-renewable-energy-2023-12-02

cclxviii https://www.spglobal.com/commodityinsights/en/market-insights/latest-news/energy-transition/120223-cop28-fifty-oil-and-gas-companies-sign-net-zero-methane-pledges

cclxix https://www.voanews.com/a/us-vp-harris-announces-3-billion-pledge-to-green-climate-fund/7381503.html

cclxx https://www.thenews.com.pk/print/1134364-message

cclxxi Ibid.

cclxxii https://www.cop28.com/en

[cclxxiii] Ibid.
[cclxxiv] Ibid.
[cclxxv] https://www.statista.com/outlook/co/digital-connectivity-indicators/united-arab-emirates
[cclxxvi] Ibid.
[cclxxvii] Ibid.
[cclxxviii] https://hedayah.com
[cclxxix] https://sawabcenter.org
[cclxxx] https://u.ae/en/information-and-services/justice-safety-and-the-law/maintaining-safety-and-security
[cclxxxi] https://ra.ac.ae/en/about-rabdan
[cclxxxii] Ibid.

www.ingramcontent.com/pod-product-compliance
Lightning Source LLC
Chambersburg PA
CBHW080850120626
46546CB00008B/2762